The MADNESS
of
Michele Bachmann

The MADNESS
☆ ☆ ☆ of ☆ ☆ ☆
Michele Bachmann

A Broad-Minded Survey of a Small-Minded Candidate

Ken Avidor, Karl Bremer,
and Eva Young

WILEY
John Wiley & Sons, Inc.

Published by John Wiley & Sons, Inc., Hoboken, New Jersey
Published simultaneously in Canada

Design and composition by Forty-five Degree Design LLC

For general information about our other products and services, please contact our Customer Care Department within the United States at (800) 762-2974, outside the United States at (317) 572-3993 or fax (317) 572-4002.

Wiley also publishes its books in a variety of electronic formats and by print-on-demand. Some content that appears in standard print versions of this book may not be available in other formats. For more information about Wiley products, visit us at www.wiley.com.

ISBN 978-1-118-19767-7 (cloth); ISBN 978-1-118-22627-8 (ebk);
ISBN 978-1-118-22821-0 (ebk); ISBN 978-1-118-22995-8 (ebk)

Printed in the United States of America

10 9 8 7 6 5 4 3 2 1

CONTENTS

ACKNOWLEDGMENTS

The authors thank the many people who helped to make this book possible: the bloggers and journalists in Minnesota and elsewhere who have reported about Michele Bachmann's antics; the government workers who make data about candidates and public officials accessible to the public; the many nonprofit organizations that assist in bringing that data to light; our readers for their tips, suggestions, and comments; and those who must remain anonymous (you know who you are).

We also thank Stephen S. Power at John Wiley & Sons for his assistance in distilling a mountain of material from our blogs into book format in record time.

Most of all, the authors thank their long-suffering families and friends who endured more than a decade of listening to us discuss this subject endlessly and suffered through countless Michele Bachmann videos and broadcasts.

For more tales of Michele Bachmann and continuing stories mentioned in this book, follow the authors' blogs online:

Dump Bachmann Blog:
http://www.DumpBachmann.com

Lloydletta's Nooz (Eva Young):
   http://Lloydletta.blogspot.com

Ripple in Stillwater (Karl Bremer):
   http://www.RippleInStillwater.com

Vennes Info Blog (Ken Avidor):
   http://VennesInfo.blogspot.com

Putting the Pieces Together

Getting Michele Bachmann's story on record has always been *Dump Bachmann*'s primary goal. Equally important has been getting it right—and, as often as not, we've gotten it first.

Dump Bachmann was the first to get Bachmann's most hateful and misinformed antigay rhetoric on the record with the posting of her infamous 2004 speech at EdWatch Minnesota, "The Effects of Gay Marriage on Education." It was *Dump Bachmann* that first exposed to the world her theocratic campaign speech at the Living Word Church in 2006, in which she talked of being called by God to run for office and preached that women should be "submissive" to their husbands. In both cases, it was Bachmann's own words that did her in.

That would prove to be the case time and time again during Bachmann's political career—hoisted with the petard of her own words and record.

Bachmann's proclivity toward inflammatory and fact-free statements, hypocrisy, and mishandling the truth has drawn frequent comparisons to former half-term Alaskan governor and vice presidential candidate Sarah Palin. So naturally, we wondered whether her—and, for some of us, our—hometown of Stillwater, Minnesota, was about to suffer the fate of Sarah Palin's Wasilla, whose city hall James Carville famously compared to a south Louisiana bait shop.

The national and international press did indeed head straight for Stillwater. Some didn't even bother to visit Stillwater but smeared it from afar, such as *Rolling Stone*'s Matt Taibbi, who called it "a Midwestern version of a Currier & Ives set piece, complete with cozy homes, antique stores—and no black people. In short, the perfect launching pad for a political career built on Bachmann's retro-Stepford image."

In defense of my own hometown of Stillwater, I've had to inform the media that if they are looking for the typical Bachmann Tea Party voter, they are more likely to find him or her elsewhere in Minnesota's 6th Congressional District, because Bachmann has failed to carry Stillwater in any of her three congressional races. In fact, not until she moved to ultraconservative West Lakeland Township, which went for Tea Party Republican Tom Emmer over Democrat Mark Dayton for governor by a margin of more than 2:1 in 2010, did Bachmann ever manage to carry even her own precinct.

So I steer them to Wright County on the west side of the district, the home of Bachmann's hateful antigay "minister" pal "Bradlee Dean" and failed gubernatorial candidate Emmer, where Bachmann won handily in virtually every precinct.

I also recommend that they visit the northern Twin Cities suburb of Anoka, where Bachmann went to high school. The Anoka-Hennepin School District is fast gaining a reputation as one of the most hostile school districts in the state to gay students. Two lawsuits were filed in 2011 against the district, alleging harassment of students based on sexual orientation. Nine teenagers in the district have committed suicide in the last two years, many of them gay or perceived to be gay and sometimes bullied. So that might be a good place to start if the media are looking for what shaped Bachmann's virulent homophobia.

Perhaps we should be thankful that Bachmann chose to kick off her presidential campaign in Waterloo, Iowa, where she lived the first twelve years of her life, rather than in Stillwater. Because the record is clear on one thing: even though Bachmann has called Stillwater home her entire political life, it has never been Michele Bachmann's base of political support.

Read on to find out about Michele Bachmann's true believers, and what a cast of characters it is: from grifters and money launderers to high-flying preachers and low-life ministers, and, of course, Michele and Marcus Bachmann leading the parade. Absent this compilation produced by the *Dump Bachmann* crew during her political career, Michele Bachmann would be starting her presidential campaign with fewer fellow travelers and substantially less baggage on her ride.

Here you will find the baggage the national media are finally pulling out of the line and carefully inspecting: Marcus Bachmann's Christian counseling clinic, her amazing paucity of legislative accomplishments, the convicted money launderer who was once Bachmann's biggest campaign contributor and is now under indictment for fraud, the Bachmann family farm that has harvested more than a quarter-million dollars in federal subsidies, the heavy-metal homophobic hate "minister" who Michele has prayed for, her repeated and flagrant abuse of public office for personal gain, and a career built solely on government paychecks.

We're happy to remind her—and the American people—of all of them.

CHAPTER 1

Bachmann's Fellow Travelers

Some folks say using "guilt by association" on a presidential candidate is unfair . . . not Michele Bachmann:

> Why isn't it appropriate to ask about the formative rela-
> tionships he's had? The types of relationships that may
> have influenced Barack Obama's views on public policy
> and on government decision-making? Why is the media
> more intent on learning the type of plumbing license
> Joe the Plumber has than on exploring the obvious
> questions about Barack Obama's formative relation-
> ships with people such as the Rev. Jeremiah Wright and
> Bill Ayers—people with views far outside the main-
> stream, where most voters find themselves?

During the 2008 election, Michele Bachmann repeatedly called on the media to "investigate" the "formative associations" of Barack Obama.

The *Dump Bachmann* blog answered Michele Bachmann's call for an investigation; however, we turned the focus of our investigation on the formative associations of . . . Michele Bachmann.

The Admiral

The Admiral blogs at *Lake Minnetonka Liberty*. Back in 2009, the Admiral wished someone would assassinate President Obama:

> Somebody please! Do a Sirhan Sirhan on this pompous ass, willya?

The Admiral ranted about Congressman Barney Frank:

> One of the men responsible for the financial collapse, Barney "Fudge Packer" Frank has the audacity to call Scalia a homophobe? First off, homophobe is just one of those made up liberal labels, we all know how liberals like to make up and assign labels to everything. Hey! Fudge Packer, do America a favor, hang yourself. It's the right thing to do. Fruity bastard.

The Admiral wanted to purge the GOP:

> We don't want Democrat-lites polluting our party, we don't want "moderates" interested in compromise and appeasement by "reaching across the aisle in a bipartisan way." We want and need more people like Jesse Helms who wasn't afraid to say, "NO!" and didn't back down.

Enough is enough! Time to jettison the dead weight and bring in the real conservatives.

The Admiral thinks his congressman is a "wimp." The Admiral likes Bachmann—and according to the Admiral, the admiration is mutual:

> Since February I've had 3 or 4 direct communications with Michele Bachmann. Not her staff, but her. She's been more than helpful in giving me information and fulfilling any request that I may have, and I don't even live in her district. Regardless of how you may feel about her, she's a very gracious and accommodating person. She even granted me an interview request. And I can't get the time of day out of my own representative!

Bachmann has had only one town hall meeting with constituents since she was elected to Congress. But according to the Admiral, she has time for an extremist bigot who wishes somebody would assassinate the president. The Admiral still used violent language as recently as June 14, 2011, when blogging about President Obama: "This asshole of a president needs to be hung [*sic*] for treason."

Barb Anderson

Barb Anderson is a researcher for the Minnesota Family Council and a member of the Parents Action League (PAL), a shadow group formed to oppose "the Gay Agenda" in the Anoka-Hennepin School District.

The Parents Action League is worried about "the pro-gay activist teachers," "an increase in pro-gay curriculum materials," and "the health risks to students who are affirmed and labeled as 'gay' and who may participate in homosexual acts."

The Parents Action League has put a lot of effort into hiding who its members are. There are no names associated with the group, though Barb Anderson, a Minnesota Family Council employee, has been active with promoting antigay hysteria within the Anoka-Hennepin School District. Some of Anderson's letters to the editor are quoted on the PAL website.

Anderson was a guest on hate-monger Bradlee Dean's radio show. On the show, she gloated about how as one person, she has become very powerful within the Anoka-Hennepin School District. Barb Anderson is also the vice president of Janet Boynes Ministries.

Barb Anderson and her husband are big contributors to Michele Bachmann's campaigns.

In addition, Anderson is one of Michele Bachmann's contributors who endorsed the following proclamation of the Alliance for the Separation of School and State (ASSS): "I proclaim publicly that I favor ending government involvement in education."

Chris Baker

Chris Baker, a former radio host on KTLK, wanted to roll out a special welcome party for protesters to the 2008 Republican National Convention in St. Paul, Minnesota.

> So we've been talking about police protection during the upcoming convention when all those stinky protesters are coming. There seems to be a big debate over whether or not police officers will be able to wear helmets, carry shields, use pepper spray and Tasers on this crowd. You know, I'll tell you what works on a crowd like this—a machine gun, that always works very well.

Baker's sidekick chimed in, "Mow 'em down, baby!"

"You must have order, you cannot have a civilized society without order and if that means cracking a few skulls, so be it," Baker said. "A good ole boy network is what you need, and hand out some ax handles."

Bachmann appeared on Baker's show a bunch of times. The most memorable Bachmann quote from 2009 was: "We're running out of rich people in this country."

Former Minnesota State Representative Mark Olson (R-Big Lake)

While in the State Senate, Bachmann worked closely with GOP Representative Mark Olson in the House on his wacky wingnut crusades: the marriage amendment, Personal Rapid Transit, monkey-wrenching real transit. Bachmann and Representative Olson coauthored a bill inspired by Christian revisionist historian David Barton to support faith-based history in the public schools. In an audio clip from Bachmann's weird speech at the 2006 "Gala" for Bradlee Dean's ministry, she talked about the bill she and Olson championed in the Minnesota Legislature.

Bachmann also supported Olson's bizarre Rapid Transit boondoggle. Like Olson, Bachmann opposed reality-based transit such as the very successful Hiawatha Light Rail Line and the Northstar Commuter Line.

Olson had an anger-management problem. Early in his legislative career, he lost his temper at a legislative aide in an incident that was unbecoming; he was reprimanded by his caucus leader.

Five days after Olson was reelected in 2006, he was arrested for repeatedly pushing down his wife, Heidi, during an argument. According to a media report,

"State Representative Mark Olson was arrested Sunday and is in Sherburne County Jail facing charges of domestic abuse," Sherburne County Sheriff's Department chief deputy Scott Gudmanson said.

"Sherburne County authorities were called to the Big Lake Township home Olson shares with his wife, Heidi, at 20945 Sherburne County Road 43 about 5 p.m. Sunday," Gudmanson said. "Sherburne County asked Blaine Police Department to arrest Olson at a residence in Blaine."

Olson was convicted of one count of misdemeanor domestic assault with the intent to cause fear. Sherburne County District Judge Alan Pendleton sentenced Olson to two years' probation and required him to pay $400 in fines, as well as court costs.

Olson refused to plead at his arraignment and refused to leave the legislature. He was ejected from the Minnesota GOP House Caucus, but he continued to rant and rave on the House floor while other legislators cringed. During one session, Olson was caught on video raving about suicide and "death, death, death!"

After his conviction on one count of domestic assault, Olson declined to run again for his House seat and instead announced he would run for the Minnesota Senate District 16 seat vacated by Betsy Wergin. He was endorsed at the Minnesota SD16 Convention last summer and again recently after he lost the primary. The Minnesota GOP Senate Caucus wants nothing to do with Olson. Even Republican operative and former Bachmann campaign consultant Michael Brodkorb and Senator Norm Coleman threw Mark Olson under the bus.

And where was Michele Bachmann's condemnation of her ol' pal Representative Mark Olson? Where was Bachmann's "titanium spine" when it comes to denouncing the Minnesota GOP's poster boy for domestic violence? . . . (sound of crickets)

Olson lost his race for the Senate as a write-in candidate. Right-wing blogger Gary Gross of *Let Freedom Ring* had this to say about Representative Mark Olson:

> I'd say that getting convicted of Domestic Assault-Misdemeanor-Commits Act With Intent to Cause Fear of Immediate Bodily Harm or Death fits most people's definition of depravity or vile, shameful, or base character.
>
> I'm disgusted with Mr. Olson. It's apparent that Mr. Olson picks and chooses which rules, laws and promises he'll obey and which ones he'll ignore. What type of lawmaker picks which laws he'll abide by and which he'll ignore? Does Olson think that he's above the law? For that matter, does he think he should be exempted from keeping his promises?

Mark Olson returned to the capital as a lobbyist for a would-be Personal Rapid Transit [PRT] vendor proposing a $100 million pod transport project in Coon Rapids.

Bradlee Dean

Bradley Dean Smith, aka Bradlee Dean, is the longhaired, tattooed head of what used to be called the You Can Run But You Cannot Hide Ministry and has been renamed You Can Run But You Cannot Hide International. He is also the drummer for the heavy metal Christian band Junkyard Prophet. Bradlee Dean made headlines when he gave a prayer that questioned President Obama's belief in Christianity, while dressed in a tracksuit at the Minnesota Legislature. Bradlee Dean and Larry Klayman sued MSNBC host Rachel Maddow and *Minnesota Independent* reporter Andy Birkey. (More about Bradlee Dean in chapter 6).

Janet Boynes

Michele Bachmann's ex-lesbian sidekick Janet Boynes is a promoter of the "pray-away-the-gay" movement and a close friend of Michele and Marcus Bachmann. Boynes writes books, appears on Christian radio and television shows, and gives lectures about how she went from gay to straight with the help of God.

She testified at a Minnesota Senate hearing that legalized gay marriage would have dire public health consequences: spreading AIDS and "gay bowel syndrome."

Here's Boynes's endorsement of Bachmann posted on the right-wing blog *Look True North*:

> I've known Michele for 4 years, and consider her a good friend. During the RNC convention, talk show host Laura Ingraham broke her rule of no endorsements to support Michele Bachmann's re-election campaign. I was invited to the event, and it was great that Laura saw in Michele what I have these past four years: that her heart is right and she is a woman of integrity.
>
> It breaks my heart to see the condemnation by the media who have taken Michele's words out of context in her interview with Chris Matthews (who we all know is a liberal Obama cheerleader). They are all trying to shut her campaign down.
>
> But not if I can help it. And those of you who know Michelle's [*sic*] heart. You can judge her from the video or judge what she's done these past two years for her district. I choose the latter, and hope you will too. Michele cares for people and doesn't want them taken advantage of. She stands strong for conservative values, and liberals (with the media's help) are making this molehill into a mountain to help defeat her.

I'm Janet Boynes, and I approve Michele Bachmann's message 100%. Please give her your support to get her re-elected.

Andrew Breitbart

Andrew Breitbart runs a bunch of sleazy right-wing websites that spread sensational news and gossip. Breitbart's websites are responsible for infamous escapades like the ACORN videos in which his reporter James O'Keefe dressed up as a pimp, and the video of a speech by U.S Department of Agriculture employee Shirley Sherrod that was edited to make her appear to make a racist remark. In 2011, Sherrod announced she was suing Breitbart for defamation.

Bachmann, of course, is a proud member of the rogues gallery that infests Breitbart's website, Big Government.

In an interview with Michele Bachmann by columnist and radio host Ben Shapiro posted on Breitbart's Big Government website, Shapiro suggested that Barack Obama was the worst president in U.S. history.

> *Shapiro:* Is President Obama better or worse than Jimmy Carter.
>
> *Bachmann:* Worse. Easily worse.
>
> *Shapiro:* I agree. So far, you'd have to say he's the worst president in United States history . . .
>
> *Bachmann:* No question. No question.
>
> *Shapiro:* . . . with the possible exception of James Buchanan.

In a video featuring Andrew Breitbart, he obsequiously praised Michele Bachmann: "This is a true warrior. This is a person you'd

13

want to march to battle with. This is not a person who is looking at polls to decide what the right thing to do is. This is a person with a moral compass."

Marcus Bachmann

Marcus Bachmann is Michele's husband and would be the first "First Dude" in the White House. Marcus runs Bachmann & Associates Inc., a Christian counseling clinic. Marcus denies reports that his clinic practices pray-away-the-gay "reparative therapy" on homosexual patients. *Psychology Today* had an entry, since removed, on their website on Marcus Bachmann's counseling clinic that said yes on whether the clinic has "Gay/Lesbian expertise." The entry also claims that Bachmann & Associates will counsel on "gay/lesbian issues." Marcus Bachmann gave a presentation titled "The Truth about the Homosexual Agenda" at the antigay Pastors' Summit. Bachmann & Associates also takes Medicaid reimbursement and many other major health insurance plans, while not providing health insurance to its own employees.

In a November 20, 2006, *Star Tribune* article titled "Bringing a Touch of Haute to the U.S. House," reporter Kim Ode quoted Michele Bachmann describing the fashion help she gets from Marcus:

> Shopping help comes from another quarter, as well. Before Vice President Dick Cheney's visit this past summer, Bachmann's husband, Marcus, hit the stores—"he's got a good sense of style"—and came home with "a sleek, simple hourglass dress with a yoke collar in winter white." He even bought a matching coat and shoes. "I just slipped it on."

Marcus also goes on "dad dates" with his daughters and helps pick their prom dresses.

Jason Lewis

Jason Lewis is a right-wing radio talk show host, a failed congressional candidate, and a special friend of Michele Bachmann. When Bachmann launched her campaign in Waterloo, Iowa, in July 2011, Jason Lewis gave the warm-up speech.

Lewis came to Bachmann's defense when *Star Tribune* reporter Eric Black (now at *MinnPost*) reported Bachmann's remarks to a *Saint Cloud Times* reporter about a secret Iranian plan to carve up Iraq. Lewis was incensed that Black learned of the interview from the *Dump Bachmann* blog.

In a tirade lasting four minutes, Lewis ranted about the "angry lesbians and radical pacifists" of *Dump Bachmann* and how they "planted" the story in the newspaper and that there was no difference between *Dump Bachmann* and the *Star Tribune*. Lewis finished up his screed by praising *Dump Bachmann* for getting the word out about his favorite congresswoman:

> I'm just tellin' you folks that this is the way a hit job starts. The anti-partisan, radical left, Bachmann looney tunes, plant a story in a local media, Drudge grabs it, puts it on his website, Rush Limbaugh reads it, and all of a sudden Michele Bachmann has been tarnished for saying something that everybody has been saying for months. Great job for the Dump Bachmann folks, because they got their lackeys disguised as journalists at the *Strib* to do their dirty work. In fact, they didn't even wait for a quote—a quote from Bachmann.

Lewis is now a columnist for the *Star Tribune*, the very newspaper he accused of being in cahoots with the angry lesbians and radical pacifists of *Dump Bachmann*.

Larry Klayman

Bradlee Dean's lawyer Larry Klayman appeared on Michele Tafoya's WCCO radio show on July 27, 2011, to talk about his defamation lawsuit against MSNBC. Klayman said he and his client Bradlee Dean and Michele Bachmann don't want children "indoctrinated" in the "homosexual lifestyle" because it is a "very unhappy lifestyle and an unnatural lifestyle and something that God did not intend to occur." Klayman added that he believes homosexuality is "perverted" and explained what the lawsuit is really about:

> What she [Maddow] said, and this is what is going to end her career. Her career is over, Michele. What she said is that Michele Bachmann and Bradlee Dean and other conservative Christians are bloodthirsty, that they want bloodletting in the culture war, and Christians are not satisfied that they have not killed enough lesbians and gays.

Regarding Maddow's career, Klayman was less than prescient. Fewer than two weeks later, MSNBC signed Maddow to a new multiyear contract long before her current contract had ended.

According to his January 2011 column for *World Net Daily*, Klayman is a close pal of Michele Bachmann who was "unafraid to be vilified by the left." Klayman continued to gush about Bachmann:

> If you need to understand one thing about Michele, its [*sic*] not just that she is articulate, charismatic and one

of the two most attractive conservative women in national politics today, but she is a mother who has raised not only her own children, but 23 foster children—yet still pursued her ambitions and career goals. Michele is the real deal. She may be modest in physical height, but she stands tall on principles.

Klayman transcribes another encounter with the congresswoman that reads like it was copied from a Harlequin bodice-ripper:

I became reacquainted with Michele last fall when I visited her in her office in the Rayburn Building. As I waited in the lobby, I remember her "bouncing" out of her office like an energetic, enthusiastic staffer, quickly walking over to me and with a warm smile holding out her hand. Looking into her eyes, I told her how nice it was to meet her. In a quick response she quipped, smiling, "Larry, I met you many years ago at CNP!"

The CNP Klayman refers to, the Council for National Policy, is a group of conservatives that gathers in private four times a year to discuss policy.

Klayman invited Bachmann and Alan Keyes to a press conference on November 17, 2010, to support the People's Mujahideen Organization of Iran (PMOI, also known as the MEK), asking that they be removed from the U.S. State Department list of Foreign Terrorist Organizations.

James O'Keefe

Back in 2009, Bachmann praised Breitbart-brat James O'Keefe at a right-wing freak show called the "How to Take Back America

Conference." "Defunding the left is going to be so easy," said Bachmann, "and it's going to solve so many of our problems." She praised James O'Keefe III and Hannah Giles, the people behind the ACORN sting. "Hannah and James used Saul Alinsky's 'Rules for Radicals'—that's the community organizer's bible—against ACORN! Brilliant!"

Bill Pulkrabek

Bill Pulkrabek is one of Michele Bachmann's early mentors. Pulkrabek managed Bachmann's first campaign for the state Senate.
In 2009, Pulkrabek gave this quote to the City Pages:

> "I don't think she has any weaknesses," says Bill Pulkrabek, Bachmann's former campaign manager, now a Washington County commissioner. "DFL activists are blinded by their hatred for this woman. That's because she's not afraid to throw gas on the fire. She's not afraid to whip up our side."

Pulkrabek was also quoted in a recent AP profile of Bachmann:

> "Early on, Bachmann showed potential as an articulate and magnetic speaker," said Bill Pulkrabek, a Republican leader who helped assemble the school board slate.
> "People had been predicting her demise since Day One: 'Oh, she's a radical, she's too far right, she's too outspoken, she's too inflammatory,'" Pulkrabek said. "The fact of the matter is, with the exception of the first race, she wins."

Pulkrabek, a Washington County commissioner, once referred to homeless people as "jackasses." Pulkrabek was arrested and jailed on Memorial Day 2011 on suspicion of felony domestic assault by strangulation and misdemeanor fifth-degree assault. He was charged with misdemeanor domestic assault for allegedly choking his girlfriend with his forearm and dragging her down the stairs by her hair, according to the Woodbury, Minnesota, police report.

GOP blogger Andy Aplikowski took note of Pulkrabek's bad temper in this post from 2005:

> Going in, I thought Ron had it. I really did. Heck I was campaigning for him, without being asked. I truly felt that it was not right to make a change at this time considering the options. Pulkrabek showed the fact that he was not strong enough to be a party leader. His speech was all over the place, and he came across well, bent. He had an axc to grind and he did it. His message was not fully developed. He just wasn't happy with the Eibensteiner [sic]. Obviously the message of the day, but not enough alone. He got emotional during his speech and lost his cool.

John A. Stormer

A favorite author of the right-wing nut John Birch Society is also a fan of Michele Bachmann. John A. Stormer of Florissant, Missouri, the author of the highly popular (among the black helicopter crowd) 1960s anticommunism screed *None Dare Call It Treason*, gave Bachmann's congressional campaign $225 in the 2005–2006 election cycle.

None Dare Call It Treason, published in 1964, sold 6 million copies when it came out, largely through John Birch Society chapters and their communist conspiracy–prone members. The book's chief premise was that the United States was losing the Cold War because communist subversives had heavily infiltrated it. Stormer's updated edition, *None Dare Call It Treason . . . 25 Years Later*, and another book, *None Dare Call It Education*, currently are available through the John Birch Society bookstore, American Opinion Book Services, and probably can be found on the Bachmann family bookshelves.

Stormer is a retired minister and Christian school superintendent and the past president of the Missouri Association of Christian Schools. He's also a past member of the Council for National Policy described by the *New York Times* as "a secretive club whose few hundred members include Dr. James C. Dobson of Focus on the Family, the Rev. Jerry Falwell of Liberty University and Grover Norquist of Americans for Tax Reform."

Stormer has been linked to violent extremist groups in Missouri.

According to a 1999 report by the Missouri Citizen Education Fund, Stormer was a U.S. Taxpayers Party (USTP) national committeeman. "The USTP has become a clearing house for dissatisfied groups on the far right—members of David Duke's Populist Party, Randall Terry's Operation Rescue, the militant Christian Right, and the militia Movement," the report states.

> Stormer holds prayer sessions in Jefferson City for Missouri legislators. He also contends that tolerance of homosexuality and abortion is bringing God's judgment on America in the form of natural disasters. (*St. Louis Journalism Review*, November 1995)

Stormer and Bachmann are connected in other ways beyond his campaign contributions to her.

Stormer has signed the proclamation of the Alliance for the Separation of School and State (ASSS) to abolish all government education. Bachmann took more than $51,000 from signatories of the ASSS proclamation.

Stormer spoke at an EdWatch conference in St. Louis, a group that Bachmann has spoken to on many occasions. Fellow CNP member and heavy Bachmann contributor John Scribante is a board member and a former president of EdWatch.

Mary Kiffmeyer

Mary Kiffmeyer was elected to replace Mark Olson in Minnesota House District 16B. Kiffmeyer had previously served two terms as Minnesota's secretary of state. A legislative audit found that she overpaid her staff by $190,000 and claimed excessive reimbursement for mileage. Kiffmeyer was defeated by Mark Ritchie in 2006.

Kiffmeyer, like Bachmann, attended and gave a speech at the 2006 fund-raiser for Bradlee Dean.

Mary Kiffmeyer also had to defend writings about "racial purity" on her think tank Minnesota Majority's website.

Kiffmeyer said that the page dealing with health care and its mention of racial purity must be understood in context. That phrase, she said, is simply descriptive.

"That's a genetic term," said Kiffmeyer, who is a nurse by training. "It does matter when you are doing medical studies."

Drew Emmer, the communications director for the organization, said that Kiffmeyer is the organization's executive director, and Jeff Davis, who has been active in pushing for a Minnesota antigay marriage amendment, is the president (*St. Paul Pioneer Press*).

Mary Kiffmeyer is married to Ralph Kiffmeyer. A former member of the Minnesota House of Representatives, Ralph Kiffmeyer tried and failed to pass legislation that would outlaw the sale of sex toys, earning him the sobriquet "Anti-Dildo Crusader."

Phyllis Schlafly

Phyllis Schlafly is America's best-known female antifeminist and antigay proponent. Schlafly is most well known for her vigorous and successful campaign opposing the Equal Rights Amendment (ERA), based largely on the argument that the ERA would require same-sex bathrooms. According to her website, in her book *The Supremacists*, "Schlafly reveals the astonishing scope of judicial ambition. Without any constitutional mandate, judges have banned the public recognition of God, redefined marriage, undermined national sovereignty, released a flood of pornography, institutionalized feminist dogma, interfered in elections, and handicapped law enforcement." Schlafly has a gay son and believes married women cannot be raped by their husbands. Schlafly's Eagle Forum Political Action Committee has contributed $26,000 directly to Bachmann's political campaigns from 2005 to 2010 and has spent thousands more on behalf of her campaigns.

Orly Taitz

Orly "Queen of the Birthers" Taitz once posed for a picture with Michele Bachmann and was miffed that it went viral on the Internet.

> Shortly after I posted this picture with Congresswoman Michelle [*sic*] Bachmann, it was re-posted on a number of Obama propaganda Marxist disinformation blogs. One of them "Obama conspiracy theories" was calling it "Birds of a feather" and posted this comment above. Apparently they compared picture I took with Michelle [*sic*] Bachmann to an invitation to spend a day in NY with Bill Clinton, which I posted previously. If these

bloggers don't understand a difference between the two, they are really brain-dead.

Tony Perkins

Family Research Council president Tony Perkins has been condemned for speaking to America's leading white supremacist organization, the Council of Concerned Citizens, and to former Ku Klux Klan Grand Wizard David Duke. Bachmann featured Tony Perkins as a keynote speaker on April 20, 2005, at her anti-gay marriage rally on the steps of the Minnesota state capitol building. The *Nation* magazine's April 26, 2005, web issue detailed Perkins's unseemly association with the CCC and the KKK:

> Just four years ago, Tony Perkins spoke before the Louisiana chapter of the CCC. This is the successor to the racist White Citizens Councils, which fought integration in the south in the 1950s. And in 1996, when Perkins was running a campaign for a Republican U.S. Senate candidate in Louisiana, he paid former KKK Grand Wizard David Duke $82,500 for his mailing list and was fined $3,000 by the Federal Election Commission for trying to hide his payment to Duke.

David Strom

Former Taxpayers League president David Strom once called Michele Bachmann a "moderate." On Channel 5's *At Issue*, he referred to Michele Bachmann and Cheri Pierson Yecke as "moderate women."

In Strom's *Our House Blog*, he blamed liberals for "failing the body politic" for attacking Bachmann personally. Strom failed to see how Bachmann's attack on the personal relationships of gay people could provoke such a response:

> I defy anyone to find an example of Bachmann attacking any of her opponents for their private sexual activities. It doesn't happen. Bachmann has a passionate position on a matter of legitimate public policy debate (yes, it is a legitimate matter of debate—in fact, if it weren't a legitimate matter of debate, the proponents of gay marriage would lose immediately because huge majorities oppose them at the moment), but she NEVER EVER attacks her opponents on matters of personal behavior or temperment [*sic*]. She sticks to the arguments.

Strom fails to mention that one of Bachmann's arguments was that being gay was "from Satan." Strom complained the opponents of the marriage amendment were nasty to question Bachmann's motives and her honesty. Strom also vouched for Bachmann's humanity:

> I've personally seen Michele reach out to her opponents on gay marriage and engage them on a very basic human level, disagreeing on the merits, but treating them with respect.

Treating people with respect by attacking their right to marry the person they love?

Robert Battle

Robert Battle is the pastor of the Berean Church in St. Paul. The *New York Times* quoted Battle saying the following about his pal Michele Bachmann:

"She stood up as a Christian," said Bob Battle, pastor of the Berean Church of God in Christ here. "She made her point of view known, and she gave Christians a voice."

In a letter to the *Pioneer Press*, Battle defended Michele Bachmann:

> Upon reading your editorial endorsements in Minnesota House races last month, I was troubled by the editorial staff's opinion that same-sex marriage is a "non-issue" in Minnesota, and its characterization of state senator Michele Bachmann as "divisive" and "hard right."

Battle wound up his opinion piece by invoking the memory of Martin Luther King to support his own long-standing antigay bigotry:

> In "Letter from Birmingham City Jail," Dr. Martin Luther King stated, "A just law is a man-made code that squares with the moral law or the law of God." Clearly marriage as between one man and one woman fits these criteria. And Bachmann is right in her dedication to these principles.

Appalling . . . but, just what you would you expect from a fellow traveler of Michele Bachmann!

CHAPTER 2

Bachmann's Antigay Crusade

In June 2003, the Supreme Court overturned the Texas Sodomy Law in a 6–3 ruling. Reaction from religious-right groups was to change the subject from sodomy laws to gay marriage, which at the time was unpopular. The Massachusetts Supreme Judicial Court ruled that prohibiting gays from marrying was unconstitutional under the state constitution. Shortly after this, Michele Bachmann introduced her constitutional amendment to ban gay marriage and "legal equivalents."

As we document in this chapter, Michele Bachmann's crusade against gay marriage included radio appearances, hysteria-laced e-mails to "Death Penalty for Homosexuals as Prescibed [*sic*] by the Bible," signs at an antigay rally at the state capitol, and an e-mail bragging about shutting down the legislature over this "earthquake issue."

27

By the time she ran for Congress in 2006, Bachmann didn't even campaign on the gay marriage issue in her congressional campaign—she campaigned on taxes, immigration scares, and "Drill, baby, drill." If campaigning on the gay marriage issue could have helped Bachmann, she'd have done it—but she didn't. Bachmann's winning by a plurality in the most conservative, gerrymandered district in the state was not a referendum on gays.

Senator Bachmann's Crusade during the 2004 Legislative Session

During the 2004 legislative session, Michele Bachmann sent out e-mails with videos and made frequent appearances on Christian radio and her church and home school networks to promote the Bachmann amendment. An example is her March 20 appearance on Jan Markell's *Understanding the Times* radio show (Olive Tree Ministries) on KKMS 980 AM. Michele Bachmann told Markell's listeners to visit the mnvoter.com website, which had a three-minute video explaining "the problem, the solution, and also telling people there's a rally that will be held this coming Monday, March 22." Bachmann urged Markell's listeners to let legislators know that her amendment was an important issue. In addition, Bachmann noted that "the largest rally last year at the capitol was the gay rally."

Bachmann ramped up her fearmongering:

> Because, Jan, this is an earthquake issue, this will change our state forever. The immediate consequence if gay marriage goes through is that K–12 little children will be forced to learn that homosexuality is normal and natural and that perhaps they should try it. And this will take away the civil rights of little children to be pro-

tected in their innocence—so it will take away the rights of parents to control and direct their child's education and step on their sincerely held religious beliefs.

This is a serious matter because it's our children that's the prize for this community. They are specifically targeting our children. Jan, you're right. Our people are perishing for lack of knowledge.

During the rally, signs such as "Death Penalty for Homosexuals as Prescibed [*sic*] in the Bible" and "No Homos as Leaders" were prominent. Bachmann exhorted the crowd to "storm the capitol" in order to persuade "Democrat" senators to support her amendment.

Shortly after this event, the *Dump Bachmann* blog debuted, to report on Senator Bachmann's crusade against the LGBT (lesbian, gay, bisexual, and transgender) community.

The following correspondence sent in May 2004 from Senator Bachmann to her Senate e-mail list is just one of many fearmongering missives she sent over the years, claiming that the sky was falling for one reason or another, but more often because of gay marriage.

In these e-mails, Bachmann repeated the same stories and anecdotes. Often, they were war stories such as this:

> On the morning of December 7, 1941, local St. Paulite Orville Ethier was aboard the USS Ward, a boat manned by 82 Navy reservists from St. Paul, when a small Japanese sub appeared near the entrance to Pearl Harbor. The Ward fired two shots, one of which struck and sank the sub, which constituted the first American shots of World War II. The commander of the Ward relayed a message about the incident back to military headquarters in Honolulu. The message stated, "We have attacked, fired upon and dropped depth charges upon submarine

operating in defensive sea area." The message, sent more than an hour before the 8 a.m. attack on Pearl Harbor, went unheeded.

The point she was trying to make was that gay marriage was just as bad as the Japanese navy's attack on Pearl Harbor:

> You are a type of Orville Ethier—a patriot looking to secure American freedoms. The question is, will the Senators of Minnesota act like the Honolulu military headquarters and ignore your message? Today we face perhaps the greatest attack on the family in our lifetime. Now is OUR time to stand up and send a message to avert an equally impending disaster. Please visit www.mnmarriage.com to read my recent column on the threat that legalized gay marriage poses to our civil and religious liberties and to tax-exempt organizations in particular.

Bachmann sent a follow-up e-mail the next day, urging her followers to e-mail pledges to their representatives at the legislature:

> The Defense of Marriage Pledge attached to yesterday's email is intended for State Legislators to sign and state their support as a "Defender of Marriage." Please ask your State Legislators if they have yet signed this pledge. It is not necessary for the general public to sign this pledge.

The foes of same-sex marriage didn't rely only on Chicken Little e-mails to rally their forces. On a September 12 talk radio show *Dump Bachmann* learned of an antigay marriage Truth Truck. On the local radio show *Garage Logic*, the guest host Dave

Thompson discussed the Truth Truck, which displays a sign showing two gay men kissing and the slogan "Want Gay Marriage? Vote Democratic." Jeffrey Davis, the sponsor of the truck, called in to the show and claimed that Senator Michele Bachmann had inspired the truck. *Dump Bachmann*'s Eva Young called Jeffrey Davis. Young asked Davis whether Bachmann or the Minnesota Family Council had helped him with the website content or design, and he denied that. He also said he was legally independent of the Republican Party of Minnesota—and that coordination would have been illegal (true). He also mentioned that some Republicans had told him he was making the party look bad. He wouldn't name the people who said that. He said there are about two hundred donors to his organization, and that he has personally put around $25,000 into this effort. He said the rest of the donors were in his report—but that a few donors had contributed most of the funding.

Davis said his main concern was that gay marriage would lead to church ministers being put in jail for quoting antigay bible verses (such as Leviticus 18:20). He referred to a bill (C-250) in Canada that he claimed would make sections of the bible "hate literature," but the text of that bill does not say this. Amnesty International Canada wrote a brief in favor of this bill, stating, "a conviction will result in only the clearest cases and most egregious circumstances. Moreover, Bill C-250 would not prevent people from believing what they wish" (*Christianity Today*, 2004).

As Senator Bachmann and her supporters became more strident and shrill, she still lacked support for her amendment. The senator from Stillwater soldiered on. By March 2005, *Dump Bachmann* described her as a "voice in the wilderness."

Bachmann was the only sponsor (later joined by senators Mady Reiter and Michael Jungbauer) of the Bachmann amendment in the Senate. Representative Dan Severson took over from Representative Mary Liz Holberg as chief author of the House bill. Former senator and Democratic pundit Ember Reichgott Junge on Channel 5's *At Issue* attributed a Bachmann quote to Holberg. According to Reichgott Junge, Holberg confronted her about this and was not happy to have the Bachmann statement attributed to her.

Bachmann was quoted in the alt-weekly City Pages, saying, "Bills were deliberately not taken up because of the marriage issue. We had lost the battle, but encouraged one another that our God would be victorious in the end."

Bachmann bragged that her amendment was the single cause for what became dubbed the "Do Nothing Legislature" failing to pass a bonding bill.

Letter from Senator Michele Bachmann

On May 17, 2004, Michele Bachmann sent out a letter declaring the day was "a momentous day of change for America, but our God is mightier still." Bachmann proceeded to describe what happened on the Senate's final day of the session. She recalled how the session ended Sunday morning in "a thunder of confusion" and that it was "all over the issue of letting the people vote on marriage."

Bachmann claimed the "number one story" for the end of session was "the praying people, their clear pro-family witness for Christ, and their strength of numbers." Bachmann described her contribution:

> We tried for 21 hours to get the marriage bill on the Senate floor for debate and a vote, but were prevented from achieving that goal. The Senate refused to recognize me when I stood requesting to speak on any bill. Other Senators tried to speak and tried to yield their time to me so I could speak, but the Senate President

ignored me and continued to pound his gavel at the desk.

Bachmann's pleas were ignored, and the session ended in her words "with a thud." After the conclusion of the session, Bachmann's letter described meeting with "the faithful gathered with their signs" who consoled each other about losing the battle and "encouraged one another that our God would be victorious in the end." Bachmann concluded her letter by telling the people of Minnesota to keep praying because "as of today, homosexual marriage is legal in Massachusetts and that imposes a real threat to Minnesota's definition of marriage and to our civil and religious liberties."

The next day Bachmann was at the Family Research Council Press Conference pushing for the Federal Marriage Amendment.

Bachmann sounded a bit like Jerry Falwell when he said, "I really believe that the Pagans, and the abortionists, and the feminists, and the gays and lesbians, . . . the ACLU, People for the American Way—all of them who have tried to secularize America—I point the finger in their face and say 'you helped this [terrorist attack] happen'" (*700 Club*, September 13, 2001).

On September 16, 2004, Michele Bachmann, Marcus Bachmann, and Janet Boynes attended a MacLaurin Institute–sponsored debate on same-sex marriage between Dale Carpenter (a law professor, University of Minnesota) and Glenn Stanton of Focus on the Family. Both Michele Bachmann and Janet Boynes asked questions, but neither identified herself. Bachmann wanted to know what effect the amendment would have on families. Boynes, as always, voiced her fear that gay marriage would spread disease.

Dump Bachmann's Eva Young described what happened next. "After this event, I introduced myself to Michele Bachmann. Bachmann was extremely charming and introduced me to her husband, Marcus."

Marcus, who ran a Christian clinic, was often seen with his wife at public events and campaign appearances.

As expected, the Bachmann Amendment returned to the legislature in 2005, and Bachmann continued her antigay antics. Representative Mary Liz Holberg reintroduced her Anti-Marriage Constitutional Amendment. House File 0006 (HF0006) is a first step in the relentless effort by antigay activists to enshrine discrimination in the Minnesota Constitution. Eva Young took note of Bachmann's tireless effort to recruit religious leaders to support her amendment (*Dump Bachmann*, January 13, 2005).

From the OutFront Minnesota E-Nooz (Minnesota's statewide GLBT organization):

> Predictably, Senator Michele Bachmann has announced her intention to introduce her amendment bill in the Senate once again this session.
>
> Senator Bachmann has already enlisted eager voices to help her in her quest for discrimination. She has planned a press conference for today with the Reverend Bob Battle, in "honor" of the Reverend Martin Luther King Jr., purportedly to claim that he would not have stood with us in this fight. Yet Rev. King's support of openly gay civil rights activist Bayard Rustin, the organizer of the 1963 March on Washington, suggests otherwise. In November, Rev. King's widow, Coretta Scott King, was quoted as saying, "Freedom from discrimination based on sexual orientation is surely a fundamental human right in any great democracy, as much as freedom from racial, religious, gender or ethnic discrimination." Tying discrimination against GLBT people to Rev. King undermines the legacy and lessons of one of America's greatest heroes.

Battle wrote a column defending Bachmann in the *St. Paul Pioneer Press*. He was also profiled in the *Star Tribune* and said this: "This society has to make a course correction. . . . We've lost our moral dignity, lost our sense of family and morality, and we're about to go down the same path as the Roman Empire." Battle, like Senator Bachmann before him, left the Democratic Party and went to the Republicans to push his antigay animus.

March 11, 2005: Michele Bachmann was featured prominently at a capitol-steps rally supporting her "earthquake issue:" a constitutional amendment to prevent LGBT citizens from enjoying such rights as hospital visitation of lifelong partners aka the "Bachmann amendment." This rally featured Family Research Council President Tony Perkins as a keynote speaker. Perkins has ties to both Ku Klux Klan grand wizard David Duke and the Council of Conservative Citizens, another white supremacist group. Due to disastrous publicity that stemmed from the hate-filled signs of the 2004 rally, rally organizers made a concerted effort to discourage hand-designed signs.

April 7, 2005: Senator Bachmann failed to get a hearing on the Bachmann amendment and then failed to convince the Senate to break its rules and move the amendment to a floor vote. Later that afternoon, Bachmann was photographed spying on a pro–gay rights rally at the capitol while crouched behind the bushes. The photos generated blog and talk radio chatter and plenty of headlines for Bachmann.

April 9, 2005: Two days later, Bachmann and Representative Ray Vandeveer terminated a Scandia Township public town hall forum early after facing challenging questions. After the forum, two participants tried to continue their conversations with Bachmann in the women's bathroom. Bachmann ran screaming from the bathroom of the Scandia City Hall. She later filed a police report, claiming she was held against her will by two members of a "gay and lesbian activist group" after escaping a hostile audience. In fact, one of the women involved was a retired nun, and the other was the partner of explorer Ann Bancroft. Both women were constituents. Representative Ray Vandeveer, also at the meeting, declined to corroborate her bizarre version of events. The Washington County Sheriff Department investigated Bachmann's complaint and forwarded it to the county attorney's office, and it was dropped. It wasn't a good week for Senator Bachmann. (This incident became known as "Bathroomgate" and warrants its own chapter in this book.)

April 15, 2005: Eva Young debated Michele Bachmann about the Bachmann amendment on Joyce Harley's show on KKMS. During the debate, Bachmann discussed a court case in Oregon where the Oregon Supreme Court held that the marriage licenses of three thousand gays/lesbians from a county in Oregon were null and void. County Supervisors in Multnomah county had "issued licenses of their own accord, much the same way that San Francisco mayor Gavin Newsome did in San Francisco. . . . The intervening factor is that now there is a constitutional marriage amendment that the voters of Oregon passed last November. . . . We may have had a very different result from the Supreme Court of Oregon but for the constitutional amendment going through." Bachmann stated that constitutional amendments were needed so "the courts will follow the constitution. When they don't, courts will do whatever they so choose." Bachmann failed to mention that constitutional bans on same-sex marriage also preclude legislatures from passing legislation to allow gays to participate in the institution of marriage. Young countered Bachmann by pointing out the language of her amendment that not only banned marriage between gays but also included "legal equivalent" language:

This legal equivalent language, it's vague, and this will be litigated in the courts—the same courts that do those "activist decisions" that you're [Senator Bachmann] criticizing. My other question is about activist judges because supposedly the reason for this amendment is because of activist judges. Well I'm wondering what you think about the activist judge who made the decision to overturn the decision the City of Minneapolis made to offer domestic partner benefits to their employees? The city wanted to do that. The voters in the city of Minneapolis want to offer domestic partner benefits. But there was a judge who decided it was against state law. Michele Bachmann stated that the language was not vague, but failed to back that up. She also did not respond to Young's question asking her about the Judge who overturned City of Minneapolis–provided Domestic Partner benefits.

At the end of the debate, Young pointed out that signs such as "Death Penalty for Homosexuals" were prominent at the 2004 rally for the Bachmann amendment and that Senator Bachmann and Governor Tim Pawlenty failed to speak out against those signs. Bachmann responded that for the record she did speak out against those signs. After the debate Young searched for examples of where Bachmann had spoken out publicly against those signs and failed to find any evidence.

April 24, 2005: There is no better example of the deep-seated animosity Michele Bachmann carried toward gay people than this letter from Fred Comb about the senator refusing to shake hands with him.

Comb, a constituent of Michele Bachmann's, had an appointment for a meeting with her on the day of the 2004 OutFront Rally. He was on a skiing vacation with his son and called Bachmann's office the day before the meeting to confirm that the meeting was on. He did not want to fly back early with his son, if there would be no meeting. At that time, Bachmann's office told him the meeting was still on. So Fred and his son cut short their vacation in order to meet with Senator Bachmann. The following morning, someone from Bachmann's office left a message on Fred's voice mail stating that Bachmann had an emergency outside the building and would not be able to make the meeting. Other constituents of Bachmann reported to Fred that she was seen alone in her office at the meeting time.

This was his account:

> My Senator is Michele Bachmann (lucky me) and she actually met constituents today. . . . I sat next to her in the meeting and when it was my turn to speak, I introduced myself and extended my hand, as I always do. To anyone! I held my hand out for what seemed like eternity and I watched her hands rise from her lap as she turned them palm side up, looked at them, and put them back in her lap. My hand still extended to force a response, she said, "My husband has pneumonia and I don't want to catch anything." Yeah right. She did not allow anyone from outside her district in the room except for two EX-GAYS who were there to protect her and defend her positions. I bet she thinks I'M the ass for holding my hand out for so long!!!
>
> In short, Michele Bachmann was RUDE, and not only that it was and is my opinion she LIED to me. She said, "My husband has pneumonia and I don't want to catch anything." If that's true and she refused to shake my hand because she didn't want to "catch

anything," then you tell me, why did she shake other hands and hug others moments after the meeting?

These are the types of stories that describe Michele Bachmann's character.

September 17, 2005: Michele Bachmann took her antigay dog-and-pony show on the road to Hutchinson, Minnesota, and *Dump Bachmann*'s Eva Young was there.

Michele Bachmann was late to the event because she came by plane, and the plane was late. It is still not clear who paid for the plane and whether she flew by corporate jet.

When she arrived at the event, she had her ex-lesbian, African American sidekick Janet Boynes in tow. After Bachmann's speech, Eva Young challenged Bachmann during the Q and A about several of her points. For example, Bachmann ranted on about Canada's so-called hate speech law (C-250). Eva Young pointed out that law had nothing to do with marriage equality and would not be constitutional in the United States because it violates the First Amendment. Eva Young asked Bachmann if she had read the First Amendment, and Bachmann said that she had read it. Eva Young suggested Bachmann reread it. Bachmann also talked about how the U.S. House of Representatives passed a hate crimes law. That law was not about hate speech, but rather was about preventing brutal murders such as that of Matthew Shepard, who was tied to a fence post and beaten to death, or of Billy Jack Gaither, who was burned alive.

Eva Young reported, "Bachmann then brought up the 'hate crime' of Jesse Dirkhissing who was raped and murdered by two gay men. The Dirkhissing case was an appalling case. There are similar cases of teenage girls getting victimized in similar ways (by men). I'm sure Bachmann brought up the Dirkhissing case to suggest that all gay men were like the perpetrators in that case."

Bachmann talked about how both she and her children have gotten death threats because of what she has been doing.

Janet Boynes talked to Eva Young after the presentations. Boynes said she wanted to get together for coffee sometime. She said that she read Eva Young's blogs regularly, and she thought Young was too hard on "poor Michele"—whom Boynes claimed was a very nice person. Young told Janet that she didn't go after Bachmann personally.

Janet Boynes shared her tragic personal story at the meeting. She grew up in an abusive family. Several male family members sexually abused her. She talked about "living in the lesbian lifestyle" for eleven years, and then she was "saved" and is now no longer a lesbian. She said she was single and wanted to know if any of the men in the audience were looking.

Bachmann's campaign against the rights of gay people went dormant from the time she was elected to Congress until her announcement of her decision to seek the Republican Party nomination to be the candidate for president of the United States.

Bachmann Takes the Marriage Vow

In July 2011, Bachmann signed the Family Leader's theocratic pledge titled "The Marriage Vow—The Declaration of Dependence upon Marriage and Family." The Family Leader will only endorse a candidate who signs the pledge.

The Family Leader's pledge is seven pages long, with footnotes. A bizarre quote:

> Slavery had a disastrous impact on African-American families, yet sadly a child born into slavery in 1860 was more likely to be raised by his mother and father in a

two-parent household than was an African-American baby born after the election of the USA's first African-American President.

Candidates were required to pledge "fidelity to one's spouse" and "respect for the marital bonds of others." Of course, the Family Leader's pledge contained a clause about Bachmann's "earthquake issue": "Vigorous opposition to any redefinition of marriage," including bigamy and polygamy and, of course, same-sex marriage. There was the obligatory antiabortion clause: "Humane protection of women and the innocent fruit of conjugal intimacy."

Candidates are required to have "recognition" that married people "enjoy better health, better sex and longer lives" and to underscore this bizarre statement, another equally bizarre clause required "recognition that robust childbearing and reproduction is beneficial to U.S. demographic, economic, strategic and actuarial health and security."

Candidates were also required to reject "Shariah Islam."

The irony-deprived document contained this punch line: "Fierce defense of the First Amendment . . ."

After getting pushback from antigay African American ministers, the Family Leader removed the language suggesting that African American children did better under slavery than they do under Barack Obama's administration. Michele Bachmann denied reading the slavery language when she signed the pledge. This is rather strange because the slavery language was the first paragraph on the first page of the pledge.

Bachmann then signed the National Organization for Marriage pledge on August 4, 2011, committing herself to the following:

- Support and send to the states a federal marriage amendment defining marriage as one man and one woman
- Defend DOMA in court

- Appoint judges and an attorney general who will respect the original meaning of the Constitution
- Appoint a presidential commission to investigate harassment of traditional marriage supporters
- Support legislation that would return to the people of D.C. their right to vote for marriage

Michele Bachmann has come full circle.

CHAPTER 3

Bachmann's Mean Streak (and Other Campaign Problems)

Michele Bachmann has a reputation for being a voracious campaigner and a formidable fund-raiser. That may be true, but in her wake, she's left more than a few casualties: honesty, transparency, accuracy, integrity, party loyalty, and key supporters.

In a heavily Republican district, Bachmann's campaigns should have been cakewalks. Instead, she has always treated them like cliffhangers, resorting to dirty, vicious, and disingenuous campaign tactics—even against fellow Republicans—and incessant desperate appeals for donations. That Bachmann continues to employ these campaign tactics in her presidential crusade is no surprise. That they continue to work for her, is.

Most of Bachmann's major contributors live outside the 6th Congressional District, which may explain her obvious disinterest in her constituents once she's elected; most of the early money in her first congressional campaign came from the wealthy enclaves around Lake Minnetonka and the western suburbs of Minneapolis. Now that she's running for president, Bachmann has all but given up the pretense of representing anyone but Michele Bachmann.

The following vignettes from Bachmann's political career should have served as signposts of what was to come. Unfortunately, few were paying attention.

Whom Does Bachmann Really Represent?

Michele Bachmann set her political career afloat on a tide of money from outside the 6th Congressional District that she was running to represent. In 2005, the year before her first congressional election, 78 percent of the itemized campaign contributions she raked in came from outside the 6th CD. In fact, in the last quarter of 2005, Bachmann vacuumed up $84,823 in itemized contributions, and $77,033 of that—a whopping 91 percent— came from outside the 6th CD.

Said Eva Young, a sponsor of DumpBachmann.com, in a press release:

> That's unheard of even in today's climate of out-of-control, special-interest campaign spending. Clearly these wealthy contributors pouring money into Bachmann's campaign from outside the district are a special interest. They expect something in return for their large

contributions besides representation, because they can't even vote for her.

Bachmann took in $264,099 in itemized individual and Political Action Committee contributions in 2005. Of that amount, carpetbagging contributions from outside the 6th CD totaled $205,752. Another $49,683 came from unitemized contributions, the source of which cannot be determined.

The vast majority of Bachmann's itemized contributions in 2005 ranged from several hundred dollars up to the maximum allowed—$4,200 total for the primary and general elections. Bachmann bagged $3,000 from Phyllis Schlafly's Eagle Forum PAC, and a total of $5,000 came in from Barry Conner, a wealthy Georgia real estate developer who advocated the abolition of all public education, and his wife Bridget Conner.

Why would someone like Bachmann, who proclaims to be such a friend of education, be taking thousands of dollars from a wealthy out-of-state contributor who wants to abolish public education? The Conners surely expect something for their largesse.

Young also noted that two major donors to Bachmann's campaign, Stacy Taylor and John Scribante, served on the Board of Governors of the radical-right organization the Center for National Policy (CNP), and at least one of them—Scribante—still is affiliated with the group as of this writing.

This isn't really surprising, though. The CNP's roster of past and present members and directors reads like a who's who of the radical religious right, including some of Bachmann's other fellow travelers: James Dobson, Phyllis Schlafly, Grover Norquist, Tony Perkins.

Concluded Young:

> When you look at the big picture of where Michele
> Bachmann's financial support is coming from, you have
> to wonder who she really will represent. The numbers
> speak for themselves—and it's not the 6th Congres-
> sional District.

Ethical Lapses

Bachmann bullied her way through the 6th CD GOP endorse-
ment process in 2006. The pseudonymous Republican activist
"Tony Garcia" reported the ethical lapses in a series of posts at his
Always Right, Usually Correct blog.

In a January 6, 2006, post, Garcia reported on a "deceptive"
push poll used by the Bachmann campaign. Push polls are phone
campaigns designed to sound like independent political polls that
in reality are simply political campaigns spreading misinformation
or other negative material.

A March 19, 2006, post reported on Bachmann campaign
shenanigans at the Senate District 52 GOP convention:

> "Bachmann . . . Not Enough Character to
> Represent DECENT Republicans"
>
> A bird told me that Michele Bachmann scored big at
> the SD 52 BPOU yesterday. Somehow, through a vot-
> ing block that controlled the majority of the delegates
> at the convention, Bachmann supporters were able to
> change the rules of the convention at will to satisfy their
> own whims. It seems one thing that the Bachmann bloc

wanted to do was move the election of delegates early in the agenda so they could all leave afterwards. Their only desire was to be delegates at the 6th Congressional District.

They were told what slate of delegates to vote for so that all of the slate would be ensured election as delegates. This slate, according to the source, were all friends and fellow church goers of Michele Bachmann.

OK, yes, this is how the system works. I should say, yes, the system allows this. But is this REALLY the mentality we want to send to Washington?

Garcia went to say something about Bachmann's rumored malingering:

"Bachmann Too Weakened to Hold Commitments"

It seems that Michele Bachmann discovered at 7:30 pm Saturday night that she needs to rest from her surgery three weeks ago and was unable to hold to her commitments. I have talked to many people in the medical community who confirmed that "rest" after three weeks is indicative of either someone who is using their condition as an excuse (or for sympathy) OR someone whose health is very poor.

To give extra weight to this, my wife's boss had the same surgery. He was the same age, a bit out of shape in comparison and was back to full strength in less than a week. His job, more stressful and more hours than Bachmann's without question.

Here's another post from March 20, 2006, from the *Checks and Balances* blog:

"Vandalism and Theft of Lawn Signs at Forest Lake
Senate District 52 Convention"

Sometime between 1:30 am and 7:00 am Saturday
morning an individual or individuals decided to commit
campaign terrorism at Forest Lake High School before
the Republican Senate District 52 convention. It is our
understanding volunteers for the Rep. Phil Krinkie
(R-53A, Lexington) and Rep. Jim Knoblach (R-16A, St.
Cloud) for Congress campaigns completed their campaign signs placement in the early morning hours and
left only to return the next day to find all of their work
gone and even some damage to the auditorium ceiling.
In the place of the Krinkie and Knoblach signs [were]
Bachmann ones.

A police report was filed and we understand the
police are reviewing a video surveillance tape that shows
the perpetrator or perpetrators. This is Sen. Michele
Bachmann's (R-52, Stillwater) home district and early
speculation is some of her zealous supporters may have
been involved. We are not sure if the Bachmann campaign is involved, but it is just curious that the Krinkie
and Knoblach signage was removed and replaced by
Bachmann's. It could be an indicator of the person's
preferences in this race. The Jay Esme campaign placed
their signs before the start of the convention.

In addition to this we understand as the delegate slates
for the Congressional convention were advanced, the
Bachmann (campaign) failed to include loyal supporter
Rep. Matt Dean (R-52B, Stillwater) on their slate. This
was a great surprise to the delegates and a delegate who
was offended by the result stepped down to make sure
Dean had a spot.

Here is Republican activist Garcia's comment on the Bachmann campaign's "hijinks": "She runs away from potentially tough questioning, her campaign supporters seem to be involved in illegal activity (vandalism and theft of political signs is something the state wants to make into a FELONY) and stacking the vote to gain a distortion of support . . . this is not a person of character no matter what her positions on issues are."

Here's what Garcia said in a March 30, 2006, post:

> I have been critical of the slate-fixing (within the rules, but slimeballish nonetheless) by the Bachmann campaign. There is a long term consequence to her tactics.
>
> First, what is she doing?
>
> In a nutshell she mobilized many people to attend the caucuses with one intention: become delegates to become delegate [*sic*] to endorse Bachmann. The mobilization part is great. The problem is that these people are not party activists. They are robots being led to do one thing: endorse Bachmann.

Garcia went on to describe the effect Bachmann's delegates would have on the party:

> Bachmann's lemmings are succeeding in one thing . . . kicking out as many people as possible that do not support Bachmann. The people that are getting kicked out to the streets are the longtime grassroots people. The people who man the executive committees, the chairs, secretaries, treasurers and even state legislators. That leaves these single-minded drones in those positions. Since their sole purpose of being a delegate and being in the process is to endorse the least electable candidate, their objective will be completed by mid-summer.

They will not be filling and or performing the roles they are supplanting. They will also have chased away a few of the activists from continuing their role (myself and a few others that I have talked to will be either inactive or leave the party as of the convention if Bachmann wins).

I know, I am assuming quite a negative aspect on these people. From what I have heard from many eyewitness accounts the Bachmann sheep are rude, impolite, nasty and disinterested except for voting for each other.

Another post from Garcia, from April 6, 2006, described how Bachmann avoided questions about her ethics:

I do not know what it was like before I got involved in politics (about 1995), but I have noticed since I became involved that almost every time someone tries to invoke the 11th Commandment (according to Ronald Reagan, "Thou shalt not speak ill of any fellow Republican"), it is because they (or their candidate) have a lot they don't want discussed. Other times it is someone who has thrown a ton of "mud" and just as the retaliations are about to make them look bad they say, "Hey, remember the 11th Commandment. I'm sorry. Let's move forward."

Michele Bachmann has had the most misleading campaign. Now that she is being called to the carpet for her lies, distortions and half-truths she sends out a message in her newsletter.

"In our interests to see the campaign for the endorsement remain positive and focused on the issues, we've set up a website encouraging candidates, campaigns and the public to keep the messages positive. Check it out and sign Ronald Reagan's 11th Commandment: Thou shall never speak badly of another Republican. [At this point, Tony Garcia's blog post is linked to a now-defunct website titled keepitpositive06.com.]

"Remember to spread the word too, because Republicans have to stick together this year."

Michele, positivity includes the truth (which your campaign and you as an individual seem absent of).

Bachmann is the latest addition to the "Reagan's Commandment, so you don't talk bad about me." She has the most legitimate dirt against her . . . so it comes as no surprise that she suddenly wants everyone to follow "Thou shall NEVER speak badly of another Republican. Run on your own merit."

The reason I say this Commandment is abused is that the people like Bachmann distort facts, brazenly lie and then want everyone else to limit their responses to, well, no response. The least moral people in the party try to invoke this "commandment" upon others. The most moral people in the party simply live it.

After Bachmann won the endorsement on May 6, 2006, Tony Garcia followed up with these comments:

I am guessing the anti-Bachmann crowds (from the ethics-over-party segment of the Right and from the Left) are expecting some more scathing words from here. I will say that I am trying to follow up on a lead I was given. If it comes through, it will result in an interview that will be a very big story in the election. Until that story either falls through or comes through, there will be little from me about Bachmann.

Unfortunately, Garcia's alleged lead never materialized into anything, but he went on to describe the strong-arm tactics Bachmann used at the convention:

> Sorry, the responsibility of the delegates was to take that kind of stuff into consideration. Electability, I believe, is the general category. Ethics is another major category (one that the GOP has been casting aside recently). Each candidate was asked if there was anything in their backgrounds, past or present, that would embarrass the GOP should it be made public. Bachmann answered "No" and the committee knew that was a lie.

Apparently, the embarrassment was Bachmann sticking the taxpayers with her cable TV bill. Garcia continued to describe something remarkable—that delegates were afraid of Bachmann:

> They had the opportunity to not forward Bachmann's name for endorsement and from what my source inside that committee reported, that was close to happening. The only reason it didn't was for fear of their own personal safety. The exact wording was, "We would not make it out of this building alive," and was mostly tongue in cheek. I don't think they actually meant they'd be killed.
> You had the chance to put forward a candidate that did not have the baggage—most of which you already knew about. Instead the GOP endorsed Bachmann and with it lost a good number of conservative supporters.

And then Garcia posted this on his blog on April 8, 2006:

> Well, I had one last hope that at least to a person's face she would be honest. I was wrong. She flat out lied.

Here's how the conversation went between her, her husband and me.

Michele [as she was leaving the auditorium after her speech]: Hi, Tony.

Tony: Hello, Senator Bachmann. I have a question for you.

Michele [stops walking and faces me]: OK.

Tony: In your lit piece about your Taxpayer's League Score you are using outdated 2004 information. Why did you not use the information released last September?

Michele: No, that is a lie from Krinkie's campaign.

Tony: I'm talking about YOUR lit piece using outdated information.

Michele [starts to walk away]: You should look it up for yourself at the Taxpayer's League Website. My information is straight from there.

Tony: I understand that. My question is why are you using outdated information?

Michele kept walking away, turned back again, looked, and continued.

Tony: Ms. Bachmann, why are you using outdated information for your literature?

Michele: I don't know.

Tony: Is that the answer I quote tomorrow on the air?

Michele: You quote whatever you want.

Tony: Thanks, but only what you actually say.

Michele's husband [muttering and barely audible, so I could be wrong about this]: Asshole.

Michele's husband, then shouting back: You're inappropriate.

Tony: I'm sorry, I don't understand. How is trying to understand your campaign's distortions "inappropriate"? Is seeking the truth "inappropriate"?

At that point one of her volunteers got in the way, "Is there a problem?"

Tony: Yes, I want to know why your candidate is using misleading information on her literature.

Volunteer: I don't know, I'm just a volunteer.

Tony: Oddly enough Michele doesn't know why she is doing that either. That is a problem in a candidate.

By then Michele and her appropriate (what the hell?) husband were gone. I went back to get more donuts from her table. (Dammit, make them spend their money!!)

Garcia continued,

Not only did she try to lie directly about the literature pieces, not only is she a nasty person behind-the-scenes to people who cannot help her, but she is a poor excuse for a candidate. She is the GOP's version of Cynthia McKinney.

She is a coward and cannot handle tough questioning. When we were going to have her on our show back in September there was a lot of activity from her opposition trying to organize many callers to ask her tough questions. She called and said she will hang up if we take any calls.

In 2007, after reporter Eric Black left the Minneapolis-based *Star Tribune* newspaper, he recalled on his blog a bizarre incident that revealed Bachmann's "mean streak" from the May 6 convention:

> I was covering the convention and was at a press table in the lobby. A crowd gathered around Bachmann, her entourage and [a] woman.
>
> By the time I got there, the woman was verging on tears, but was continuing to ask what specific form of retaliation she had to fear.
>
> Bachmann portrayed an eerie calm and maintained an expression with which I later became more familiar from covering her at other stressful moments. The smile never left her face and her gaze was steady, eyes open very wide. I heard her say "you will pay, you will pay, you will pay" in answer to the woman's insistent questioning, but as far I could hear, she never specified how.
>
> I half-heartedly tried to talk to the woman as her husband led her away in tears, but he asked me to give her space to calm down, and I did. I didn't see her again that day to follow up.

Unfortunately, Eric Black decided not to report that incident in the *Star Tribune*, but we are grateful he later chose to relate the story of Bachmann's mean streak.

Bachmann's Mean Streak

It will be interesting to see whether the national press will also choose not to report Bachmann's lack of ethics and her mean streak.

Dump Bachmann's Eva Young interviewed Michael Gerster, a campaign staffer with Bachmann opponent Phil Krinkie, on May 7, 2006, at the 6th Congressional District Convention in Monticello, Minnesota. Gerster offered some revealing insights into Bachmann's character.

EY: I'm interviewing Michael Gerster, who is a big supporter of Phil Krinkie.

MG: I'm on the campaign staff.

EY: The reason I find this rather notable is I found your picture on Michele Bachmann's website. And the caption was "Michele Bachmann with a veteran."

MG: OK I was not aware that it was on the website. She knows my position now about using my image. Yesterday they had my picture along with another veteran that happened to be chairman of her district. And she did not have permission to use either one of our images. And this happened to be for a posthumous award ceremony for the other man's father. And in the picture he was getting a little teary eyed accepting the award. And neither one of us wanted that picture displayed. We requested and finally insisted that they remove the picture. A number of people were asking me did I drop the Krinkie campaign because I'm all of a sudden pictured in two areas and so we're getting used to this—that we have to correct certain issues in this campaign.

EY: There was Senator Bachmann's other claim—that she had the best taxpayer league voting record—

MG: Oh—if you'd look at the taxpayer league during the timeframe that she wanted to mention, she had 100%—but she forgot to put in 2005 where she was at 77, 75 somewhere in that neighborhood.

Watch "Interview with Michael Gerster 5/7/06," on YouTube.

A Constituency of One

Michele Bachmann gained a reputation in the Minnesota State Senate for using her office to promote the interests of one constituent: Michele Bachmann. A 2008 examination of official mailings from Bachmann in her first six months in Congress showed that she carried those habits to Washington.

On Michele Bachmann's congressional website, she pledged to uphold the "American Taxpayers Bill of Rights," which calls on House conservatives to "Restore fiscal discipline and find innovative new ways to do MORE with LESS. . . . If families in America can tighten their belts, so too can bureaucrats in Washington."

Yet when it came to Bachmann's self-promotion at taxpayer expense, there was no fiscal dieting to be found. An examination of congressional mailing expenditures from the first six months of 2007 showed Bachmann to be the runaway big spender in the Minnesota delegation, doing less for her constituents with more tax dollars to promote herself.

Bachmann's oversize four-color glossy mailings were the subject of much debate in the 6th District. Most recently, a Stearns County constituent questioned the expenditures for Bachmann's puffery in a *St. Cloud Times* editorial. Not surprisingly, Bachmann's office was not forthcoming with an explanation of the costs; however, all members of Congress must file quarterly reports of their offices' expenditures—including details of mass mailings to constituents conducted under the franking privilege. That information eventually is published in a Statement of Disbursements for the House of Representatives.

The most recent Statements of Disbursements that were available in early 2008 when this investigation took place covered only the first two quarters of 2007. Only four members of the Minnesota delegation—Bachmann, Keith Ellison, Jim Ramstad, and Tim Walz—reported significant mass mailings of more than ten thousand. The House defines mass mailings as "unsolicited mailings of substantially identical content to 500 or more persons in a session of Congress." Representatives Jim Oberstar and Colin Peterson reported minor mass mailings, and Betty McCollum and John Kline reported no mass mailings during the period covered.

Based on those reports, the cost for Bachmann's first mass mailing last year was 46 cents apiece for printing and postage—more than double the 22 cents apiece that mailings for Walz and Ramstad cost and significantly higher than Ellison's per-piece cost of 28 cents. The biggest difference was in the production costs of the mailings. Bachmann spent a total of $32,589 with the Franking Group for mass mailings totaling 136,465, for a production cost of 24 cents each—far beyond what her colleagues in either party spent.

Ellison spent $31,358 with Gold Communications for mass mailings, totaling 265,522—a production cost of just 12 cents apiece. Walz's figures show only $2,210 spent on the printing of 101,017 pieces, for a meager production cost of 2 cents each. Ramstad paid Catterton Printing $15,295 for mass mailings totaling 300,017—a production cost of only 5 cents each.

One of Bachmann's mailings that landed in our mailbox in the fall of 2007 was typical of her misrepresentations. It announced that Bachmann was "Fighting Waste and Controlling Spending." Bachmann boasted that she cosponsored the "Family Budget Protection Act. . . . Among other things, the bill would establish a commission to investigate all federal programs and compile a list of potential savings from waste, fraud and abuse." That sounded an awful lot like what the Government Accountability Office and the Office of the Inspector General already do, but Bachmann wanted to create another bloated federal commission to investigate it?

Then Bachmann voted against the appropriations bill for the Office of the Inspector General, and when Bachmann had an opportunity to strengthen the integrity of the Inspector General's

Office on October 3 with a vote on H.R. 928, the "Improving Government Accountability Act," she was one of only 11 members who voted against it. Bachmann later claimed she really meant to vote yes on H.R. 928, but the House record still shows Bachmann voting no. Nice try, Michele.

Then there's the item in her mailer about how Bachmann was "Working for Affordable Health Care." "Congresswoman Michele Bachmann is working to provide commonsense solutions to give more Americans access to affordable health care," the poster-sized mailing claimed.

Sure thing—unless you were a poor kid on the State Children's Health Insurance Program (she opposed it). Or Bachmann & Associates employees (they got no employee health insurance benefits). Or Bachmann campaign workers (they got no health insurance benefits in her 2006 campaign either).

And what Bachmann mailing would be complete without a staged photo of Michele and someone in uniform? Bachmann was shown at a veteran's bedside as she "talks with Marine Corporal Rhea Curtis of St. Paul about her military service." It's a safe bet, however, that Bachmann didn't talk with Corporal Curtis about her vote against a measure that would ensure that Curtis's next tour of duty in Iraq could not exceed the length of time she spent between tours.

Bachmann's Court

Besides her periodic promotional mailings, Bachmann had only one public, in-person town hall meeting in her district from the time of her election in 2006 until September 2011. She has forsaken those for what are called "tele-town hall meetings." *Dump Bachmann* contributor Karl Bremer related his experience with Bachmann's new form of constituent contact in a 2008 post:

Last week, I felt honored, like the Queen invited me to her court.

Well, not really. But after seven years of representing me in the state legislature and Congress, I finally got my first call from Michele Bachmann, inviting me to engage in a question-and-answer session with her.

Okay, not exactly. I got an anonymous robo-call from somewhere telling me to stay on the line and I could participate in a tele-town forum with the congress-woman. A few seconds later, I became party to a conversation between Bachmann and another caller.

Well, sort of. I could hear their conversation, but I couldn't participate in it. Eventually, robo-voice advised me to press "star-three" to signal that I wished to ask the congresswoman a question myself. So I did, and thus began a 25-minute wait through an endless stream of friendly callers that ended abruptly without me ever getting to talk to Michele.

Welcome to constituent service, Bachmann style.

Our 6th District congresswoman isn't known for her robust communication with constituents—at least those not on her list of supporters. In fact, Bachmann has nurtured a reputation over the years for not com-municating with constituents at all, unless it serves to promote herself or her agenda in some way. Rare is the constituent who disagrees with Michele Bachmann and receives even an acknowledgement of a letter, e-mail, or phone call.

In that spirit, Bachmann has not had one public town hall meeting in the district since being elected. And when she has appeared on local talk radio call-in shows, she has refused to take calls.

A tele-town hall is more to Bachmann's liking, and a

lot less messy. She can screen every caller's name and address before allowing them to ask a question, and simply reject or keep on interminable hold those she doesn't want to talk to. She can have staff at her side awaiting her commands to get answers to questions, rather than having to think on her feet before a live audience. No more worries about getting ambushed at a public meeting by an angry constituent—or having to shake hands with any homosexuals. And no more dealing with those mean media people who are always beating her up.

The calls are supposedly made at random from constituent lists. But amazingly, while Bachmann won in our district with only 50.3 percent of the vote—barely half—every one of the seven or eight callers who was allowed to ask a question while I was eavesdropping was clearly a supporter.

In between the softball questions and plaudits for visiting Iraq, Bachmann had ample opportunities to remind us who she was and that she has five kids and twenty-three foster kids and a small business, so she and her husband know what it's like to provide food for themselves and raise a family. Kind of like the little commercials you get while you're on hold with a credit-card company.

Some of the questions begged for a follow-up. But that's the beauty of a tele-town hall, at least for politicians like Bachmann. If you don't like the caller's question, you can just ignore it, answer with something totally irrelevant, and move on to the next one with no consequences.

Like the Hugo school teacher who asked Bachmann how local schools could get more funding without going to property taxpayers for levy after levy. Bachmann responded first by making up some inflated figures about the state's share of school funding (it declined during Bachmann's tenure in the legislature from 86.7 percent in 2003–04 to 82.7 percent in 2006–07), and then launched into a disjointed rant about how "politicized" public schools are today. The poor teacher is probably still scratching his head.

To be fair, in the hands of a politician truly interested in expanding his or her reach to constituents—and not just cultivating their supporters—tele-town halls could be a useful tool in addition to regular in-person town hall meetings. They afford the opportunity to have at least some semblance of contact with their representative for those who otherwise could not—or would not—venture out to a live town hall meeting.

But if its early proponents—Bachmann and her GOP mentor in the Second District, John Kline—are any indication, I fear it will be used for just the opposite.

In Bachmann's case, it's clear that the tele-town hall is simply another tool with which to further isolate herself from her constituents, tightly control the dialogue, and pursue the agenda of her choice, rather than theirs. Indeed, why concern yourself with such mundane matters as school funding when there are liberals and homos lurking in your children's classrooms?

Kline has admitted that's a motivating factor in his decision to use them, saying live town hall meetings have become nothing more than "partisan battlegrounds." In other words, his opponents can show up there.

Other aspects of these tele-town hall "events" are still murky. Are they considered official public events or campaign events? If public, is a complete transcript available for the entire event? Are records of accepted versus rejected callers available? Are callers screened, and if so, by whom and based on what criteria?

Republicans—in particular George W. Bush—have mastered the Orwellian art of controlling their public audiences in order to project only positive images of their appearances, to the point of having suspected antagonists arrested simply because of the T-shirts they were wearing. But even troublesome T-shirts are a thing of the past with tele-town halls.

Whether she's hiding from constituents in a town hall restroom or behind the bushes at a state capitol rally, Michele Bachmann long has shown a similar disdain for those who do not march lockstep with her. With tele-town halls, she now has yet another means by which she can avoid them.

Marcus Miles

Bachmann hasn't been above getting her husband, Marcus, some "driving around money" while he worked for her campaigns. She may wish to shield Marcus from the prying eyes of the national media as she seeks the presidency, but both she and Marcus have some explaining to do about a $6,230 payment from her 2006 campaign to Marcus for "mileage reimbursement."

The payment was made on December 15, 2006, and was reported on Bachmann's year-end Federal Election Commission (FEC) statement from 2006. It covered the period of November 28, 2006, to December 31, 2006. Curiously, Marcus's last name was misspelled on Bachmann's own FEC report.

Based on the federal mileage reimbursement rate of 44.5 cents/mile at the time, that payment represents exactly 14,000 miles. That's a lot of miles that Marcus put in for Michele's campaign in thirty-four days—418 miles a day, to be exact—especially considering that Marcus claimed them a month after the 2006 election was over. It would be interesting to see Marcus's mileage logs from that busy month on the road.

DumpBachmann.com thought the expense was a bit suspicious at the time and noted the sizable disbursement on February 14, 2007. As usual, it was ignored by the mainstream media, and nothing more was ever heard about it.

Then, on Bachmann's next FEC report for First Quarter 2007, a mysterious entry showed up: a February 22, 2007, receipt to the campaign from Marcus Bachmann for the exact same amount as the earlier mileage payment—$6,230. The entry was identified as "Offsets to Operating Expenditures," which according to FEC rules includes refunds, rebates, and returns of deposits. An aggregate total of $6,530 was listed in the same entry. The additional $300 shown in the aggregate total for Marcus Bachmann's campaign "donations" was most likely for receipt of a donation from "Marcus Bachman" [sic] to Michele's campaign for $300 for "personal use of vehicle" dated December 11, 2006.

Was this refund from Marcus Bachmann an admission that the "mileage reimbursement" and the vehicle use donation were erroneously paid to him, and if so, what prompted it eight days after *Dump Bachmann* reported it, if not *Dump Bachmann*?

Bachmann's campaign didn't respond to a request for an explanation of Marcus's mileage mystery. Maybe the FEC should ask for one.

Getting the FEC Involved

In 2005, Michele Bachmann sent out a fund-raising appeal that included a letter from Renee Doyle, the president and founder of "nonprofit" EdWatch Minnesota. EdWatch is a 501(c3) nonprofit organization. An organization that is classified as a nonprofit is strictly prohibited from campaigning for a specific candidate.

The letter from Renee Doyle repeatedly mentioned EdWatch and listed EdWatch's address at the bottom of the letter. It was signed "Renee T Doyle, Founder and President, EdWatch Inc." At the bottom of the letter it said "Prepared and Paid for by Bachmann for Congress."

Dump Bachmann encouraged readers who received the EdWatch Minnesota mailing requesting contributions to Bachmann's campaign to file an FEC complaint against Bachmann and a complaint with the IRS about EdWatch. *Dump Bachmann* contributor Karl Bremer did just that. This is his story of the outcome.

When Bremer filed a Federal Elections Commission (FEC) complaint against Michele Bachmann in September 2005, he never expected to be the subject of lies and character assassination by Tom DeLay's leading attack-dog lawyer, Donald F. McGahn II.

Bremer's complaint alleged that a solicitation for support for Bachmann was sent out by the anti–public education nonprofit group EdWatch in violation of FEC rules. A similar complaint was registered with the IRS.

The FEC determined that the complaint merited a full investigation; however, following the FEC investigation, Bremer's complaint was not upheld. It wasn't until recently, though, that he discovered the extent to which Bachmann and her hired gun went to smear him in their response to the FEC—which included filing false statements.

Yet first a little background on the lawyer for the Bachmann for Congress campaign.

Donald F. McGahn II made a name for himself as a campaign lawyer for former Texas congressman Tom DeLay, who himself was indicted for his alleged role in a campaign finance scheme.

He also served as a campaign finance lawyer for DeLay's scandal-ridden ARMPAC.

Some references.

Among his other achievements, McGahn once browbeat some Houston TV stations into not running anti-DeLay ads, threatening that they contained allegations that were "actionable." So the role of attacking the messenger was nothing new for McGahn.

McGahn also represented numerous other Republicans and the National Republican Congressional Committee (NRCC) before the FEC. At the time that he was representing Bachmann before the FEC, McGahn was on a $25,000 retainer with the NRCC. (For the record, Karl Bremer filed his notarized complaint on his own behalf.)

In McGahn's response to the FEC on behalf of the Bachmann for Congress campaign, he began by describing Bremer as "a paid Democratic-Farmer-Labor operative," citing "Exhibit 3" that characterized Bremer as a "writer for the House DFL [Minnesota Democratic-Farmer-Labor Party] media office."

That was the first lie for the big-shot lawyer. Bremer hadn't worked for the House DFL Media Office since 2002.

McGahn described Bremer as a "media gadfly," presumably because of his extensive publication history in thirty years as a professional writer, and included a number of Bremer's op-ed columns and letters in local papers as "evidence." There was even one on Mark Kennedy in there. Bremer guesses that McGahn simply got carried away.

"More specifically," McGahn continued, "Bremer has been labeled an 'anti-Bachmann agitator' and a 'Bachmann opponent.'"

So, being an opponent of a politician made Bremer's complaint suspect? How many FEC complaints are filed against candidates by their supporters?

The $25,000-a-month counselor couldn't even spell his client's name right: "He is a participant in a web blog entitled Dump

Michelle Bachmann [*sic*]," wrote McGahn, with ten pages of exhibits from DumpBachmann.com included as evidence. "This blog has publicly encouraged readers to file complaints against Bachmann, and sets forth an outline of what ultimately became the complaint in this matter. And of course, after the complaint was filed, it was quickly added to the *Dump Michelle* [*sic*] *Bachmann* website. Thus, this current complaint should be seen for what it is: a vindictive political vendetta filed by a paid Democrat [*sic*]operative against Bachmann, designed to get headlines at her expense."

That was Lie Number Two for McGahn.

In a footnote, McGahn even went so far as to suggest that DumpBachmann.com might be in violation of some law: "The blog itself appears problematic. In addition to expressly advocating the defeat of Michelle [*sic*] Bachmann, a DFL operative appears to be involved to a significant degree, and appears to exercise at least some control over the blog. This takes the blog out of the protection afforded by FEC Advisory Opinion 2005–16."

Those were Lies Number Three and Four (Bremer never had any control whatsoever over DumpBachmann.com). Yet the Bachmann-DeLay defender used these fabrications to imply illegal behavior on Bremer's part or on the part of DumpBachmann.com.

Don McGahn was a familiar face at the FEC and no doubt made plenty of friends over there. In fact, McGahn was being considered in 2005 as an interim appointment to the commission. He would have fit right into the Bush administration's approach to oversight and accountability.

Discussing how FEC commissioners are chosen, McGahn told an interviewer in 2003 that "it's not like other agencies because you have . . . the fox guarding the hen-house. You gonna appoint your guys to make sure you are taken care of. The original intent was for it to be a glorified Congressional committee. That's the way I see it."

Most of the Bachmann-McGahn response attacked Bremer's character, rather than his complaint. It clearly was designed to portray this to the FEC—falsely—as the actions of a "paid Democrat operative" against a Republican in an attempt to color their opinion of the complainant. That sounded a lot better than saying a constituent filed the complaint on his own behalf.

But Bachmann and McGahn really should have been more careful, because lying to the FEC is a serious matter.

Verification of Bremer's employment as a paid DFLer at the legislature was a no-brainer; it could have been cleared up with one phone call or website check at the legislature. Yet Bachmann, who was serving in the State Legislature at the time, and her Tom DeLay–defending lawyer couldn't be bothered with the facts. So they made them up instead as the basis of their smear campaign and used this misinformation repeatedly in their response.

Whether that had any bearing on the FEC's rejection of Bremer's complaint, we'll never know. Meanwhile, Bremer let the FEC's Office of General Counsel decide whether lying to them in a sworn affidavit constituted a violation of the law, because even congresswomen ordained by God and $25,000-a-month lawyers weren't above the law.

Pepsi's Homosexual Agenda

One had to wonder what the virulently antigay EdWatch Minnesota would have thought about Bachmann taking thousands of dollars in campaign contributions from gay-friendly Pepsi.

Among the biggest donors to Michele Bachmann's 2008 campaign was the Bernick family of St. Cloud, Minnesota, the owners of the Bernick Companies, one of the state's largest Pepsi-Cola distributors. Charles Bernick, CEO, dumped a last-minute $1,000 into Bachmann's coffers on November 1, 2008. That was in addition to the $4,600 Bernick gave to Bachmann in 2007; the $2,000 he gave in 2006; the $2,750 that Bernick manager Jason Bernick has given to Bachmann since 2006; and the $4,500 Bachmann has received from Pamela Bernick since 2006. Bachmann also took $1,000 from the Pepsi-Cola Bottlers Association PAC in 2008 and $500 in 2006.

Yet Bachmann must not have gotten the memo from chief homobigot Don Wildmon at the American Family Association (AFA), who had just sent out a desperate appeal to his supporters to help him fight PepsiCo for their "support for the homosexual agenda."

In an e-mail dated November 14, 2008, AFA founder Wildmon warned,

> Pepsi has given Parents and Friends of Lesbians and Gays (PFLAG) a half-million dollars to help push the homosexual agenda in the workplace. PFLAG is a political advocacy group that promotes radical homosexual political causes like same-sex marriage, hate-crime laws, and gay adoption.
>
> Pepsi has a long tradition of financial support for homosexual groups. According to Jacqueline Millan, director of PepsiCo Corporate Contributions, "We are delighted to continue our partnership with PFLAG . . . (in) promoting the necessary message of inclusion to untapped groups . . . and that is a crucial step toward building a healthy working environment."

Wildmon said that he twice wrote to Pepsi asking the company to "remain neutral in the culture war," but "Pepsi didn't care enough to respond to the AFA letters." As always, Wildmon asked his flock to support their efforts to fight the homosexual agenda with a tax-deductible donation.

Did Bachmann return the dirty Pepsi money from Bernick and the Pepsi PAC that was clearly designed to advance the homosexual agenda? Did she wash her hands after accepting all of those Pepsi-tainted checks? Of course not.

Bachmann owes her antigay supporters an explanation.

Bachmann's Legacy

Michele Bachmann was caught lying about her record—again—in September 2010. This time it was about her support for the 2008 "Legacy Amendment"—the constitutional amendment passed overwhelmingly by Minnesota voters that raised the state sales tax by 0.375 percent to provide a dedicated fund for the outdoors and the arts.

Bachmann had used her opponent Tarryl Clark's State Senate vote to put the amendment on the 2008 ballot as evidence that Clark "loves taxes" and voted to raise taxes on State Fair corn dogs and deep-fried bacon. The charge was the basis for one of Bachmann's campaign ads that claimed Clark also voted to raise taxes on color crayons for kids.

Yet as first reported on *Dump Bachmann* on September 6, 2010, Bachmann herself supported the corn-dog-tax-raising amendment.

Minneapolis-based *Star Tribune* outdoor writer Dennis Anderson stated in an October 23, 2008, column that Bachmann appeared at an August 2008 Game Fair in Anoka and spoke of her support for the Legacy Amendment. She even displayed blaze-orange placards in her booth at the Game Fair, urging "Sportsmen Vote Yes" on the amendment, Anderson wrote.

In the September 12, 2010, *St. Cloud Times*, Bachmann mouthpiece Sergio Gor flatly denied that Bachmann supported the Legacy Amendment: "The Clark campaign said this week that Bachmann also supported the sales-tax amendment, citing a newspaper article from 2008. But Bachmann spokesman Sergio Gor said she never supported the tax."

When informed that Bachmann claimed he was lying about her support for the amendment, Anderson responded in an e-mail:

> I'm telling the truth, as a thousand or so other people can attest. She expressed her unqualified support for the amendment over the PA system at Game Fair in August 2008. (*Star Tribune* outdoor writer) Ron Schara was the interviewer. . . . Of course, that doesn't mean she didn't tell other people just the opposite.

Once again, the truth and Michele Bachmann appeared to be perfect strangers.

A footnote: The Legacy Amendment garnered 217,501 votes in the 6th Congressional District in 2008, while Bachmann herself received only 187,814 votes. In other words, 29,687 more 6th District voters voted to raise taxes on themselves than voted for Bachmann.

Bachmann's Duck-and-Cover Strategy

It should have come as no surprise to anyone who paid any attention to Michele Bachmann during her second term in Congress that her campaign strategy with regard to debates in 2010 would follow the old nuclear attack films shown to grade schoolers in the 1950s: duck and cover.

The Teabagging congresswoman had shown nothing but contempt for her constituents and anyone but the most accommodating and fawning media since her infamous appearance on Chris Matthews's *Hardball* that almost derailed her reelection in 2008.

Once secure in her $174,000 government job for another two

years, Bachmann thumbed her nose at media requests for interviews and clarifications of her half-truths and outright lies. She holds the record at the Pulitzer Prize–winning "PolitiFact" of the *St. Petersburg Times* newspaper for Pinocchio-like behavior.

Bachmann held only one public meeting during her entire five years in Congress at which constituents had the opportunity to address her, unfiltered by screeners and staff. Instead, the invisible congresswoman has opted for the safety of one-way communication through faceless "tele-town hall" meetings during which she and her handlers determine which constituents and questions she will respond to.

During the 2010 campaign season, Bachmann predictably ignored invitations to debate her two opponents, DFLer Tarryl Clark and IP candidate Bob Anderson, until public pressure from even the normally reticent mainstream media became too great. Less than a month out from the November 2 election, Bachmann cowardly agreed to a mere three debates—none of which were before a live audience and only one of which was even in her district.

The most glaring example of how Bachmann abrogated her duty to represent the 6th Congressional District was the October 7, 2010, debate sponsored by the Minnesota Broadcasters Association that was scheduled to be broadcast from WCCO's television studios—again, insulated from a living, breathing audience of her constituents.

According to Jim du Bois, the president and CEO of the Minnesota Broadcasters Association, Bachmann was first contacted about the MBA debate in late August—at least five weeks prior to the scheduled debate. And then they waited. And waited. And waited.

The response? Crickets.

Further attempts to get Bachmann to commit to a debate sponsored by the organization that represents Minnesota's broadcast community were futile. "We never did receive a response from Congresswoman Bachmann's office," said du Bois. "We kept open the option of going with the debate with just two of the three candidates, but we weren't really sure we could get it done within the timetable WCCO had." Eventually, explained du Bois, "we waited so long that WCCO's window went away. . . . It came up to the wire and we lost the opportunity to debate."

Was Bachmann so busy with her congressional duties that she couldn't find time to even respond to the MBA, much less debate? Hardly. As it turns out, she had other priorities that superseded such menial obligations before the unwashed masses.

Bachmann was scheduled to offer her "insightful critique" at the "Reclaiming America: The Taking Back Congress Tour" sponsored by wing-nut radio WWTC at Orchestra Hall that same night—a half-block away. Clearly, the choice was easy for Bachmann: spend a night debating her opponents in the most expensive congressional race in America or spend a night hobnobbing with the likes of Hugh Hewitt, Ed Morrisey, and Dennis Prager at a $225-per-VIP soiree.

This isn't the only debate Bachmann skipped out on. She couldn't even find the time to respond to an invitation from the *Stillwater Gazette*, her hometown newspaper, to a debate it sponsored on October 12, 2010, before a live audience in Stillwater. Yet that may be more understandable. Even her neighbors have rejected their local darling in her last two congressional elections, and facing that crowd could get a little uncomfortable.

Sadly, Bachmann's duck-and-cover strategy may have worked. The three debates to which she did agree were held during the last week of the campaign, giving little time for voters to digest their results before heading to the polls on November 2. Instead, they had to settle for hearing from their congresswoman in a multimillion-dollar barrage of ugly TV commercials and a blizzard of glossy brochures in their mailboxes.

Better to keep 'em dumb all over.

Bachmann's Sloppy Bookkeeping

Michele Bachmann's sloppy—or deliberately deceitful—campaign bookkeeping has continued to this day. Twice in 2011, Bachmann was found to be using a false address on official government filings. This time it was on two Federal Election Commission (FEC) receipts for "mileage reimbursement."

Bachmann's old Stillwater address where she hasn't lived for three years was reported on two campaign disbursement receipts that her campaign filed with the FEC. One was for $74.80 on February 3, 2011; the other was for $562.51 on February 7, 2011. Both were for payments to Bachmann. It would seem to be hard to explain how a candidate's own campaign could still be using a 2008 address for the candidate on 2011 FEC reports—particularly when one of the disbursements to the candidate required a "receipt, invoice or cancelled check."

Federal election campaign laws state that "The treasurer of a political committee shall keep an account of . . . the name and address of every person to whom any disbursement is made, the date, amount, and purpose of the disbursement, and the name of the candidate and the office sought by the candidate, if any, for whom the disbursement was made, including a receipt, invoice, or cancelled check for each disbursement in excess of $200."

It may take a complaint filed with the FEC to determine what address was listed on the receipt, the invoice, or the check that Bachmann provided to her campaign for her reimbursement. The FEC frowns on candidates filing false information, and it looks especially bad when the information is the candidate's own address on a reimbursement receipt.

It's not likely the current owners of Bachmann's old house would be happy to find out that she's been using their address on her legal filings, either, because this isn't the first time. Bachmann listed the same phony address on her annual state lawyer's registration filed on July 11, 2011.

CHAPTER 4

Bachmann's Record of Nonachievement

This section is a chronological record of the gaffes, blunders, lies, chicanery, and shenanigans that make up Bachmann's record as a Minnesota state senator and congresswoman. It is a bizarre record for a presidential candidate. Early on in the life of the *Dump Bachmann* blog, we received this message from a commissioner in the Jesse Ventura administration about the then senator Michele Bachmann:

> She will manipulate, fabricate, restate, obfuscate, misrepresent, misquote, mistreat and use whatever tactic she thinks she might be able to get away with to make

77

her point. Sen. Bachmann knows no ethical boundaries and has no discernible conscience except that whatever moves her agenda forward is acceptable because her agenda is "right" and everyone else is wrong.

Senator Bachmann believes in "scientific creationism" (an oxymoron, if ever there was one) as passionately as she believes in anything. She has also spoken quite often about the need to ensure that children are given "all sides" of the origin question but that "scientific creationism" is the only true one because it comes from God!

Stillborn in Stillwater

In 2003, Bachmann proposed a bill that mandated the certification of stillbirths. In a February 20, 2003, article from the *Stillwater Gazette*, Bachmann explained that her bill (Senate File 191) would require the deaths of fetuses older than five months to be catalogued and the names of the parents to be recorded. Bachmann claimed that it was out of respect for the parents:

> Bachmann said she decided to work on the legislation after she was approached by a woman who had given birth to a stillborn baby. The woman told Bachmann that there was a coalition of families that was surprised to learn that they were not able to get a certificate of record for their stillborn child.
>
> "They wanted to be able to recognize that a child had been born," Bachmann said.
>
> "They wanted to have something, obviously it's not a live birth, but they wanted to have something that recognized that their child existed and was born. So,

they came and asked if I would be willing to carry this legislation."

The bill was similar to legislation in other states dubbed "Missing Angel" bills, which was promoted disingenuously by the foes of legal abortion. As always, Bachmann expressed confidence that the bill would become law:

> "We are now in the process of requesting a first hearing," Bachmann said. She expects the hearing to happen in the third week of March. She does not anticipate any resistance to the bill, she said, because it does not have a financial impact on the state.
>
> "I think from a policy point of view, it's good to recognize that a part of our human family existed and to make a memorial of that. So I can't imagine any reason why anyone would resist this bill."

The certificate of stillbirths could have been interpreted as an inroad to reverse abortion rights, which Bachmann totally denied:

> Bachmann said no anti-abortion groups asked her to write the bill. "I am pro-life . . . but this is not phrased in any way to be a pro-life bill. This is a measure for grieving families to help them deal with grief."

Yeah, right—by forcing them to do paperwork. Yet Bachmann herself apparently wasn't eager to do the work (sound familiar?) to advance the bill through the legislature:

> For Bachmann to have her bill heard in the Senate, a House legislator will likely have to file a bill similar to it in the House. As of the Monday, February 17 deadline, a bill had not been introduced in the House.

"We could hear it, but if there is no House File, then it's half a bill," he said. "It is sort of an unwritten rule, that if there is no House File, then there's really no sense in hearing a Senate File." Bachmann still has plenty of time to organize a House File, he added.

Reporters need to ask whether Bachmann will push for a similar bill if she is elected president. Similar laws that mandated certification of stillbirths were created by the regime of Nicolae Ceausescu.

The legislative laziness of Senator Bachmann was legendary, as was her relentless self-promotion. Karl Bremer took note of this in a letter to the editor published in the *Stillwater Gazette* on March 3, 2003:

When I think of State Sen. Michele Bachmann, *hard working* aren't the first words that come to mind. Self-serving maybe, but not hard-working.

Bachmann has the lightest workload of any state senator. Although she serves on only three committees, two of them meet at exactly the same time. That means Bachmann only attends a maximum of four committee meetings a week. The rest of her colleagues' calendars, with the exception of two in leadership positions, are filled with anywhere from six to 11 committee meetings a week.

According to the Secretary of the Senate's office, senators are "strongly discouraged" from requesting assignments to committees with conflicting schedules. An aide in Bachmann's office says she often attends committee meetings in lieu of the senator. Is this the kind of representation Washington County voters elected in November?

When Bachmann's not skipping committee meetings, she's promoting herself with meaningless resolutions—six of them already this session, dealing with such matters as a missile defense system and the federal estate tax. Bachmann is well-versed in the art of authoring these self-serving public relations gimmicks. In her first two years in office, she authored 21 of them—10 percent of all the resolutions proposed by the entire 67-member Senate during that period. When you add up the cost of drafting, printing, voting on and recording these resolutions, the cost to taxpayers for promoting Michele Bachmann starts to look like real money.

When Michele Bachmann's lease is up in four years—after all, she says she's just renting the office—the voters of Senate District 52 should evict this deadbeat tenant and elect someone who at least pays the rent.

Increasingly, Bachmann's Marriage Amendment overshadowed her service to constituents in her district. Karl Bremer wrote the following letter, published in the *Stillwater Gazette* on July 1, 2004:

On April 27, Sen. Michele Bachmann issued a press release praising the inclusion of $4.5 million in the state's bonding bill for classroom and technological improvements at Century College in her district.

"I plan to lobby diligently for the inclusion of this important project in the Senate bonding bill," Bachmann pledged.

On May 6, Bachmann voted against the bonding bill that included the money for Century College. And ever since, Bachmann has threatened to work to defeat any bonding bill if she does not get a vote on her already-dead proposal to write discrimination into the state Constitution with an amendment to ban gay marriage.

So much for our senator's "diligent lobbying."

Bachmann does not represent the values of Stillwater and the St. Croix Valley but, instead, a shrill minority of religious extremists on a crusade to codify their fundamentalist beliefs into law. It's time that the silent majority reject this charlatan's homophobic agenda at the ballot box, wherever she runs for office.

Annus Horribilis

Apparently, 2005 was a banner year for Senator Bachmann. Let's take a look at Bachmann's record of "accomplishments" in 2005.

January 28: Senator Bachmann, always vigilant for our safety, went after one of the most serious homeland security threats Minnesotans face today: light-rail scofflaws. Her bill would have made it a petty misdemeanor for anyone who was caught trying to catch a free ride on the rails (Bachmann, Nienow SF1919). Rep. Ray Vandeveer, who represented half of Bachmann's Senate district, made a video of Michele Bachmann asking passengers on the Hiawatha LRT whether they paid their fare. This bizarre video, with a soundtrack using the *Star Wars* theme, was shown to a House Transportation Finance Committee hearing on Thursday, April 14. Committee members joked and laughed after the conclusion of the video.

February 3: Bachmann authored the first of six resolutions—more than one-third of the entire Senate's—this one to honor the birthday of Ronald Reagan, a president who never won an election in Minnesota.

February 8: Following up on her obsession with Reagan, Bachmann proposed legislation to designate I-494 and I-694 as the "Ronald Reagan Beltway" and require scarce highway funds to be spent to design and erect signs. It died without a hearing.

February 18: Bachmann introduced the "American Heritage Education in Minnesota Public Schools Act," which would mandate that schools teach about "America's founding documents . . . including documents that contributed to the foundation or maintenance of America's representative republican form of limited government, the Bill of Rights, our free-market economic system, and patriotism."

March 3: In a direct rebuke to state senator Michele Bachmann, the Minnesota Senate reaffirmed that its chambers were not to be used for commercial purposes. This came days after Bachmann was caught using the Senate chambers as a backdrop for a testimonial and endorsement video of a commercial right-wing video production company. That prompted the State Senate to amend its rules to prohibit such crass commercialism of the Senate chambers. The business for which Bachmann filmed the commercial endorsement was a public relations/media firm that worked for Bachmann on her "Defense of Marriage" legislation that went nowhere.

Senate Majority Leader John Hottinger (DFL-Mankato; (Minnesota Democratic-Farmer-Labor Party) delivered a smackdown to Bachmann on the Senate floor when he proposed—and then later withdrew—an amendment to the Senate rules prohibiting commercial use of the Senate chambers.

> "When I was first alerted to that [Bachmann's commercial], I was amazed. I was incredulous that someone would think that was an appropriate usage of the Senate chambers," said Hottinger on March 5, 2005. "I talked

to a number of people and I found no one—no one—who would think it would be a proper thing to use the Senate chamber to make a television ad or an Internet ad for a commercial company."

Yet Hottinger then withdrew his amendment, because he wanted to avoid "filling the rules with things that are so obvious as this." He noted that Senate rules already prohibit using Senate hearing rooms for commercial purposes.

"I don't know why Sen. Bachmann chose to be using the Senate chambers to advance a commercial business purpose when it's barred by our rules in hearing rooms. I mean, how much common sense does it take to understand if you can't use the less-than-sacred hearing rooms for commercial business purposes, then you shouldn't be using the Senate chamber for commercial business purposes?" Hottinger asked.

He continued to lambaste Bachmann for her lack of judgment.

She didn't bother to ask anyone "Is this within the rules of the Senate, within the decorum, within the history, within the traditions, within the standards?" She didn't ask. And had she asked, of course she'd been told "No, we don't use that kind of commercial purpose to promote some group that we support for financial gain." . . . It shows how far we have stooped to think we need to have rules on something so obvious and so clear.

Even Senator Mady Reider (R-Shoreview), normally a faithful ally of Bachmann's in the Senate, conceded that Bachmann's abuse of the Senate chambers was in bad taste.

"Good taste would probably say we not use it for commercial purposes," Reider testified.

Bachmann, of course, made no apologies for turning the Senate chambers into a commercial soundstage. In fact, using her own bizarre logic, she denied it was even a commercial.

"This was not a commercial as I had understood it. This was going to be a video ad that the company has on their website, and that's what this was about," Bachmann told her colleagues.

Instead, Bachmann once again played the victim card and claimed she was being vilified for supporting Minnesota businesses and jobs.

Hottinger saw through Bachmann's smokescreen, however, noting that the commercial Bachmann made was for work the company did on Bachmann's failed legislation.

"It's not about jobs or economic development. If that's the argument, any company can come in here and make a commercial."

Hottinger's amendment was reintroduced by Senator Dave Kleis (R-St. Cloud) and passed on a 58–7 vote. Bachmann voted for the measure, despite her refusal to admit wrongdoing.

March 11: Michele hit her stride with her marquee issue: writing discrimination into the state constitution. Her capitol-steps rally supporting a constitutional amendment to prevent some citizens from enjoying such rights as hospital visitation of lifelong partners featured a speaker with ties to both Ku Klux Klan Grand Wizard David Duke and another white supremacist group.

March 29: Bachmann extended the long arm of the legislature into the classroom again with the introduction of the "Free Speech for Faculty and Students Bill of Rights." Citing Joe McCarthy–like allegations of liberal college professors tormenting and flunking conservative students, Bachmann encouraged students to rat out their leftie profs. She failed to get a hearing for the bill—or another Senate author.

April 7: Bachmann failed to get a hearing on her constitutional discrimination bill and then failed to convince the Senate to break its rules and move her bill to the front of the line for a floor vote. That afternoon, Bachmann was caught on film spying on a pro–gay rights rally at the capitol while crouched behind the bushes. The photos generated extreme Internet notoriety and plenty of headlines for Michele, but not the kind she was hoping for that day.

April 9: Two days later, Bachmann ducked out of a public forum early and ran screaming from the bathroom of the Scandia City Hall. She filed a wildly exaggerated police report claiming she was held against her will by two members of a "gay and lesbian activist group" after escaping a hostile audience. Representative Ray Vandeveer, also at the meeting, declined to corroborate her bizarre version of events. The Washington County Sheriff Department investigated Bachmann's complaint, then forwarded it to the county attorney's office and it was dropped. (See chapter 9, "Bachmann's Bathroomgate.")

April 26: Bachmann introduced a resolution designating May 5 as a "day of prayer" in Minnesota. By the end of this month, she needed all of the prayers she could muster to salvage her reputation as anything but a wing-nut.

November 12: Bachmann appeared at a 6th Congressional District GOP candidate forum, where she declared, "There's a movement afoot that's occurring, and part of that is this whole philosophical idea of multicultural diversity. Which on the face sounds wonderful. Let's appreciate everyone's cultures. Guess what? Not all cultures are equal. Not all values are equal."

While protecting Minnesotans from the evils of light-rail free-loaders, liberal professors, and monogamous gays, Bachmann somehow found time to raise $179,276 in itemized contributions for her congressional campaign through September 30. More than 71 percent of that came from carpetbagging contributors outside the 6th CD. That included $3,000 from antiwoman crusader Phyllis Schlafly and $5,000 from wealthy Georgia real estate developer Barry Conner, who advocated the abolition of all public education, and a sizable amount from the proceeds of the Tom Petters Ponzi scheme. This, from the candidate who in 2002 pledged to be "the voice of the people, not the big-money, outside interest groups."

Creating a Presumption

Bachmann, a former high school cheerleader, preferred grandstanding to lawmaking and could always be counted on to adopt the right-wing, theocratic cause du jour, as was the case of her bill that was inspired by the Terri Schiavo case. Terri Schiavo was a Florida woman who suffered a heart attack that resulted in massive brain damage. She existed in a vegetative state from 1990 until, after a prolonged legal battle between her husband and her parents, her feeding tube was removed and she died in 2005. Right-wing politicians, including President Bush, sought to impress their theocratic base by interfering in the case and proposing legislation that would give the government a greater role in end-of-life decisions.

Not surprisingly, Bachmann introduced her own Terri Schiavo bill in the Senate (S.F. No. 2184—"A bill for an act relating to health; creating a presumption directing nutrition and hydration sufficient to sustain life").

A year later, in a debate with Patty Wetterling, Michele Bachmann gave her opinion of Schiavo's condition: "From a health point of view, she was not terminally ill."

Unity Doesn't Work for Bachmann

In the 2005 video described earlier in this chapter, filmed on the Senate floor and produced by Unity Works, Bachmann warns about same-sex marriage, calling it "evil":

> [In]May, homosexual and lesbian activists who live here in Minnesota will be able to travel to Massachusetts to have their same-sex relationships declared marriages by the state of Massachusetts. Upon returning here to Minnesota they will be able to demand legal recognition through our state court system and at that point an activist judge could very well rule in their favor and then strike down Minnesota's current defense of marriage law. If we allow this to happen, group marriage, polygamy, and things much worse may not be far behind. . . . Without this amendment, Minnesota could have gay marriage imposed on us in 2004. . . . Edmund Burke was right when he said, "All that is necessary for evil to triumph is for good men to do nothing." Now is the time for all of us to act for the good of the next generation.

This video is available on YouTube.

Senator Bachmann had a $2,500 expenditure in her campaign finance report to Unity Works Video. She also did the endorsement for Unity Works Video—filmed from the State Senate chambers. Unity Works removed the Michele Bachmann references from its website sometime after February 3, 2005. The endorsement video showed a number of videos that were used in Bachmann's e-mail video campaign to get people to come to the capitol for the Bachmann amendment rally and also to raise funds for her campaign.

Bachmann Itemized

When Bachmann was not grandstanding on fundamentalist issues or demonizing minorities, she was helping herself to the taxpayers' money to pay for cable TV bills.

According to public data from the Minnesota Senate Office of Fiscal Services, Senator Bachmann requested reimbursement from the Minnesota Senate for cable television at her home in Stillwater. Bachmann submitted an itemized Comcast bill for reimbursement that listed the following cable service.

> Standard Cable (includes basic 1 $8.96, Expanded Basic $30.51, Basic 3 $3.32) $19.99 (discount subtracted), paid on February 11, 2005.

This reimbursement request was received by Senate Fiscal Services on February 2, 2005, and paid on February 11 for service from November 29, 2004, through December 28, 2004, and was signed by Laura Folland.

> Standard Cable (includes basic 1 $8.96, Expanded Basic $30.51, Basic 3 $3.32) $24.69 (discount subtracted), paid on December 15, 2004.

This was submitted on December 9, 2004, and paid on December 15 for cable service from October 29, 2004, through November 11, 2004, and was signed by Eileen Lunzer.

Bachmann submitted a nonitemized Comcast bill for reimbursement on three occasions:

- February 11, 2005: $125.00
- June 1, 2005: $102.11
- March 14, 2005: $76.38

The outrageous abuse of taxpayer dollars was exposed on DumpBachmann.com. Eva Young said, "It's particularly offensive when a self-described fiscal watchdog like Bachmann is caught feeding at the public trough. It certainly makes you wonder what other household bills of Senator Bachmann's the taxpayer is picking up."

Bachmann's use of taxpayers' money to pay her cable bills is a prime example of her blatant hypocrisy. Her pilfering from the public purse is just one strand in the web of unethical actions she has undertaken to advance her career and line her pockets.

The *Star Tribune* took note of the brewing scandal:

> Signaling a bitter fight brewing between Republicans in the Sixth District congressional race, a longtime supporter of a GOP gay rights group is questioning the expense statements of same-sex-marriage opponent Michele Bachmann.
>
> Eva Young, active in the Log Cabin Republicans, said a supporter of a Republican competing with Bachmann for the party's endorsement next month told her about Bachmann's expense statements from a cable firm. Young would not identify the supporter or the candidate.

Bachmann told the *Star Tribune* she sought reimbursement for her TV expenses because she used cable TV to watch school board and other government meetings on local public access stations. The controversy over Bachmann's cable bill would again resurface at the 6th Congressional District Republican Convention in 2006.

Bachmann Relieved

Also in 2005, "Assistant Minority Leader Michele Bachmann" was relieved of her leadership position by Senate Republicans. Bachmann spun the demotion as a "purge of conservatives" in this press release:

> SAINT PAUL—A fight to the finish over whether to raise taxes has led to the removal of Senator Michele Bachmann, (R-Stillwater) from her State Senate leadership position as Assistant Minority Leader in charge of Policy for the Senate Republican Caucus.
>
> "My constituents are my first priority, and they've consistently supported me fighting tax increases. I think they'd agree that I've been very faithful to their wishes," said Bachmann.
>
> "Unfortunately, I felt at the end of the recent legislative session that I was fighting an uphill battle on my constituents' behalf," said Bachmann. "It became especially clear on the final day of session when I offered an amendment to remove the cigarette tax from the Health and Human Services budget bill that my philosophical differences with the minority leader were just too deep for him to allow me to continue in a leadership position."
>
> "Today the fallout was finalized—I was stripped of my leadership position," said Bachmann. "It's a shame that the anti-tax message is lost on the leadership when it so resonates with our constituents."
>
> "What's most discouraging is that in the end, I supported final passage of the HHS budget bill because of its strong pro-life language recognizing fetal pain, and still the minority leader was not satisfied," said Bachmann.
>
> "For five years, I have consistently fought tax increases and have been an advocate for the unborn," said Bachmann. "Though my advocacy has cost me my leadership position, I will continue to fight against tax increases

and for the well-being of those who cannot speak for themselves. The upside of today's event is that I can be completely committed to thinking about my constituents' concerns."

In the future, Bachmann would use the same excuse whenever she was caught in a tight spot. Bachmann would always play the victim . . . and a compliant news media always let her get away with it.

Enough to Make You Sick

Also in 2006, team *Dump Bachmann* began to focus attention on Michele Bachmann's hypocrisy on another of her trademark issues —health care. In a letter to the *Woodbury Bulletin*, Karl Bremer noted that Michele Bachmann was fond of bringing up her family's Christian counseling business in discussions about health care. The Bachmann Clinic employed about thirty people, for whom the Bachmanns provided no health-care benefits. Michele Bachmann also did not provide health-care benefits for her campaign staff:

> You might call Bachmann's plan faith-based health care—you just pray that you don't get sick.
> Bachmann is opposed to government involvement in health care, calling it "socialized medicine." But under whose plan is Bachmann's family insured—her State Senate taxpayer-subsidized plan? Are any of the employees of Bachmann & Associates, or Bachmann's congressional campaign on the state-subsidized MinnesotaCare program because they can't get health insur-

ance from their employers, the Bachmanns? If the free market is the answer to all our health care problems, as Bachmann contends, what role should businesses like Bachmann & Associates and multimillion-dollar congressional campaigns play in that market to ensure that their employees remain healthy and not a burden on the taxpayers?

Michele Bachmann, a frequent critic of "Obamacare," provided zero health benefits for her own employees. It's enough to make you sick.

Here Lies

In 2006, Karl Bremer and *Dump Bachmann* took note of another legacy of Bachmann's shoddy stewardship of her district, the closure of the Stillwater Boomsite Rest Area:

> This National Historic Monument on the St. Croix River has served many generations of Minnesotans as a state highway rest area, picnic spot, hiking location and place of respite for boaters on the river. Today, the Boomsite Rest Area is barricaded, overgrown with weeds and vandalized—the victim of the bankrupt "no new taxes" policy of our Republican legislative delegation and Republican governor.
>
> The bronze plaque noting the site's historic significance is gone—either stolen or removed by MnDOT. Perhaps a new one should be erected in its place that reads: "Here lies the legacy of Matt Dean, Michele Bachmann, Ray Vandeveer and Tim Pawlenty."

Eminently Bachmann

This is from Michele Bachmann's campaign website:

> Like most Americans, I was dismayed by the Supreme
> Court's decision. Moreover, I have long been concerned
> about the abuse of eminent domain powers in Minnesota,
> such as the case of the Albrecht family's Shady Birch
> Resort in Washington County and the case of the
> Salokar family farm in Wyoming, which was taken to
> make way for a sewage treatment plant but was then
> sold at an enormous profit to a private company. That
> is why I am drafting legislation in the Minnesota Senate
> to reform our state eminent domain laws.

One bill drafted by Senator Bachmann would expressly prohibit
the use of eminent domain if the effect is the transfer of private
property to a private owner.

Nonetheless, in 2006, Bachmann, allowed William Hawks, an
eminent domain advocate, to host a fund-raiser featuring Vice
President Dick Cheney. Hawks is the owner of a company called
Crown Hydro, which had been trying for years to secure a location
and permits for a small hydroelectric plant on the Mississippi River
near St. Anthony Falls. Thus far, it had been unsuccessful.

Crown Hydro received a Federal Energy Regulatory Commission (FERC) license for the proposed 3.4-megawatt plant in 1999,
when the powerhouse was to be located in the basement of the old
Crown Roller Mill on the river. When Crown Hydro failed to
reach a lease agreement for the property, it proposed to locate its
powerhouse on the remains of the Holly and Cataract Mill foundation in Minneapolis's Mill Ruins Park on the east side of West
River Parkway and sought an amended license from FERC in
2002.

The Minneapolis Park Board intervened in the FERC license hearing and opposed the move, saying that "the relocated power-house and water conveyance components of the project would cause irreparable damage to Mill Ruins Park and to the goals of the Park Board and the City of Minneapolis in their development of recreational facilities and historic preservation activities in the project area." The board further charged that Crown Hydro had failed to negotiate for use of the park board's land, despite the board's attempts to initiate talks. Even the nearby neighborhoods the power plant was supposed to serve opposed the project.

Crown Hydro requested—and was granted—repeated extensions on its FERC permit application. In its final request on October 26, 2004, Crown informed FERC, "Crown would still prefer to work out a lease with the Park Board, but has not dismissed the possibility of exercising eminent domain in accordance with applicable law in the event there is no ability to enter into an agreed-upon lease."

FERC was unimpressed with Crown's threat to take public park land and finally dismissed Crown's application for an amended license in February 2005. Crown requested a rehearing on the matter, and it was denied again in June 2005. Then Crown appealed the FERC's decision to the 8th Circuit Court of Appeals.

William Hawks evidently was a guy who won't take no for an answer—even to the point of picking up the cudgel of eminent domain to get his hydroelectric plant. Yet what was even more offensive is that he was willing to use eminent domain to take public park land—a historical site, no less—to achieve his goal.

The Bachmann fund-raiser at William Hawks's Lake Minnetonka palace, which was nowhere near the 6th Congressional District Bachmann sought to represent, raised several questions that people should have asked of the candidate: How does this square with Bachmann's oft-repeated opposition to eminent domain? Or is eminent domain okay when it involves a private entity taking public land?

When Bachmann authored legislation in 2005 to rein in the use of eminent domain, she wrote, "I have long been concerned about the abuse of eminent domain powers in Minnesota. . . . That is why I am drafting legislation in the Minnesota Senate to reform our state eminent domain laws."

What did William Hawks and Crown Hydro want from Michele Bachmann in return for hosting a gold-plated fund-raiser for her with the vice president of the United States? Was Bachmann working behind the scenes to aid and abet the forced taking of Minneapolis parkland by eminent domain?

Michele Bachmann again showed her hypocrisy on the issue in 2007. The *Saint Cloud Times* had a story about Koch, a refining company, asking big government to use eminent domain to condemn private property to make way for one of its nasty pipelines. The company started condemnation proceedings against Central Minnesota landowners who had not signed agreements allowing the new oil pipeline to cross their property. Where was Michele Bachmann?

Bachmannomics

During her campaign in 2006, Bachmann touted her expertise on economics. Karl Bremer gave this assessment of her economic acumen: "Representative Michele Bachmann is kind of like the old Magic 8 Ball. Tip her upside-down and a random and senseless response appears with no apparent connection with reality. Except the Magic 8 Ball actually made more sense than our congresswoman from the 6th District."

Speaking before the Stillwater Rotary recently, Bachmann gave a laughably rosy report on the economy. The *Stillwater Courier* wrote,

Bachmann noted the improved health of the country's economy since tax cuts went into effect in 2003, saying that the country's economy has tripled its growth rate since then. Previous to the tax cuts, the country was losing jobs; now it is adding jobs to its employment rolls, she said. "That's what happens when you stimulate the economy from the private sector."

Such stimulation makes an economy "recession proof," she said, marked by "competition and prosperity."

Just two days later, the state's economic forecast was released, and contrary to Bachmann's smiley-face economy, the *St. Paul Pioneer Press*'s headline blared, "It's Official: Minnesota's Economy Is Sick." The state was facing a $373 million budget shortfall, which the governor said reflected a national economic slowdown, and state economists said there was a 35 percent chance of recession.

Further contradicting Bachmann's happy talk, the budget forecast reported that 2008 would bring two years of negative employment growth for Minnesota.

Bachmann claimed that short-term national debt was under control but that "the long-term debt literally keeps me awake at night." She could have thanked her president whom she so dutifully supported for her insomnia. The national debt under eight years of President Bush rose from $5.7 trillion when he took office in January 2001 to more $10 trillion when he left office in January 2009. With the help of the Bush-initiated war in Iraq, the national debt continues to rise at the rate of nearly $1 million a minute.

Bachmann pitched her bill for the 100 percent tax deductibility of health-care expenses. That, she claimed, would "level the health care playing field for all Americans." She didn't say what it would do for those taxpayers who did not itemize. In the next breath, however, Bachmann touted her proposal for a flat tax, under which all income tax deductions would disappear. So much for the level health-care playing field. What Bachmann giveth, Bachmann taketh away.

Bachmann told her audience that many small businesses couldn't afford to provide health insurance for their employees. Yet it wasn't likely that she told them that her own family's business—a Christian counseling clinic in Lake Elmo with about thirty employees, many of them doctors—was one of them. Perhaps, with her health-care tax-deduction bill, our congresswoman was looking out for the Bachmann clinic employees who had to pay for their own health insurance.

The self-proclaimed fiscal conservative railed against government assistance programs of any kind and voted against the farm bill. Yet she happily collected federal farm subsidies on her family's farm in Wisconsin.

Bachmann also appeared in district newspapers to take credit for federal grants to local fire departments. The problem was, Bachmann voted against the 2008 appropriations bill for the Department of Homeland Security, which provided the grants.

She Couldn't Give a SCHIP

In 2007, Bachmann said she would rather have been at the White House with the president than voting on State Children's Health Insurance Program (SCHIP). Republican senator Norm Coleman called SCHIP "a vital safety net filling the void and protecting against increased numbers of uninsured children." Republican representative Jim Ramstad said he supported SCHIP because "We have a moral obligation to cover all our children."

But the God-fearing 6th CD congresswoman Michele Bachmann? She called the vote on SCHIP "ridiculous"—mainly because it appeared to have gotten in the way of an afternoon rendezvous at the White House with the president. To demonstrate how far out of the mainstream Bachmann was swimming in those days, even arch-conservative senator Orrin Hatch of Utah, a coauthor of the measure Bush vetoed, called the legislation "a true compromise."

Bachmann, who as a government employee virtually her entire professional life has been the recipient of government-provided health care, made her ridiculous assessment of SCHIP on failed congressional candidate Jason Lewis's radio show.

"I was supposed to be at the White House this afternoon meeting with the president," Bachmann pouted. "It got canceled because of this ridiculous SCHIP vote. But I'm gonna go back there Wednesday."

Bachmann repeatedly referred to getting "beat up" over her vote to sink the SCHIP:

> The Democrats want to delay the SCHIP vote to overturn the president's veto that he issued this morning. They want to delay it two weeks, and I'll tell you why. They want to beat up on enough of us so that we will change our votes. So they want to give themselves and Moveon.org two weeks to beat up on us. Tonight at 7 o'clock in St. Cloud, they're planning a big demonstration at my office in St. Cloud to beat up on me. They'll bring all the local media out so that I'll cave and switch my vote on SCHIP, which is just not going to happen.

Bachmann continued with the black helicopters whirring overhead: "Let me tell you, they will spare no expense. It'll be millions of dollars. They rent a mob—like this protest they're going to have tonight at my office."

"Who's leading the protest?" Lewis interrupted, on hearing this revelation about rented mobs. "Who's organizing it? Do you know?"

"Uhhh," Bachmann stammered, "I don't know. Undoubtedly, MoveOn will have their fingers in it. But it's the D-Triple C—the

Democrat [*sic*] congressional committee, the Democrat [*sic*] National Party, probably working hand-in-glove . . ."

Bachmann was lying. In fact, neither Moveon.org nor any Democratic Party organizations had anything to do with the protest at Bachmann's St. Cloud office. It was organized by Americans United for Change. Other participants included "faith leaders, local families, Iraq Campaign, SEIU MN State Council, and USAction," according to the group's press release. There were no reports of "rented mobs."

Bachmann and Lewis also perpetuated the lie that the SCHIP legislation would provide health coverage to children in families earning $83,000 a year.

"This is not health care for poor people," Lewis blustered.

"No! Are you kidding me?" Bachmann laughed. "We're talking people making $83,000 a year—that's rich people in Minnesota."

Actually, that sounded more like a middle-class Minnesota couple making $41,500 each in their jobs. Bachmann's congressional salary alone was $165,200. And Bachmann's solution to what she perceived as a phony health-care crisis?

> We could turn around the health care quote crisis in our country in a month's time," Bachmann says. "All we have to do is some simple changes in the federal tax code. You change it and then all of a sudden, guess what—this crisis is going to go away.

That, and a little pixie dust.

Doing Less with More

Michele Bachmann's staff salaries skyrocketed by 26.4 percent in 2009, while her staffers double-dipped as campaign consultants.

Although Representative Michele Bachmann developed a reputation as a champion for cutting government spending, her own 2009 congressional staff salary budget mushroomed by $176,868—a whopping 26.4 percent—compared to her 2008 staff budget, even though her congressional workload didn't change.

At the same time, Bachmann's national media profile took a dramatic jump in 2009 due to her frequent cable TV appearances and campaign speaking engagements around the country.

Were taxpayers subsidizing Bachmann's campaign expenses and increased media exposure with a congressional staff that grew at more than twice the rate of anyone else's in the Minnesota delegation? That was hard to tell, because a number of Bachmann staffers also worked as consultants to her campaign.

In 2009, four top staffers in Bachmann's Washington office—including former chief of staff Michelle Marston and communications director David Dziok—collected $66,000 in campaign consulting fees while they were also drawing congressional salaries. Bachmann also added yet another staff person whose salary was split between her office, her campaign, and another congressman.

Although this double-dipping practice was legal, it has been relatively rare. In fact, among the Minnesota delegation in 2009, only two part-timers on Representative James Oberstar's congressional staff worked simultaneously on his campaign staff.

Such commingling of official staff and campaign staff made it difficult to determine when a person's congressional duties ended and campaign duties began, leaving the system ripe for abuse. Instead, according to a spokesperson with the House Committee on House Administration, House staffers usually took a leave of absence from their House position to go full time into campaign work.

Without examining the time sheets for Bachmann's staff, it was difficult to determine whether placing congressional staffers on the campaign staff simultaneously came at the expense of conducting official legislative business or constituent services for Bachmann's district.

According to the House Committee on Standards of Ethical Conduct, "Employees who do campaign work while remaining on the House payroll should keep careful records of the time they spend on official activities and, separately, on campaign activities, and demonstrate that campaign work was not done on official time. There is no set format for maintaining such time records."

Bachmann's office did not respond to a request for payroll records for staffers who worked congressional and campaign jobs simultaneously. In defense of Bachmann's 26 percent increase in her office workers' salaries, Bachmann's apologists pointed to her seventh-lowest staff salary budget in the Minnesota delegation as proof that Bachmann was prudent with tax dollars (Erik Paulsen was the lowest); however, those numbers didn't tell the whole story.

Bachmann, along with Republican freshman Paulsen, had fewer committee assignments than anyone else. Every member of the Minnesota congressional delegation other than Bachmann and Paulsen either chaired a committee or had at least two and some-

Minnesota Congressional Staff Salary Increases

Member	2008	2009	Increase
Bachmann	$667,516	$844,384	26.4%
Walz	$816,458	$906,677	11%
Ellison	$900,349	$986,420	9.5%
Kline	$880,628	$943,552	7.1%
Oberstar	$1,185,003	$1,260,012	6.3%
McCollum	$962,399	$996,294	3.5%
Peterson	$1,004,809	$1,022,875	1.7%
Paulsen	N/A	$749,791	N/A

times three committee assignments and several subcommittee assignments. Bachmann and Paulsen each sat on a lone committee and only three subcommittees. Fewer committees meant less work and, consequently, less staff was needed.

Yet even that light schedule seemed to be too demanding for Bachmann. The *Minnesota Independent* found that Bachmann missed four times as many committee votes as her Minnesota colleagues Paulsen and Keith Ellison on the House Financial Services Committee. According to the *Minnesota Independent's* analysis, three-quarters of those missed votes occurred on days when Bachmann had national media appearances.

In Congress, it appeared that Bachmann was continuing her long-standing tradition of doing less with more.

Party Girl

While Bachmann's constituents had to settle for tele–town hall meetings and mailboxes stuffed with frankly self-promoting junk mail, their congresswoman was partying away in D.C.

When Michele Bachmann admitted in 2009 that in her more than three years in Congress, "I don't have substantive bills that I have been able to pass," the second-term congresswoman blamed it on her being a "fairly new freshman" in a "deep minority." A look at Bachmann's social calendar, however, suggests that if she had spent more time on legislating and less time on the D.C. cocktail-party circuit, she might have actually gotten something accomplished.

The Sunlight Foundation's Party Time project documented the political partying scene in Washington through invitations to political fund-raisers it received from a network of connected sources. In addition to a searchable database of party beneficiaries, hosts, venues, and types of entertainment, copies of actual party invitations were available to be downloaded from the site.

Although Party Time didn't document every party that was thrown—only the ones it received invitations for—it served as a good barometer for who was throwing down, and among the Minnesota congressional delegation, Bachmann was the clear party animal.

In 2009, the Party Time website featured invitations to twenty-seven Bachmann parties since she was elected, all but two of them in 2008–2009. No one in the Minnesota delegation even came close to that kind of carousing. Colin Peterson and James Oberstar—both powerful committee chairs—showed only eleven invitations, as did Keith Ellison. Betty McCollum and Tim Walz had only seven invitations apiece by their names. John Kline was even less sociable, at five. And Erik Paulsen, who perhaps hadn't had time to learn the ways of Washington yet, had only three. Al Franken showed only three—one at his own home—and a modest four invitations showed up for Amy Klobuchar.

Bachmann's favorite venue for putting the squeeze on lobbyists and PACs was only one block from the U.S. Capitol at the exclusive Capitol Hill Club, "a refined and elegant environment for your business, political, and social activities." She held at least seven fund-raisers there in 2009 alone, fetching $1,000 per PAC and $250–$500 per individual, and at least another three in 2008.

Described as a "national social club for Republicans," the Capitol Hill Club's membership was by invitation only and required the sponsorship of at least two members. The candidate's name and the names of the sponsors were posted in the lobby for ten days and then the candidate's application was presented to the Membership Committee and the Executive Committee for final approval. According to a 2008 *Harper's* article, successful applicants paid a $1,000 initiation fee ($300 for members of Congress) and $125 a month in dues ($62.50 for members of Congress).

Stated the club's website: "In a recent speech to Club members, a respected Republican leader said 'There's no place in this town where the ratio of impression to value comes at a lower cost.' As a member of the Capitol Hill Club, you will enjoy the opportunity to associate with the men and women who shape the future of our country. Whether here for business or pleasure, at the Capitol Hill Club you are part of the excitement of Washington."

When Bachmann wasn't being "part of the excitement of Washington" at the Capitol Hill Club, she had to settle for partying with the hoi polloi at the more public digs of Finemondo or the Sonoma Restaurant and Wine Bar, where she held at least four fund-raisers in 2008 and at least five more in 2009.

Sometimes Bachmann's supporters offered up their own quarters for her parties, as with the June 17, luncheon with Pete Sessions at the National Rifle Association's offices. Other times Bachmann took advantage of a more recent phenomenon: the free or discounted use of a lobbyist's private townhouse.

According to a January 31, 2008, *USA Today* article, this growing trend allows lobbyists, corporations, and labor unions to offer lawmakers a free or low-cost venue for fund-raisers just a few steps from the capitol. This perk doesn't necessarily show up on campaign expense reports.

"It's a nice added bonus to say, 'Hey, we're going to host it at our house,'" Jeffrey Shoaf, chief lobbyist of the Associated General Contractors of America, told *USA Today*.

Bachmann was the beneficiary of the Associated General Contractors townhouse herself at a June 3 reception for her featuring John Boehner. In 2008, she took advantage of the lobbyist-owned townhouses of Rupli and Associates and Bartlett, Bendall & Kadesh to raise campaign cash.

Sometimes Bachmann wasn't the beneficiary of these soirees but, rather, a featured guest designed to draw the big checks. She added marquee value to at least four such events in the past two years, according to Party Time.

The Promised Land

One month when you didn't find Bachmann going to lobbyists' fund-raisers was August, when Congress was in recess. Not because she wanted to spend that month in her district meeting with constituents, but because that was when she took her annual excursion to Israel, courtesy of Jewish organizations affiliated with lobbyists for Israel.

Bachmann—and her family members—enjoyed free trips to Israel in 2007, 2008, and 2009, to the tune of $44,380.

In 2007, Michele and Marcus jaunted off to Jerusalem and Tel Aviv, with the American Israel Education Foundation picking up the tab again, which included luxurious $436 per night rooms at the David Citadel Hotel. Cost: $17,796.

In 2008, Bachmann and her husband, Marcus, traveled to Jerusalem, this time courtesy of the Jewish Community Relations Council. The cost of the trip: $7,170.

In July–August 2009, Bachmann and her daughter, Elisa, traveled to Jerusalem on the dime of the American Israel Education Foundation, living like royalty at the $500-a-night, five-star David Citadel Hotel. The cost of the trip for Michele and Elisa Bachmann: $19,414.74, covered entirely by the Jewish group, which is affiliated with the powerful pro-Israel lobbying group AIPAC (American Israel Public Affairs Committee). They each even got a nice photo album from their hosts as a memento of their junket.

MIA

Meanwhile, as Bachmann topped the Minnesota delegation in parties and free trips to Israel, she also topped the delegation in missed votes. As of February 2010 in the 111th Congress, Bachmann had missed 11 percent of her votes, placing her 25th worst among 435 members. The average for all members was 3.8 percent.

Bachmann's absentee voting record reached an astonishing 58.7 percent from June to September 2011, roughly the period since she announced she was running for president, during which she missed 145 of 247 votes.

None of this came as a surprise to those who tracked Bachmann's political career since the beginning. She had a reputation as a lazy legislator while serving in the Minnesota State Senate, more interested in promoting herself and her narrow extremist agenda than in doing anything beneficial for her constituents. As with her congressional career, where Bachmann had only one committee assignment, she carried a lighter committee load in the legislature than just about all of her Senate colleagues and passed nothing of significance during her tenure there, either.

When Bachmann arrived in Washington in 2007, one of her first pronouncements was to lambaste House Speaker Nancy Pelosi for extending the congressional work week from three days to five.

> "So now we have very limited opportunities to meet with people back in Minnesota," Bachmann groused. "Unless you're rich enough to take time off of work and have money to buy an airplane ticket to come to DC, your opportunities for meeting with your local congressman are greatly diminished."

From 2006 to 2009 Bachmann found time to make a national name for herself through countless appearances on conservative TV and radio shows and with coast-to-coast speaking engagements, while holding only a single public town hall meeting in her own district.

The moral of the story? If you lived in Minnesota's 6th District and wanted to meet with your congresswoman Michele Bachmann, there was no point in waiting around for her next town hall meeting. You'd have had a far better chance of catching her if you'd headed over to the Capitol Hill Club instead with a $500 check in hand.

The Public Trough

Michele Bachmann continued to feed at the public trough in 2010. Bachmann is a champion for critics of runaway government spending, but she has also been a champion at running away with more than her share of the government pie for much of her life.

The most recent example of Bachmann's hypocrisy on government spending was her headline-grabbing proposal to freeze all federal employees' pay, eliminating a scheduled pay raise in 2011. No law requires federal employees—including members of Congress—to accept pay raises. Yet Bachmann has happily pocketed every one of hers. She watched her federal salary increase from $165,200, when she took office in January 2007, to her current paycheck of $174,000 a year. That's a pay raise of 5.3 percent in three years in office. Not bad, considering what most of her constituents have seen their salaries do in the last three years.

Yet Bachmann's congressional salary is only one part of the government trough from which she feeds. Let's take a look at how Michele Bachmann has benefited over the years from government spending.

Bachmann went to public schools in Minnesota and graduated from Anoka High School in 1974 and Winona State University in 1978. After she completed her postgraduate degrees, she went to work as a tax collection lawyer for the Internal Revenue Service from 1988 to 1993, where she drew a nice federal salary for five years.

Bachmann was elected to the Minnesota State Senate in 2000, where she drew a state salary for another five years. She even managed to bill the taxpayers for her home cable television for a few months. Bachmann also was one of the State Senate's perennial top recipients of taxpayer subsidies for political campaigns every year she served there, raking in a total of $96,722 in taxpayer subsidies for her campaigns from 2000 to 2005.

Then in 2006, Bachmann hit the jackpot and was elected to Congress, where she more than quadrupled her government salary and beefed up her government benefits. After serving five years, she became vested in the congressional pension plan, again courtesy of the taxpayers. That's still not all, though.

There's the Bachmann family farm in Independence, Wisconsin, of which Michele and her husband, Marcus, own up to a $250,000 share. The Bachmann farm enterprise has harvested more than a quarter of a million dollars in federal farm subsidies between 1995 and 2006, thousands of that going into Michele's pocket.

The Bachmann & Associates Christian counseling clinic in Lake Elmo, owned by Michele and Marcus Bachmann, has taken in nearly $30,000 in state funds since 2007 and more than $100,000 in Medicaid payments. The Bachmanns also undoubtedly collected some sort of government payments for the twenty-three foster children that she claims they have taken in.

We're not even counting the times Bachmann has tried to improperly bilk the taxpayers for her personal gain and gotten caught as when she tried to turn Washington County Adopt-a-Highway signs into permanent campaign signs by illegally using her State Senate title on them. So, the next time Michele Bachmann trots out her shopworn platitudes about reducing the size of government and weaning people off Social Security and Medicare, just remember: Michele Bachmann has never met a government check she hasn't liked—or cashed.

Hawaiian Lyin'

When Bloomberg reporter and former *Time* magazine White House correspondent Margaret Carlson called Michele Bachmann the first week in February 2011 for a comment on the people's uprising in Egypt, Carlson wrote that Bachmann's office told her the Minnesota congresswoman "wouldn't be giving any interviews this week while she concentrates on district work."

Yet according to the Grassroot Institute Hawaii, Bachmann was scheduled to give a luncheon talk at the Ala Moana Hotel in Honolulu that day—4,476 miles and 80 degrees F from the subzero temperatures that her constituents in Minnesota's 6th District woke up to on the morning of February 2, 2011.

According to the Grassroot Institute website, Bachmann's $35-a-head luncheon was sold out. The Grassroot Institute Hawaii was founded in 2001 and said its mission was "to promote individual liberty, the free market and limited accountable government." The institute promised that the speech from the "potential 2012 presidential candidate" would offer "great insight into the 2011 congressional session."

With millions of freedom-loving Egyptians clamoring for democracy, Michele Bachmann was noticeably quiet on the massive revolt under way there. After all, "freedom" is the lynchpin of virtually everything the 6th District Minnesota Republican says or does. Bachmann, a fervent supporter of Israel and a frequent traveler to Israel on the Israelis' dime, gave no clues about where she fell on the goings-on in Egypt.

In Iran, Bachmann threw her support behind the People's Mujahideen Organization of Iran (PMOI, also known as the MEK), whose goals include the replacement of the current Khamenei-Ahmadinejad regime in Iran with a democratic and secular government. Bachmann asked that the terrorist group be removed from the U.S. State Department list of Foreign Terrorist

Organizations. According to the *Guardian* newspaper, however, there may be a good reason why the MEK is considered a terrorist organization.

"There is a strong credibility gap between the group's rhetoric and its past actions, especially its associations with Saddam between 1986 and 2003," the newspaper wrote.

> According to the Council on Foreign Relations, MEK directly participated in the savage reprisals against those who rose up against the Iraqi tyrant in 1991. Indeed, the extent to which it functioned as an effective arm of Saddam's totalitarian regime is demonstrated by the fact that, when it surrendered to US forces in 2003, it had "2,000 tanks, armoured personnel carriers, and heavy artillery pieces."

The *Guardian* also raised the possibility of blowback in return for U.S. support for the MEK: "Ironically, before its split with Ayatollah Khomeini, its leaders worked closely with Iran's theocratic government, directly participating in the 1979 takeover of the U.S. embassy in Tehran. This raises the obvious risk that if Britain and America covertly, or overtly, support MEK, it could then cut a deal with Tehran and turn its guns on Europe and America."

Banks, Blastocysts, Big Oil, and Big Pharma Big Winners in Bachmann's First Hundred Hours

Although much was made of Representative Michele Bachmann's performance at President Bush's 2007 State of the Union speech—when, as he walked through crowds of legislators afterward, she clutched his shoulder and wouldn't let go, drew him in for a kiss and a hug, then got an arm around him and patted his back repeatedly, all while he paid her no attention at all—the real embarrassment was her first hundred hours in Congress.

Even before she took office, Bachmann joked that during her congressional tenure, "My No. 1 goal is to not go to jail." Yet one of the first votes Bachmann took was against House Resolution 6, which expanded prohibitions against influence-peddling and the acceptance of gifts from lobbyists, which included sporting and entertainment tickets, junkets to posh resorts, and travel on private jets. The legislation was a direct response to members of the last Congress who—yes—did go to jail.

House Resolution 6 was also intended to bring much-needed restrictions and sunshine to the congressional practice of "earmarking" funds for pet projects. It would institute a "pay as you go" policy for tax-and-spend measures. Bachmann told the *Minnesota Christian Chronicle* in 2006 that those earmarks undermined the power of state and local governments and contributed to the need to raise taxes. "I'm running for the right reasons, and will fight for fiscal responsibility in the U.S. Congress," Bachmann pledged. Yet despite Bachmann's bluster about fiscal responsibility, she rejected those measures as well. House Resolution 6 passed anyway, 232–200.

This is what candidate Michele Bachmann said about homeland security when she was campaigning in 2006: "The horrific attack on 9/11 demonstrated that terrorists can bring the battlefield to our shores. For this reason, we must remain continually vigilant and ready with a broad-based strategy that includes . . . more effective and efficient homeland security."

Yet when it came time to pass the first bill of the 110th Congress, H.R. 1: "Implementing the 9/11 Commission Recommendations Act," which would have, among other things, required inspection of all cargo arriving in U.S. ports, Bachmann voted no. The bill passed by a margin of more than two to one, 299–128.

The House's second bill, H.R. 2: "Fair Minimum Wage Act," was intended to gradually raise the minimum wage to the grand sum of $7.25 an hour by 2009. Bachmann, who advocated abolishing the minimum wage altogether, predictably voted no. The bill passed overwhelmingly, 315–116.

H.R. 3: "Stem Cell Research Enhancement Act" was meant to require the secretary of Health and Human Services to conduct and support research that utilizes human embryonic stem cells, regardless of the date on which the stem cells were derived from a human embryo, provided that they were voluntarily donated from fertility clinics. Yet Bachmann voted no, preferring that those potentially life-saving embryos from fertility clinics be thrown away instead, as they later were under President Bush's order. That didn't sound very "pro-life." The bill passed anyway, 253–174.

Bachmann loved to be photographed with seniors, but when she had to choose between seniors and pharmaceutical companies, Bachmann sided with Big Pharma. H.R. 4: "Medicare Prescription Drug Price Negotiation Act" was intended to require the secretary of Health and Human Services to negotiate with pharmaceutical manufacturers the prices that may be charged to prescription drug plan sponsors and Medicare Advantage organizations, which could reduce the prices of some drugs for seniors. Bachmann voted no again, but the bill passed handily, 255–170.

The banking and financial industry was Bachmann's biggest campaign contributor outside of single-issue groups, so perhaps it should have come as no surprise that she put their interests ahead of college students when she voted against H.R. 5: "College Student Relief Act." The measure was designed to amend the Higher Education Act of 1965 to reduce interest rates for student borrowers.

Bachmann called the bill to reduce student loan rates "anti-student" because it helped only those who had graduated and not those currently in school.

Huh?

The measure passed by an overwhelming margin without Bachmann's help, 356–71.

Bachmann's abysmal voting record in the first hundred hours was predictable, based on her state senate record. Perhaps that's why those who knew her best—the voters in her hometown of Stillwater—rejected her in November 2006 and in her two subsequent reelections in 2008 and 2010.

Hypocrite Bachmann and Her Secret "Letter-Mark" Requests for Socialist Stimulus Pork $$$ Revealed

Michele Bachmann repeatedly claimed President Obama's stimulus act (American Recovery and Reinvestment Act of 2009) was a "failure." A January 12, 2010, *Townhall.com* blog authored by Bachmann was titled "Stimulus is not creating jobs." Even as Bachmann, the founder of the House Tea Party Caucus, was blasting the president's bill as a wasteful barrel of pork, she was quietly trying to bring some stimulus bacon home to her own district.

In October, the online news site MinnPost revealed six letters, obtained through a Freedom of Information Act request, that Bachmann sent to Transportation Secretary Ray LaHood urging stimulus funding for transportation projects in the 6th District.

In one of those letters, Bachmann requested $690 million for a bridge over the St. Croix River. In a September 15, 2009, letter, Bachmann specifically mentioned the job-promoting benefits of the project:

> Residents in Stillwater, which is home to more than 1,000 businesses that employ over 10,000 workers, have

been working to make this bridge a reality for decades. MnDOT estimates that the project would directly produce 1,407 new jobs per year while indirectly producing 1,563 a year— a total of 2,970 each year after the project's completion.

In another letter, she requested money to complete the Northstar Commuter Line to St. Cloud. Bachmann's request for funds for the Northstar Phase 2 project to St. Cloud is at odds with her longstanding opposition to the project. Bachmann's pals at the Minnesota Taxpayers League called Northstar a "robbery," a sentiment shared by many of Bachmann's conservative colleagues in the Minnesota Republican Party.

Bachmann responded to a request for comment on the letters from MinnPost:

> I continue to oppose the so-called stimulus package because it has been a failure. It has failed at job creation, has wasted millions on everything from "smoking cessation activities" to "tax breaks for Hollywood movie producers" and has piled a massive amount of debt on our children and grandchildren.
>
> It is my obligation as a member of Congress to ensure stimulus dollars are spent on the most worthy projects. I did just that when I supported applications for the TIGER grant program.

So, why didn't she make these requests public? Why didn't she simply ask for earmarks? Did she really think she could get away with campaigning against stimulus funding, while secretly begging for stimulus money?

Asked to comment on Bachmann's hypocritical letter-marks, Minnesota's Fifth District Representative Keith Ellison told Minn-

Post, "It would embarrass me to do it, I would be ashamed to do what Michele does, but then again she doesn't know shame."

Bachmann, as usual, was trying to have it both ways—which is probably the reason she skipped the debate on transportation in October 2010. During the election of 2008 Bachmann pretended to support Northstar when she was interviewed by the editorial board of the East Central Minnesota newspaper chain. In an editorial, endorsing her opponent Elwyn Tinklenberg, the board mentioned Bachmann's two-faced stand on funding transportation projects in the district:

> What really sealed her fate, however, was her unwillingness to later answer point-blank questions about a bridge project in St. Cloud and the Northstar Commuter Rail. We find it disingenuous that she wears a Northstar lapel pin but won't comment on whether or when the line should ever be extended to St. Cloud and Rice.

Bachmann Shocked Veterans with a Plan That Would Cut Veterans' Benefits

In January 2011, on her official House of Representatives website, Michele Bachmann unveiled a plan to cut $400 billion in federal spending that included freezing Veterans Affairs Department health-care spending and would have cut veterans' disability benefits. There was no mention of cutting her own benefits.

Veterans groups reacted with outrage, posting condemnations of Bachmann on their websites. A *Dump Bachmann* reader left this comment about Bachmann's callous disregard for the men and the women who selflessly served their country: "Apparently veterans are useful only when a photo op comes along during a campaign."

Hydrocephalus Hypocrisy

Perhaps no story about Michele Bachmann illustrates how unscrupulous and self-serving she is than the time she accepted a "Heroes of Hydrocephalus" award but voted against federal funding for research five years in a row.

The Minnesota 6th District Republican was recognized a few years back as one of the Pediatric Hydrocephalus Foundation's "Heroes of Hydrocephalus" for her sponsorship of H.Res. 373 in 2009, designating September "National Hydrocephalus Awareness Month." It's a curious honor, though, because Bachmann has voted against federal funding for hydrocephalus research at every opportunity since she was elected to Congress in 2006.

Hydrocephalus is a condition in which excess cerebrospinal fluid—a clear fluid surrounding the brain and the spinal cord—accumulates to cause an abnormal dilation of the spaces in the brain called ventricles. This dilation causes potentially harmful pressure on the tissues of the brain. The disease may be congenital or acquired and occurs in about 1 in 500 births.

"What Congresswoman Bachmann and Congressman Lance have done for the Hydrocephalus Community cannot be overstated. In just under two years, we saw September named as 'National Hydrocephalus Awareness Month,' and just this past month, a Congressional Caucus to educate and raise awareness about Hydrocephalus was created," said Michael Illions, PHF's national director of advocacy.

Not so fast, Mr. Illions. Let's take a closer look at what Congresswoman Bachmann has done for hydrocephalus research.

Federal funding for hydrocephalus research comes through the Department of Health and Human Services (HHS). The National Institute of Neurological Disorders and Stroke (NINDS) is part of the National Institutes of Health in HHS and is the leading federal agency conducting and funding hydrocephalus research.

In addition, some research may be conducted by the Centers for Disease Control and Prevention, also under HHS.

Bachmann's own 2009 resolution stated that "further research into the epidemiology, path physiology, disease burden, and improved treatment of hydrocephalus should be conducted and supported" and that "public awareness, professional education, and scientific research regarding hydrocephalus should increase through partnerships between the Federal Government, health care professionals, and patient advocacy groups."

"It is my hope that by raising awareness of hydrocephalus, we can encourage the research that will lead to new diagnoses, treatments, and cures for it, helping these children and their families live full lives without constantly fearing the worst," Bachmann wrote on her website.

Yet since 2007, Bachmann has voted against every HHS appropriations bill that funds the very research she claims to support. She cast "no" votes on the final passage of HHS appropriations for FY2007, FY2008, FY2009, FY2010, and, most recently, on December 17, 2010, for a continuing appropriations resolution for FY2011.

"It is truly humbling to receive the 'Heroes of Hydrocephalus' award, but I believe the real heroes are those with hydrocephalus, their families, and all advocates who work tirelessly every day to bring awareness to this condition. I'm glad I could play a small role in the cause by sponsoring a House Resolution designating September as 'National Hydrocephalus Awareness Month,'" said Congresswoman Bachmann.

Yes, a resolution is a small role, Congresswoman Bachmann— a very small role. Yet it could have been much larger. You could have joined another group of heroes you failed to mention: the members of Congress who actually vote their convictions for such causes and back them up with real dollars, instead of simply mouthing them for cheap publicity stunts before moving on to the next camera.

Ironically, the newly formed Pediatric and Adult Hydrocephalus Congressional Caucus will be cochaired by Minnesota congressman Tim Walz (D-1). Walz got no award, but, unlike his headline-grabbing colleague, he has consistently voted yea on federal funding for hydrocephalus research.

Yet another wrinkle to this story was first reported on the *Dump Bachmann*–affiliated *Ripple in Stillwater* blog. An inquisitive *Ripple in Stillwater* reader sent an e-mail to Michael Illions, the founder and the vice president of the Pediatric Hydrocephalus Foundation, and asked how that organization could bestow an honor on a member of congress such as Michele Bachmann, who voted against hydrocephalus research funding five years in a row.

"Your email is pretty ridiculous and should not even be dignified with an answer," Illions began, before proceeding to answer. "Only someone who would rather squabble about political viewpoints would not see the good and the progress made in the Hydrocephalus Community with Congresswoman Bachmann's involvement," he continued, before launching into some political viewpoints of his own.

"Congresswoman Bachmann did not vote specifically against funding for Hydrocephalus; as a Fiscal Conservative, she voted against an over bloated budget that used MILLIONS of dollars of tax-payer money to fund items like watching bees mate and the differences between maple syrups, just to name 2 items. [Editors note: That budget included a request from Illions himself for $4.5 million for the National Institutes of Health to conduct hydrocephalus research.]

"Had their [*sic*] been a line item veto or a budget bill that dealt specifically with health related funding requests, the outcome would have been different," Illions claimed.

If that sounds like a response from a typical Tea Partier, instead of a rational explanation from the head of a nonprofit children's organization, that's because it is. Illions is the head of a New Jersey Tea Party group called Conservatives With Attitude! The group claimed it has "the most influential and most visited political blog in New Jersey" and described its members as "home grown, rock ribbed, all American patriots that have united to bring the conservative message to the American people."

Illions plied his trade on the speaking circuit as well, appearing before such crowds as the Family Research Council and the Woodbridge, New Jersey, Tea Party, but he's long been accustomed to performing before rubes. He's also a former professional wrestler, having spent fourteen years in the ring as "A.J. Sparxx."

Now it's perfectly clear why the Pediatric Hydrocephalus Foundation would not only defend but also honor a congresswoman who has voted against their interests her entire congressional career. It has far less to do with hydrocephalus research and far more to do with Tea Party politics.

That's why it makes so little sense.

Not on the Road Again

Michele Bachmann's record of nonachievement is epitomized by her abysmal record on transportation. Bachmann has always opposed funding for rail projects such as the Northstar Commuter Rail that runs from Minneapolis to Big Lake in her district and the Hiawatha Light Rail Line in Minneapolis. She once referred to light-rail as a "black hole for money."

This is what used to be on Bachmann's State Senate campaign website:

> As your District 52 State Senator, I will work hard to add capacity to Minnesota highways. . . . This is my personal commitment to you.

> Michele believes a successful transportation policy must put an end to the diversion of scarce funds to impractical and expensive rail transit programs that will have no direct benefit for area residents and will cost millions of dollars in the future for operating subsidies. She has called for dedicating 100 percent of the sales tax on vehicles to road construction.

Bachmann said in her 2006 congressional campaign, "I want to wake up in the morning to see bulldozers" building roads. She voted against funding for Northstar in 2005 and 2006.

During the 2006 election, however, Bachmann pretended to support Northstar when she wore a Northstar lapel pin to an editorial endorsement interview with the north-suburban ECM newspaper chain. However, she was unwilling to answer questions about her support for the commuter rail line's extension to St. Cloud and Rice.

The 2008 campaign against Democratic-Farmer-Labor (DFL) opponent Elwyn Tinklenberg, a former state transportation commissioner under Governor Jesse Ventura, highlighted Bachmann's appalling record on transportation.

This is what Tinklenberg said in a 2008 video interview with *The Uptake*:

> She is about partisan polarization. She is about divisiveness. And the result is she has not been able to accomplish anything as a senator and she's not accomplishing anything, except in a negative sort of way in the district currently. We think we represent a strong alternative to that.
>
> The district is the focus of some major changes in transportation, not only in terms of improvements to the existing system, but changes in that system. Northstar

is a big issue. And I'm proud of the fact that I helped get Northstar started when I was at Anoka County. And now we're making some progress on that. It's disappointing to me that it's five years later than what it should have been. It's $90 million more than when we introduced it back in 2000. Back then, it was going all the way to St. Cloud; now it's just going to Big Lake. So we've lost time, we've lost half of the line, and we've increased the cost as result of the delays that came out of the Republican-controlled House back in 2000.

I bring a record of having to do some things in transportation, and some important things, the Hiawatha light-rail line, for example, as compared to Representative Bachmann, who, when she was in the State Senate, fought every transportation initiative that came along, has been a constant obstructionist for transportation issues in the state, and has carried that on even now in her congressional seat. She has voted three times to hold up funding for the reconstruction of the 35W bridge. And I think that represents where her priorities are in relation to transportation issues.

She hasn't been able to get anything done partly because of that kind of partisan, ideologue approach she's taken to so many issues. But also she has used what support she has given to transportation, principally PRT or Personal Rapid Transit, as a way of really distracting the discussion. . . . PRT is not something that's going to work to serve commuters. It's not something that's going to work to serve the transit interests and concerns and needs of Minnesota. And she's using it simply as a distraction. She doesn't really mean or intend to support any kind of increased funding for transit, and she's just using this as a way of diffusing the issue.

Bachmann's Future Plans

Since Bachmann threw her hat in the ring for the GOP nomination for president of the United States of America, she has missed scores of votes. Bachmann rarely visits Minnesota's 6th District, preferring to crisscross Iowa, which she repeatedly declares to be her home—all the while cashing her government paychecks.

In the event that Bachmann fails to garner a winning number of delegates, she can always change her mind. She has until June 5, 2012, to make up her mind—but it will be for a district with newly drawn boundaries that may not be as Bachmann-friendly.

Will Bachmann's neglected and forsaken constituents welcome her back—and will her new constituents want anything to do with her?

CHAPTER 5

Bachmann's Antischool Agenda

Michele Bachmann is part of a group of theocratic movements that would like to transform and undermine public education. The Bachmann children were homeschooled. Bachmann claims that she was shocked by educational materials carried into the Bachmann domicile by her public-schooled foster children. Bachmann then ran for the Stillwater school board and lost. She went on to start the New Heights Charter School and served on the board. She quit after she and other members were confronted about injecting their fundamentalist Christian beliefs into the publicly funded school's curriculum. In the Minnesota Senate, Michele Bachmann worked with a small number of right-wing, theocratic authors and organizations.

Bachmann and David Barton

One of Bachmann's early causes was the American Heritage in Public Education Act, cosponsored with Mark Olson. Olson and Bachmann told the *Star Tribune* that public school teachers nationwide were not teaching from U.S. history using original documents because students might be exposed to religious views expressed in the documents. Olson and Bachmann also said that too much of what was taught in public schools about U.S. history was negative.

What Olson and Bachmann told their supporters was different. Here is an announcement on Bachmann's old campaign website that mentioned David Barton, a theocrat notorious for his attempts to rewrite history:

> BIG LAKE, MINN. (April 11, 2006)—David Barton is coming to Minnesota's sixth district to support Michele Bachmann in her run for U.S. Congress. The nationally known author and American historian has endorsed Senator Bachmann in her congressional race and will be speaking at the Bridgeview Assembly of God Church in Big Lake on Tuesday, April 18th. The title of his speech is "God, Government and Good Citizenship."

"I'm excited for David to come speak in the Sixth District and honored by his endorsement and support," said Bachmann. "He is a fantastic and insightful writer."

Representative Mark Olson (R-Big Lake) and Senator Michele Bachmann (R-Stillwater) introduced legislation that was designed to make it easier for teachers to use such documents as the Mayflower Compact, the Federalist Papers, the Gettysburg Address, and the U.S. Constitution as part of their classroom instruction. Their bills would order school districts to "permit" teachers to read, study, and post any documents relating to the history of the United States or Minnesota.

Bachmann cited a California case in which teachers were forbidden from teaching the Declaration of Independence and some of George Washington's writings because of the references to God and religion. Under her bill, she said, "districts would not be able to limit or restrain instruction if there are religious references in any of these documents."

This was a total lie promoted by the Alliance Defense Fund (ADF), which was suing the California school district. Parents in the district were very irritated about how the Alliance Defense Fund distorted the issues and publicly called on the ADF to retract its statements.

An organization of parents at the Stevens Creek Elementary School in Cupertino, California, told the ADF that it was responsible for some of the hostility they had received because of the "incendiary headline" on the ADF website that read "Declaration of Independence Banned from Classroom." The parents group requested the headline be withdrawn and a public retraction posted regarding the false allegation regarding the banning of the Declaration of Independence from classrooms. Objecting to their classrooms becoming a "battleground," the parents concluded with this observation:

> While you may not have directly contacted the many people who felt compelled to vent their hostility toward our principal and school, we believe your organization is nonetheless responsible. This reaction was the direct consequence of the incendiary headline that can still be found on your webpage, "Declaration of Independence Banned from Classroom." We therefore ask that you stop exposing our school and our children to more harm by continuing to state what is clearly false on your website.

We request a withdrawal of your headline and a public retraction. Surely, in all good conscience, you cannot continue to falsely represent that our school has banned the Declaration of Independence from the classroom.

Your group states on its website that it supports and defends families and family values. Yet, it appears that since 2001 you have targeted schools and therefore the families that make up those schools in order to achieve what we believe is your political agenda. In a recent interview, one of your spokespersons said that you view schools as the "new battleground." Do you realize that your battleground is where we send our children? Is that the environment in which you want to fight a battle? How does learning take place in a school besieged by hate mail triggered by an incendiary and erroneous headline on your website? We wonder if your supporters realize that your actions may be tearing the very fabric you purport to weave.

We have seen firsthand that truth has been a casualty in this case. But most of all it is disturbing to see how an organization that claims to defend the truth and Christian values spreads false information about our school, its principal and our local school board. These actions can only undermine the public's trust in your organization, and may cause even some of your supporters to question your actions and your judgment.

EdWatch, the nonprofit arm of Bachmann's political campaigns, heralded the passage of portions of the law in 2005:

Governor Pawlenty signed the Minnesota Education Omnibus bill into law. Included in the 128 pages were two short paragraphs that open the door to begin reclaiming Americas [*sic*] forgotten heritage. The American Heritage in Public Education Act does two things: 1) It encourages schools to teach Americas [*sic*] Founding Principles from original sources. 2) It prevents the censorship of religious references from those sources. Teachers may now introduce their students to Americas [*sic*] uncensored Christian heritage without fear.

Bachmann Hangs Teenage Republican Student Out to Dry

In 2005, a notice was posted on the Minnesota Teenage Republican (MTR) website asking students to snitch on their liberal teachers (see chapter 1 for the entire post).

Bachmann denied any connection to the solicitation for student snitches. She said she had previously trolled for similar tales of pedagogical malfeasance from public university students to support the Freedom of Speech for Faculty and Students Bill of Rights she introduced. Yet the Republican Party of Minnesota, which hosted the Teenage Republican site, removed the link to the site when the story broke. Bachmann said she received e-mails from teachers all over the state. Bachmann was quoted in the *Pioneer Press*:

"This is like an oil tanker spill," she said. "I'm trying to contain it. How do I unring the bell?"

Translation: I'm busted. How do I spin my way out of this?

The deputy chairman of the Minnesota Teenage Republicans told the *Pioneer Press* that he posted the notice after speaking to Bachmann about her bill. He said he offered to help Bachmann by contacting the seven hundred Minnesota members of the MTR.

The stories are a bit different. If Bachmann really didn't want her scrapbook promoted to teenagers, why didn't she ask the deputy chairman not to post the request on the website?

The lesson to be learned is that people you'd think would be protecting you—adults and mentors, such as Michele Bachmann—instead hang you out to dry, rather than taking responsibility for the situation.

Bachmann Lies about Creationism in the Public Schools

The following statement from Michele Bachmann was published in the *Stillwater (MN) Gazette* on October 1, 2003. She claimed that she was misquoted about her support for teaching creationism in the public schools.

> A famous quote says, "You can't unring a bell." Similarly, once a false statement is made, it can't be fully taken back. The *Gazette* did that to me in the Monday edition by attributing views to me that I do not hold, nor did I say.
>
> Over the years, the *Gazette* has gotten plenty of quotes and information wrong about me, but I have usually let it go and tried to overlook the mistakes. This time I can't do so because the *Gazette* blew it "big time."
>
> The *Gazette* reported in a headline that I said "schools should teach creationism." That is a false statement. I told the reporter that I believe all scientific evidence surrounding an issue, in this case the study of the origin of life, should be brought into the classroom. In other words, academic freedom and balance for students should include respected, science-based critiques of evolutionary theory.
>
> The reporter also asked me my personal views on origins and I answered his question. Like the followers of

any of the leading religious faiths in America, I believe that the world was ultimately a product of design rather than a product of time and random chance.

But at no time in the interview did I say creationism should be taught in public schools, nor did I suggest my beliefs become the curriculum.

The *Gazette* wrongly placed my photo beneath a quote that did not represent my views or accurately and professionally report an interview. Both the readers and I were done a disservice.

Although Michele Bachmann claimed that the *Gazette* retracted the article, it changed only the headline. The *Gazette* stood by the rest of its reporting.

At the Republican Leadership Conference in New Orleans in June 2011, Bachmann was asked again about creationism, and this was her answer:

I support intelligent design. . . . What I support is putting all science on the table and then letting students decide. I don't think it's a good idea for government to come down on one side of scientific issue or another, when there is reasonable doubt on both sides.

Bachmann added:

I would prefer that students have the ability to learn all aspects of an issue. And that's why I believe the federal government should not be involved in local education to the most minimal possible process.

Once again, the answer you get from Bachmann depends on when and where you ask the question.

Bachmann and EdWatch

Bachmann subscribed to a number of conspiracy theories about public education and found allies at the nonprofit called EdWatch (see chapter 6, "Bachmann's Faith-Based Agenda"). She also turned her ire on work-to-school programs and the Profiles of Learning.

Bachmann Still Kissing Public School Abolitionists' ASSS

Real estate developer Barry Conner and his wife, Bridget, of Gainesville, Georgia, more than eleven hundred miles from Stillwater, Minnesota, were among the fat-cat contributors to Michele Bachmann's reelection war chest. By the fall of 2007, Barry Conner had contributed $2,300 to Bachmann's campaign on March 21 and another $2,300 on September 25. Bridget Conner kicked in another $2,300 on March 22, making a total of $6,900 from the Conner household.

Barry is also a signatory to the proclamation of the Alliance for the Separation of School and State (ASSS), a national organization that advocates for an end to all public education—not only a reduction in school funding, getting the federal government out of education, or supporting school vouchers, but ending government involvement in education entirely. The group cites a litany of shortcomings in public education to support its radical position: "Besides the on-going complaints about poor academic performance, grade inflation, and low expectations, there is also serious concern over such in-school issues as: violence, physical and emotional bullying, cheating and lying, wide-spread immorality, drugs and alcohol, worldview conflicts."

Although Michele Bachmann stated in the *Stillwater Gazette* on July 24, 2007, that public education was "my No. 1 issue," she still hauled in a total of $56,940 through September 2007 from individuals who have signed the ASSS proclamation, more than half of them from states other than Minnesota, such as Tennessee, Colorado, and Ohio:

- Barry and Bridget Conner, Gainesville, GA: $30,300
- Barbara and George E. Anderson, Champlin, MN: $18,400
- Allan and Randi Beale, Dellwood, MN: $200
- Merlyn Scroggins, Roseville, MN: $900
- Howard Phillips, Vienna, VA: $450
- Terrance Kopp, Long Lake, MN: $2,000
- Judy Shea, Minneapolis, MN: $450
- Pam and Paul Sjolund, Minnetrista, MN: $1,240
- Charles Nash, Minnetonka, MN: $100
- Jeff Myers, Dayton, TN: $500
- David Noebel, Manitou Springs, CO: $300
- Ricki Pepin, Springfield, OH: $350
- Richard Viguerie, Amissville, VA, $1,000
- Patricia Clark, White Bear Lake, MN: $150
- Rita Moosbrugger, Stillwater, MN: $600

When asked at a public forum in Oak Park Heights in October 2006 about reports that she had taken these contributions from ASSS supporters, whose number-one issue is the end of public education, Bachmann lied, saying those reports were "untrue."

Bachmann and Bullying

In 2006, Bachmann put in a rare committee appearance to share her concern that school antibullying programs might turn boys into girls and girls into boys:

I think for all of us, our experience in public schools is there have always been bullies, always have been, always will be. I just don't know how we're ever going to get to a point of zero tolerance and what does it mean? . . . One question would be what would be our definition of bullying?

Will it get to the point where we are completely stifling free speech and expression? Will it mean that— what form of behavior will there be? Will we be expecting boys to be girls? What is it exactly that we're asking for?

I don't say that as a sexist comment, but there are just differences with boys and girls when they're on the playground, when they're in the classroom.

None of us like inappropriate behavior, none of us like sassy children, but there's just a fact of life that as we grow up, we're kind of little barbarians when we're two, and our process as mothers and fathers is to civilize our children. I just don't know how we can realistically expect a zero tolerance of bullying behavior.

In 2011, Anoka-Hennepin, the largest school district in Bachmann's congressional district and in Minnesota, faced lawsuits and a federal investigation after nine students commited suicide in only two years. The reason for the high rate of suicides was blamed on the "neutrality" policy of the school district toward gay students.

Bachmann has shown no interest in or concern for the plight of bullied children in her district, despite the concern her supporters at ASSS apparently have for "physical and emotional bullying" in school.

In September 2011, an attendee at a Costa Mesa, California, political rally asked Bachmann what she intended to do about the reported high incidences of bullying gay students in her district. Bachmann responded, "That's not a federal issue."

Bachmann Claimed That President Obama Created Reeducation Camps

On April 05, 2009, *Dump Bachmann* posted a clip of an interview with Michele Bachmann on Sue Jeffers's KTLK show. Bachmann claimed that President Obama wanted to "cede American sovereignty to transnational global authorities." Bachmann later described Americorps, a national community service program, as reeducation camps for young people.

The irony, of course, was that Bachmann's son, Harrison, was employed at the time by Americorps.

CHAPTER 6

Bachmann's
Faith-Based Agenda

Much has been written about Bachmann's religious beliefs, but until recently she received very little scrutiny about how they affect what she says. Over the years, *Dump Bachmann* has taken a hard look at them and at the bizarre coterie of theocrats who support her, despite the nonprofit status of their institutions.

Generation Joshua

When Bachmann needed volunteers to help her campaign in 2006, she called on the Student Action Teams of Christian homeschooled kids from Generation Joshua, a supposedly nonpartisan, nonprofit organization.

The mission of Generation Joshua's website is very clear: the group does not believe in a separation of church and state: "Our goal at Generation Joshua is to cultivate leaders and to equip them to use their beliefs to influence the political process."

The organization claimed that the politicking was actually educational. Generation Joshua returned to help Bachmann in subsequent elections.

Pastor Mac Hammond and the Living Word Center

On October 14, 2006, Michele Bachmann appeared at Mac Hammond's Living Word megachurch. In four webcast performances we've archived on YouTube, Michele Bachmann claimed that God personally called her to run for office. Bachmann also said that she took a doctoral program on tax law, even though she had no interest in the subject, because her husband commanded her to do it, and it was her bible-prescribed duty to be "submissive" to her husband. Bachmann spoke at length about how she was not lukewarm for God but "hot." After one of the speeches, Mac Hammond said he was going to vote for Michele Bachmann, even though he didn't live in her district.

And why not? He could easily fly in.

Thanks to the excellent spadework of the *Minnesota Independent* news website, the financial dealings of the Living Word Christian Center's high-flying chief pastor, James McBryde Hammond, came under the scrutiny of the Internal Revenue Service.

The IRS began investigating Living Word Church in 2007 and sought to examine the church's financial records. When the IRS issued a summons to Living Word, the church refused to comply and the matter landed in U.S. District Court in 2008.

U.S. District Judge Ann Montgomery ruled that the IRS's

inquiry into Living Word's finances was not authorized by "an appropriate high-level Treasury official" as the law requires and dismissed the complaint on January 20, 2009. Documents unearthed by the *Minnesota Monitor* revealed a sweet deal for Pastor Mac, in which he bought private jets using loans from his church, then leased the planes back to the church at a nice profit. The church also loaned Hammond the money to buy a hangar in May 2002 and then leased that space back from him as well, along with paying for all other operating costs and staff for the jets.

According to Federal Aviation Administration (FAA) records, Hammond, a licensed pilot with Airline Transport and Commercial multiengine certifications, at the time had one private jet registered in his name—a 1986 Cessna 650 Citation III, registered to Hammond on May 8, 2003 (N700MH). That registration is valid through July 31, 2014.

He also had a 1995 Extra Flugzeugbau EA 300/L, a single-engine piston aircraft commonly used for acrobatics, registered in his name on June 20, 2002 (N43MW). That registration is valid through August 31, 2014.

A second jet registered in his name on February 2, 2000—a 1977 Cessna 501 Citation I—was transferred to Canada in 2006 and was registered to Quikjets Operating Ltd., Edmonton, Canada, on June 22, 2006. Hammond has reserved the FAA registration number from that jet—N700LW—until February 25, 2007. That same N-number was just reserved on September 16, 2011, by Jerry Savelle Ministries International in Crowley, Texas, until October 16, 2012.

A third jet—a Rockwell International Sabreliner 60—was registered to Hammond on August 24, 1999. This is the jet that appears to have been purchased on credit from the church with Hammond's first aircraft loan in July 1999, in the amount of $363,000. That loan was rolled into another aircraft loan in April 2002. There are no FAA records for this jet in Hammond's name.

Hammond received another loan from the church in December 1999 in the amount of $478,428, also secured by an airplane. This would appear to be the Citation I jet that he registered in February 2000. The going price on a 1977 Citation I is between $1 million and $1.2 million.

The church extended another loan to Hammond for $155,000 in May 2002, secured by an airplane hangar. This may have been used to help finance the purchase of his EA 300/L airplane a month later. Meanwhile, Hammond leased the hangar to the church for $3,650/month under a noncancellable lease.

The church made another loan to Hammond in March 2003 in the amount of $225,000. This loan was unsecured but apparently helped finance his Citation III jet, which he registered just two months later. Current market prices on a 1986 Citation III jet are between $3.6 million and $4 million.

LWCC defended the church's jet leases in a confidential loan document obtained by the *Minnesota Monitor*.

> [The church] believes that these lease arrangements are no more expensive than if secured from an independent provider. [The church] believes that the aircraft are important to the effective management of its ministry at the present time, and it continually reviews and assesses the economic advantages of their deployment. [The church] uses the airplanes to transport the Senior Pastor and/or staff to national events and speaking engagements, and to transport guests, speakers, educators and others to and from [the church's] Main Campus in the Minneapolis/St. Paul metropolitan area.

According to the *Star Tribune*, however, flight logs showed that Hammond also used the jets to fly to his Florida condos (purchased with loans from the church as well).

Hammond not only liked to fly in style aboard his private jets, according to the *Star Tribune*. He also liked to drive first class. The newspaper found a Lexus and a Porsche registered in Hammond's name, along with three boats.

The cockpit chaplain resurfaced in September 2011 to announce that he was joining Bachmann's presidential campaign team and may chair something called her "National Faith and Family Council," in addition to making campaign appearances with her.

Hammond revealed to his Living Word Christian Center congregation on September 25, 2011, that he has been Bachmann's "personal pastor" for some time. "She is a sister in the Lord that is as committed to his word as any of you in here are," he told his flock.

Of course, none of this may have ever come to light had Michele Bachmann not attracted the attention of the *Minnesota Monitor*, *Dump Bachmann*, and others by giving a campaign speech at LWCC and getting an endorsement from her good friend Pastor Mac at the pulpit—all broadcast on television.

So, the obvious question for reporters seems to be: What does Michele Bachmann, who never fails to remind us of her career as an IRS "tax litigation attorney," think about all of this? Isn't it time for someone to ask her?

EdWatch, the Nonprofit Arm of Bachmann's Political Campaigns

During her term in the Minnesota Senate, Michele Bachmann and other Minnesota Republicans received their talking points about International Baccalaureate (IB) and mental health screening or homosexuality from EdWatch (formerly Maple River Education Coalition). Not only did EdWatch do much of the thinking for

Bachmann, it also did some politicking on behalf of Bachmann that should have been investigated for possible violation of IRS rules for nonprofits. After Bachmann was elected to Congress, EdWatchers Renee Doyle and Julie Quist (the wife of Allen Quist, the GOP-endorsed former candidate for Minnesota governor) joined Bachmann's staff.

EdWatchers are proud of their extremist views. On the EdWatch webpage titled "Great Quotes from the War over Education," the webmaster's favorite quote is from former Minnesota Governor Jesse Ventura: "The Maple River group, they think UFOs are landing next month. Well they do! They think it's some big government federal conspiracy!"

In a speech before the Maple River Education Coalition in Bloomington on November 6, 2004, Bachmann outed a family member to drive home her point that being "in the gay lifestyle" is evil: "Any of you who have members of your family that are in the lifestyle—we have a member of our family that is. This is not funny. It's a very sad life. It's part of Satan, I think, to say this is gay. It's anything but gay."

Bachmann then went on to claim: "It's profoundly sad to recognize that almost all, if not all, individuals who have gone into the lifestyle have been abused at one time in their life, either by a male or by a female. There's been profound hurt and profound things that have happened in almost all of their lives."

The Minnetonka parents group Tonka Focus was established to defend the Minnetonka IB program from a stealth attack by the EdWatchers. The parents also exposed former Minnetonka School Board member Dave Eaton's efforts to include creationism ("Intelligent Design") in the curricula of schools in Minnetonka and other school districts. EdWatch denied supporting creationism. It used the "Santorum amendment," which has been fairly standard fare for those pushing for creationism.

Bachmann and Minnesota Teen Challenge

When Bachmann was caught with thousands of dollars of tainted Ponzi money, she donated it to Minnesota Teen Challenge. For years, Bachmann's photo and bio graced the "testimonials" web page in the company of former president George Walker Bush and Tim Pawlenty. This was her testimonial:

> MN Teen Challenge provides an environment that truly fosters spiritual growth and positive change. I had the opportunity to listen to the Teen Challenge choir and speak to the group, the whole experience was moving. Teen Challenge fills a great need in the community.

This Assemblies of God ministry apparently filled that need by insisting that Satan caused drug abuse and that only devout worship of Jesus could cure drug addicts.

In their 2001 newsletter, Minnesota Teen Challenge claimed that Pokemon, Harry Potter, and Halloween were gateways to Satanism and drug abuse. An article titled "About Witchcraft, About Halloween," claimed that Halloween is "a day totally set up for Satan" and that it is Satan worshippers' "biggest recruitment day of the year." The article claimed one Teen Challenge student who experienced being a witch would put curses on trick or treat bags and demonic symbols on Halloween candy. The Teen Challenge student went on to describe his scariest Halloween experience:

> Different moons require different sacrifices. One Halloween, we received a letter from the head church in San Diego with blood and a crow's foot on it. This meant that there had to be a human sacrifice. The leader of our group walked over to an older, unimportant man and handed him a knife, saying: "You know what you

need to do." The man took the knife and split his stomach open, letting his intestines spill out on the ground. He screamed in agony, and as he fell to his knees he cried out, "Satan, take me home!" We would never sacrifice a Christian, because that would bring glory to God. It would be disgusting. Satan was our God, and we wanted all the glory to go to him.

In the same newsletter, Executive Director Rich Scherber asked for donations to rescue "one more soul from Satan's grip."

In their October 2002 newsletter, "Drugs and the Occult, the Battle Rages at Teen Challenge," Minnesota Teen Challenge published testimonials about lives ruined by witchcraft. Parents were warned to watch for signs their children were falling into a life of devil worship if they listened to "any black metal, death metal, heavy metal, alternative metal, extreme metal or punk bands." Parents were warned to be on the lookout for books about "witchcraft, magic, sorcery, the dead, spells, rites and rituals." The examples of dangerous books included *Harry Potter*. The newsletter offered the perspective of a parent that "our children are under siege by Satan." The parent wrote that Satan knew his time was almost over and that was the reason he was going after the kids with Pokemon cards: "If he can entice a child, he sometimes can keep them for eternity.

Coincidentally, Michele Bachmann grew up in Anoka, Minnesota, which calls itself "The Halloween Capital of the World."

Minnesota Teen Challenge gambled away $27 million chasing after double-digit interest in Tom Petters's Ponzi scheme. Bachmann's pardon-pal Frank Vennes sat on the MNTC board at the time. With her donation, it seems they got some of that money back.

The group's mind-set also can be seen in Executive Director Rich Scherber's bizarre article on the *Across Pacific Magazine* website the day after the collapse of the 35W Bridge in 2007. He claimed that the Almighty protected MNTC staff and "students" from suffering the fate of scores of other motorists who were plunged into the Mississippi River.

> The Minnesota Teen Challenge program is thanking God on several fronts for His awesome protection during the bridge collapse on Interstate 35 yesterday. This bridge is located just ¼ mile from our main center and is traveled hundreds of times by many of our students and staff as the main route to the Northeast metro area. I have heard almost a dozen stories from employees and students who were on this bridge just minutes before it went down. I want to share three of the most powerful miracles.
>
> First, Jessica our admissions supervisor told me in tears how at 6:00 last night she was ready to enter the I-35 Bridge over the Mississippi. The Holy Spirit spoke to her very abruptly to turn off the freeway and go a different way home. She obeyed the Holy Spirit arguing with him all the way. Since she takes this same route every day and her commute home takes almost an hour, detouring from the freeway and not crossing over the bridge didn't make sense. Shortly after she detoured from I-35, the bridge went down. Jessica most likely would have been on that bridge.

In a different account Scherber gave to the ASSIST News Service, he claimed God also saved his daughter who drove to work over the bridge. Scherber added this anecdote to his "testimony":

> Thank God for His divine protection! Please pray for our city! Yesterday we had our Minneapolis Police Chief

Tim Dolan and members of the Minneapolis City Council at chapel. It was a powerful time and at the end we prayed together for our city and for God's wisdom on our leaders and law enforcement. Little did we know that just hours later our city would experience the greatest catastrophe in Minnesota's history. Please keep us in prayer.

Wait . . . he had the police chief and the leadership of the Minneapolis City Council in the chapel, and God didn't choose that time to warn them of the disaster to come later in the day?

Scherber insisted that his organization was Christian but not antigay (many Christian churches are open and affirming, and so are the nonprofit organizations affiliated with them). Yet Minnesota Teen Challenge invited Janet Boynes to speak to one of MNTC's women's groups. Bradlee Dean also spoke to the Minnesota Teen Challenge "students."

In a bizarre interview at the Minnesota State Fair, Scherber told the hosts of a Christian radio he believed that cirrhosis of the liver could be faith-cured and that such a miracle had happened at Minnesota Teen Challenge.

Dump Bachmann reported on Michele Bachmann speaking at a MN Teen Challenge–sponsored recovery day celebration in October 2008. The Michele Bachmann testimonial was later scrubbed from the page, as was President George Bush's; however, Bachmann's testimonial remained in the adult section of the website.

Bachmann's Pastor Problem: Bradlee Dean

Bradlee Dean is a longhaired, tattooed drummer for a Christian heavy metal band called Junkyard Prophet. Bradlee Dean, aka Bradley Dean Smith, is also the leader of a nonprofit ministry called You Can Run But You Cannot Hide International, Inc. Bradlee's ministry used to be called You Can Run But You Cannot Hide. Michele Bachmann wrote him a letter of commendation on her Senate letterhead in 2003. Bachmann also helped raise money for Bradlee's ministry and spoke at their 2006 fund-raising "gala." Bachmann praised the ministry for its controversial school assemblies. Schools booked Bradlee Dean's drug-prevention assemblies, not suspecting that the assemblies included religious sermons about abortion, homosexuality, and chastity.

Bradlee Dean and his sidekick Jake (Jacob McMillian MacAulay, aka "Jake McMillian") have a radio show called *Sons of Liberty*, on which Bradlee and Jake called for the enforcement of sodomy laws, said President Obama was a "domestic enemy," deemed a recent U.S. Marshal appointment illegal because the woman is a lesbian, claimed that Ponzi fraudster Tom Petters was not receiving a fair trial, and said that he and other "righteous men" are followed by helicopters.

So that Bradlee would not toil in obscurity, *Dump Bachmann* compiled an archive of his most bizarre rants. Bradlee created a controversy in 2010, when he regaled his listeners with the following:

> "Muslims are calling for the executions of homosexuals in America," Dean said on YCR's May 15 radio show on AM 1280 the Patriot. "This just shows you they themselves are upholding the laws that are even in the Bible of the Judeo-Christian God, but they seem to be more moral than even the American Christians do, because these people are livid about enforcing their laws. They know homosexuality is an abomination."

The Minnesota gubernatorial election was in full swing, and Republican candidate Tom Emmer was a supporter of Bradlee

Dean. *Dump Bachmann* recorded and blogged the comment, and it went viral on the Internet; however, the newfound celebrity brought more scrutiny from Karl Bremer.

Karl found that Bradley Dean Smith and his Annandale-based antigay hate "ministry" was evicted under court order from its offices in the Bass Lake Business Centre II in Plymouth for non-payment of rent. The eviction was the result of a complaint filed against Old Paths Church Ministries in Hennepin County Housing Court on June 7, 2007, by its landlord, Bass Lake Realty LLC of Minneapolis.

According to Hennepin County Housing Court records, an eviction hearing was held on June 21, 2007. A judgment against Old Paths Church Ministries and a "writ of recovery of premises" were issued the same day. Apparently, Smith had flown the coop by then, because court records state that the writ of recovery was returned six days later and had to be resent to a forwarding address. Although Old Paths Church Ministries was never served, court records state that the writ of recovery of premises was satisfied on July 5, 2007.

At the same time that Old Paths Church Ministries was not paying the rent due to Bass Lake Realty, it was operating as a self-described "sham" ministerial trust and owned a house and property in rural Annandale valued at $361,600. The house was occupied by Smith, who was paid a $45,887 housing allowance by You Can Run But You Cannot Hide International, Inc., in 2009. Smith still lived there in 2010, but the property was transferred into his name in 2009 after he and his sidekick Jake MacAulay took legal action to escape from their sham trust. It's not clear whether he currently lives there. He put the house on the market for $415,900 on March 5, 2011, and dropped the price twice to $399,900; the listing was removed on July 21, 2011.

No 2007 tax records are available for either Old Paths Church Ministries or You Can Run But You Cannot Hide International,

Inc., so it's not known what either entity's income was that year. Also unknown is the amount of rent that deadbeat tenant Old Paths Church Ministries failed to pay. Neither Smith nor Bass Lake Realty LLC returned phone calls regarding this story.

Unlike other churches, the Old Paths Church did not provide food, clothing, or shelter for the poor and needy. Bradlee Dean did not consider these acts to be beneficent works of mercy but rather the wicked deeds of socialism. . . so the tattooed pastors of the Old Paths Church traveled all the way to the governor's office at the state capitol to make that point.

Minnesota governor Mark Dayton reversed his predecessor, Tim Pawlenty, by expanding the federal Medicaid program in the state to up to ninety-five thousand more people who were currently not eligible for Medicaid or not covered by any insurance at all. Governor Dayton's signing of the bill was an occasion for Bradlee Dean and Jake to make their point in front of the cameras of an unsuspecting news media. After the signing, the governor took the unprecedented step of turning over his podium—and the microphone—to a few of the noisy Tea Party protesters present who were clamoring for an end to "Obamacare." Among them was none other than the ministry Old Paths Church/You Can Run But You Cannot Hide International, Inc. (YCR).

What was astonishing was that although MacAulay never identified himself as a "minister" or as being affiliated with any church, he blasted churches for not stepping up to the plate and providing health care for those who cannot afford it, rather than letting the government provide it through some "unconstitutional" means such as "Obamacare" or Medicare or Medicaid.

Addressing the issue of Minnesotans without health care, MacAulay asked,

> Where is the church to help these people? Because that is the church's job and duty—it's social causes. Find in

the Constitution where it's the government's job to do that. It's for nonprofit organizations. It's for the church to do what it rightfully should do.

I don't blame somebody for feeling that when the church doesn't do its job, we've got to do something. I agree we need to do something, there's no doubt about it. But when we step outside of our bounds where our Constitutional authority lies, and we start to take that authority on ourselves, because we can create an executive order, it has a ripple effect of destroying societies.

"What we need is not a strong centralized government. What we need is strong self-government of the people who will look out for each other, just like this poor woman who died," MacAulay concluded, referring to an earlier speaker's story of inadequate health care. "The church should have been looking after her."

MacAulay raised some interesting points—especially considering he was supposedly a paid ordained minister in a church himself. So, as long as he was asking, where was MacAulay's "church" in all of this?

After the investigative blog *Ripple in Stillwater* looked into MacAulay's mysterious "church," virtually nothing could be found about what it did or whom it served—other than the tens of thousands of dollars in grants it received from its sister "ministry" YCR and the $360,000 Annandale property it once owned that became the home of Bradlee Dean.

MacAulay was listed as the "agent" and "incorporator" of Old Paths Church, Inc., and YCR in filings with the State of Minnesota. The mission of Old Paths Church, its Articles of Incorporation state, "is to proclaim the Gospel of the Lord Jesus Christ, to develop Christian leadership, to perform charitable work and to otherwise function as a church." There is nothing about providing medical help for the poor, as MacAulay so eloquently demanded of his fellow church brethren.

There were no expenses reported for indigent medical services or any other kind of medical services in the tax filings, the state filings, or an independent audit of You Can Run But You Cannot Hide International, Inc. Nor were there any other expenses listed that could conceivably be related to medical services. No tax records were available for Old Paths Church, which shared the same Annandale address as YCR.

An exhaustive Internet search turned up no evidence of any "charitable work"—medical or otherwise—on the part of MacAulay's Old Paths Church, either. In fact, it's almost as if the church didn't exist at all, other than on paper. Karl Bremer also found that Bradlee Dean had ties to antigovernment, antitax groups.

The Embassy of Heaven was described in *Investigating Terrorism and Criminal Extremism*, a 2010 report by the Institute for Intergovernmental Research funded by the Department of Justice, as:

> A religious/antigovernment group in Oregon headed by "Paul Revere," the alias of a former computer analyst named Craig Douglas Fleshman. Fleshman started the Embassy of Heaven Church in 1987; it preaches a total separation from "earthly" government. Embassy members continue to make and sell the bogus license plates and other paraphernalia. Committed Embassy of Heaven adherents rarely ever show up for court dates and frequently go on hunger strikes when jailed.

"Revere" himself had a number of run-ins with the law over the years. In 1997, he and his family were evicted from their wooded property in Marion County, Oregon, for nonpayment of $16,000 in back taxes and were jailed.

Bradlee Dean was "baptized" into the extremist organization in 2002, according to his identification card verification posted on the group's website. His ID card was issued on September 30, 2003, and expired on September 30, 2010.

The Embassy of Heaven website stated,

> On file is a signed statement by Bradley Smith [Bradlee Dean] renouncing allegiance to the world and declaring citizenship in the Kingdom of Heaven.
>
> We are fellow citizens of the Kingdom of Heaven, the Government of God, which was handed to the Apostles by Jesus Christ at the Last Supper (Luke 22:29). We fulfill the Great Commission by traveling from place to place using old and modern conveyances. Our government is not of this world, and we expect to be held accountable to the laws from which we come. Our conduct is not an offense if it is not an offense in the Kingdom of Heaven.

When Smith and YCR hired Glen Stoller in 2005 to set up what they later described in court documents as "sham ministries" for YCR and its sister organization Old Paths Church, Stoller promised that part of the package would be identification cards and other materials from the Embassy of Heaven. Clearly, though, Smith had already been involved with the group at least two years prior to that.

Scott P. Roeder, who was sentenced to life in prison in 2010 for gunning down George Tiller, one of the few doctors in the country who performed late-term abortions, in a Wichita, Kansas, church during a Sunday service in 2009, also shared allegiance to the Embassy of Heaven with Smith.

The *Los Angeles Times* reported on Roeder's sentencing:

> George Hough, a clinical psychologist who evaluated
> Roeder for the defense, testified that Roeder was not
> psychologically impaired when he chose to kill Tiller,
> but was motivated by a strongly held religious belief.
>
> Hough said that beginning in his late 20s, Roeder had
> "moved increasingly in the direction of radical religion,
> Christianity," and became "obsessed" with taxes, license
> plate laws and "the true intentions of the framers."
>
> After 1992, Hough said, Roeder began to "obses-
> sively seize" on abortion and "felt an increasing need to
> take action," which culminated in the murder of Tiller.

A federal investigation was launched after Tiller's murder to
determine whether Roeder acted alone or in concert with any
organization.

According to the *Wichita Eagle*, documents from Roeder's 1996
divorce case indicate he was affiliated with the Embassy of Heaven
Church in Stayton, Oregon, in the 1990s. "Revere" wrote letters
to Johnson County (KS) court officials in 1999 and offered to pay
Roeder's back child support.

"We have faithfully informed the District Court Trustee that
Scott P. Roeder is on assignment for us in the mission field and
that we are handling his affairs," Revere wrote on August 10, 1999.

Revere said Roeder trained with the Embassy of Heaven and
received materials from them. But unlike Bradlee, Roeder never
became a "citizen" of the Embassy of Heaven.

Roeder's ex-wife, Lindsey Roeder, told the *Wichita Eagle* that
she had informed the FBI about the Embassy of Heaven. "I used
to hide their literature from Scott," she said. "He wanted to send
the title of our car to them."

Like Roeder, Bradlee Dean is also rabidly antiabortion, although there is no indication that Smith ever advocated violence against abortion providers. Smith declined to comment on his "citizenship" with the Embassy of Heaven.

Other fringe elements affiliated with the Embassy of Heaven include John Joe Gray, who has been at a standoff with law enforcement authorities at his home in rural Texas since January 2000. According to an ABC News report on September 25, 2000, Gray was pulled over for speeding earlier that year and was carrying a pistol. When police asked if he had a permit to carry a handgun, he reportedly told them 'No, sir, it's my God given right to carry.'"

A fight ensued, and Gray allegedly went for one of the officer's guns and bit the officer, according to investigators. Gray refused to appear in court, and has lived inside his armed compound with no running water or electricity ever since. He and his family have pledged to defend themselves to the death against any attempts by law enforcement to invade the compound, where adults reportedly are well-armed and two years of food is stockpiled. In a letter to authorities years ago, the family warned to "bring extra body bags" if they try.

A November 11, 1998, quote from Gray on the Embassy of Heaven website says: "I have come out of the system of the Corporate U.S. government. I use no Social Security number, do no banking, pay no income tax, do not carry license or insurance." The website states that the Gray family "denies being members of the Embassy of Heaven Church and claims to be militia."

The family told *ABC News Nightline* a decade later that "they are free and live behind the fences according to God's law." Local law enforcement, wanting to avoid another situation like the bloody 1993 siege of the Branch Davidians compound at Waco seventy-five miles away, have chosen to wait Gray out no matter how long it takes.

Another fringe element is Richard Allen Shiarla, who, according to the *Orlando Sentinel*, "found God, rid himself of most of his earthly possessions and established Embassy of Heaven Church" in Longwood, Florida, and adopted a new "Christian name," Richard Allen. He claimed his church was a sovereign nation and his church building was a foreign embassy.

In 1997, Allen sought to have his Longwood home declared tax-exempt because it served as the church's parsonage and spiritual counseling center, and the IRS and State of Florida recognized the Embassy of Heaven as a legitimate church. Baptisms were performed in his backyard swimming pool.

Some members of the church carried "passports" that identified them as citizens of the Kingdom of Heaven, abandoned their Social Security numbers, returned their drivers licenses, and drove cars with tags issued by the church.

Patrick Henry Talbert was a key associate of Gerald Payne, who along with Talbert was convicted in 2001 for running a $500 million Ponzi scheme. Talbert is serving a nineteen-year prison sentence on multiple counts of conspiracy, fraud, and money laundering for his role in the Payne Ponzi scheme.

Talbert was a self-declared "sovereign citizen" and "Ambassador of the Kingdom of Heaven," who proclaimed that ordinary laws and courts had no jurisdiction over him. He advanced that argument in court when charged in 1997 with multiple counts of racketeering, fraud, and other crimes related to a separate pyramid scheme. At one point, Embassy of Heaven leader Richard Allen Shiarla intervened on Talbert's behalf.

The Kingdom of Heaven held its own "ecclesiastical court" and found Talbert guilty of "coveting thy neighbor's property." The Kingdom of Heaven offered victims of Talbert—a dozen elderly investors—restitution if they didn't pursue state charges against Talbert. Talbert's novel defense ultimately got him a ten-year prison sentence for his crimes.

Michael Didier is a deadbeat dad in Washington who tried to avoid paying child support for his three children after his wife petitioned for separation and child support in 2004. Michael said the state lacked jurisdiction because he was a "member of the Kingdom of Heaven and served only Jesus Christ." Michael also claimed he could not pay child support because "as a church 'missionary,' he did not have an income and had taken a 'vow of poverty' that precluded him from accepting paid employment."

Yet Didier's wife told the court that he made thousands of dollars advising people on setting up churches and trusts to avoid paying taxes. According to court records, the address Didier gave the court is the same address as Glen Stoll's Remedies at Law, which organized Bradlee Dean's sham ministerial trusts. The court didn't buy it, calling Didier's reasoning "circular." Michael Didier was ruled in contempt of court and ordered to pay $4,900 in child support.

Although the Embassy of Heaven advocates checking out of government altogether, and many of its adherents have been convicted of tax evasion and other crimes, there is no evidence at this time of any illegal tax activity on the part of Bradlee Dean, YCR, or Old Paths Church.

Based on an examination of Wright County tax records for property owned by Smith, Old Paths Church, and the Family Defense League—the sham trust they established with Glen Stoll—it appears that taxes on those properties have always been paid on time and in full. Vehicles seen at YCR's Annandale headquarters also appear to be properly licensed, rather than bearing license plates from the Kingdom of Heaven. Bradlee Dean severed his ties with Glen Stoll and his illegal tax scams in 2009. It's not known whether he did the same with the Embassy of Heaven when his "citizenship" in the Kingdom of Heaven expired in September 2010.

Did creationist theme park operator Kent Hovind's conviction for tax evasion lead to Bradlee's divorce from "sham ministry" architect Stoll? Kent Hovind, along with his wife, Jo, ran Creation Science Evangelism in Pensacola, Florida. Among the group's endeavors was Dinosaur Adventure Land, a sort of cheesy theme park for creationists. Working with Stoll's Remedies at Law, based in Edmonds, Washington, beginning in 2002 the Hovinds concocted the Creation Science Evangelism Ministry under the auspices of a corporation sole, "Director of Ecclesiastical Enterprises," as trustee in 2003. Stoll issued the ministry a business license from the Kingdom of Heaven—the same Kingdom of Heaven in which Bradlee claimed citizenship.

The Hovinds' enterprise, as described in a 2009 property forfeiture proceeding filed in U.S. District Court in Pensacola, sounded virtually identical to Bradlee's "ministerial trusts" for YCR—except that Kent and Jo Hovind got caught using their ministry to evade taxes, and Kent is still serving a ten-year sentence in federal prison. Kent Hovind, known as "Dr. Dino," was convicted by a jury in 2006 on fifty-eight charges, including failing to pay payroll taxes for his employees, structuring financial transactions to avoid reporting requirements, and "corruptly endeavor[ing] to obstruct and impede the due administration of the Internal Revenue laws." Jo Hovind was convicted on forty-four counts.

Among the properties ordered forfeited to pay off the Hovinds' more than $600,000 judgment was Dinosaur Adventure Land. Stoll tried to get his hands on some of the Hovinds' property before it was forfeited, claiming to be a trustee, but was rebuffed by a federal judge. Kent Hovind is currently jailed at Jessup Federal Correctional Institution in south Georgia. He recently appealed to have his sentence vacated. Jo Hovind was sentenced to a year in prison and was released in 2009.

About the same time that the Hovinds' tax-evasion convictions and property forfeitures were making news in 2008, Bradley Dean Smith and his "co-minister" Jacob MacAulay began to take legal action to sever their ties with Stoll. Coincidence?

You Can Run But You Cannot Hide was originally established in 1999. It filed federal IRS Form 990s in 2001 and 2002. Smith established his YCR and Old Paths Church trusts with Stoll in 2005, but no federal Form 990s can be found for YCR at either the Minnesota Attorney General's Office or Guidestar.org until 2008, when it was reincorporated as You Can Run But You Cannot Hide International, Inc.

YCR's 2008 Form 990 states that "2008 is this ministry's first year of existence." Technically, that may be correct, because "International" wasn't added to the group's name until 2008, but Bradlee had been operating an organization under the You Can Run But You Cannot Hide banner for nearly a decade prior to that. What happened to YCR's taxes between 2003 and 2008? Were they ever filed? Did YCR employees pay taxes? Did the IRS even know of YCR's existence? Smith and YCR declined to comment on their relationship with Stoll or the IRS.

According to the permanent federal injunction ordered against Stoll in 2005, Stoll falsely told his customers that "church ministries are not required to notify the IRS of even their existence, much less their exemption from taxation and return filing requirements." The federal injunction stated that Stoll falsely advised his customers to take such illegal tax-avoidance steps as classifying employees as independent contractors, not reporting compensation to the IRS, and making payments to their ministerial trusts, rather than to individuals, so that income could be more easily hidden from the IRS. Court documents also state that Stoll advised and assisted his customers in transferring their pre-tax income to offshore bank accounts in the Caribbean and advised customers on how to circumvent U.S. banking laws.

"My life's an open book," Bradley Dean Smith bellowed on his antigay, hate-talk radio show on January 15, 2011. Yet when it came to anyone having a peek at the mysterious finances and real estate deals of Smith's Annandale "ministry," You Can Run But You

Cannot Hide International, Inc. (YCR), Smith went to extraordinary means to slam that open book shut.

Since *Ripple in Stillwater* began its investigation of Smith's YCR nonprofit, along with its sister nonprofit Old Paths Ministry Inc., Dean has had YCR's treasurer register a complaint with the Washington County Sheriff's Office regarding Karl Bremer's articles and had one of his lawyers send a three-page letter to the parent company of the *Minnesota Independent* complaining about coverage of his organizations by "some reporters." The letter is on the YCR website.

H. Douglas Duncan, a Lodi, California–based lawyer who prepared YCR's 2009 federal tax returns, claimed in his missive to the American Independent News Network that reporters "have engaged in baseless innuendo and supposition" in writing about YCR. "Further, they have drawn unfounded conclusions which imply that investigations and criminal proceedings were both pending and warranted. Neither is the case."

In a series of articles, *Ripple in Stillwater* examined the sham ministry trusts under which Smith had his two organizations organized by Glen Stoll of Edmonds, Washington, in 2005, as well as the curious Wright County real estate transfers between Smith, Old Paths Church, Old Paths Church Ministries, and Smith's connections to the Oregon-based antitax religious cult Embassy of Heaven. Bradlee Dean declined to comment for those articles.

Duncan defended the use of trusts as "a valid tool utilized by individuals, for profit and not-for-profit organizations," he wrote. With regard to the sham trusts set up for Smith by Stoll, he claimed that "although the trust structure was legally valid, You Can Run But You Cannot Hide International independently determined that the trusts were not in the best interest of the organization, nor were they in the best interest of the organization's nonprofit purpose.

"In addition," Duncan continued, "You Can Run But You Cannot Hide International independently determined that the information, initially provided by the promoter of the trusts, was false and that the establishment of the trusts were a result [of] fraud and misrepresentation by the promoters. You Can Run But You Cannot Hide International, at its own expense, filed a petition with the Tenth Judicial District Court to expose the fraud perpetrated by Glenn Stole [*sic*] and others."

What Duncan failed to address was why Smith and YCR secretary Jacob MacAulay needed more than three years to take legal action to get out of Stoll's sham ministry trusts. Stoll had been under a permanent federal injunction prohibiting him from promoting or selling his trusts since June 2005—the same time that he and Smith were doing business. Stoll ignored the injunction order. The Justice Department sought to have him jailed for contempt in June 2006. Stoll remains in contempt of the 2005 injunction order with at least $50,000 in fines hanging over his head.

Oddly enough, Duncan commented in a footnote to his letter that "You Can Run But You Cannot Hide International should be applauded for exposing this type of fraud and misrepresentation. Many other nonprofit organizations, previously defrauded by this scheme, now have a pattern and a court ruling upon which they can rely to assist them in reclaiming full control of the assets of their organization." He went on to liken Smith and MacAulay to unfortunate victims of a Ponzi scheme of which they had no knowledge.

Duncan was careful to note that "You Can Run But You Cannot Hide International is current on all tax reports, returns and liabilities. The tax filings by individual employees of You Can Run But You Cannot Hide International are current and there are no tax liabilities associated with those returns."

In his letter, Duncan also defended the salaries of YCR board members and employees, noting that they were "determined by an independent compensation committee in full compliance with" tax laws. According to YCR's 2009 IRS Form 990, prepared by Duncan, YCR president Smith was paid $51,303 in compensation and $45,887 in housing allowance in 2009 for a total of $97,190. YCR's secretary Jacob MacAulay was paid $42,028 in compensation and $24,869 in housing allowance for a total of $66,897 in 2009. Four other "ordained ministers" with the group received a total of $41,555 in housing allowances.

In an obvious attempt to discourage further reporting on his clients, Duncan concluded, "From this point forward any reports stating information contrary to the facts stated above are baseless, inaccurate and will have been published with the full knowledge that the reports are false." He then signed off "In support of a free (accurate and unbiased) press."

Smith Resorts to Sheriff's Complaint

Smith took his book-closing one step further when he had YCR's treasurer, Heather MacAulay of Annandale—Jacob MacAulay's wife—register a complaint with the Washington County Sheriff's Office about information she claimed had appeared on *Ripple in Stillwater*.

The sheriff's report said MacAulay was "concerned" that facts such as "where they live, what they earn, along with other information," had appeared on *Ripple in Stillwater*. Inexplicably, the report further stated that "Heather said the same information is blogged about Michele Bachmann. Heather said she is uncomfortable with this and that it is uncalled for."

As the treasurer for YCR, however, MacAulay should well know that salary information and addresses of a nonprofit's property and offices are all a matter of public record. They can be found in public property tax records, IRS Form 990s, the Attorney General's office, and the Secretary of State's office. In fact, the MacAulays' home address is listed as the registered corporate office for You Can Run But You Cannot Hide International, Inc., in its Articles of Incorporation on file with the Secretary of State's office. For the record, nothing has appeared on *Ripple in Stillwater* that can't be found in public records—and most of it is online. The Washington County Sheriff's Office sounded unimpressed with MacAulay's complaint.

Bradley Dean Smith was given the opportunity to respond to a whole series of questions about his "ministry" and relationships with antitax organizations such as Glen Stoll's and the Oregon-based Embassy of Heaven. He chose not to.

Ripple in Stillwater author Karl Bremer was happy that Smith has finally responded—sort of—through his attorney, to some of his questions. Yet he felt that Smith really should disabuse himself of the notion that sending his underlings to whine to the cops about public information being disseminated about his controversial little "ministry" is going to stop anyone from looking further into his affairs. That's really not "in support of a free press," as his lawyer would say; or much of an "open book," as Bradlee would say.

Bradlee next made headlines on May 20, 2011, when he was invited to give a prayer at the opening of a session of the Minnesota House of Representatives. Bradlee Dean strode to the podium wearing a tracksuit, his hair tied back in a ponytail. Instead of the nondenominational prayer, Bradlee offended representatives by invoking Jesus and questioning whether President Obama was a Christian. The Republican Speaker of the House apologized and took the unprecedented step of restarting the session with another minister and striking Bradlee Dean's prayer from the record.

WWTC AM 1280 "The Patriot" announced that it had dropped Bradlee and Jake's *Sons of Liberty* radio show. WWTC station manager Ron Stone told MinnPost's David Brauer (May

25, 2011) he canceled Dean's show because the hosts of the *Sons of Liberty* likened Obama to Osama Bin Laden and "did a 6-minute-long spiel in which they mocked black people, which I took offense to. For a minister to do that made no sense." The show continued to broadcast nationwide on the Genesis Communications Network (GCN). Bradlee Dean's next stunt was to announce a lawsuit against Rachel Maddow of MSNBC, reporter Andy Birkey, and the *Minnesota Independent* website. Bradlee chose another Bachmann fellow traveler, Larry Klayman, to handle his lawsuit, which mentions Bachmann by name fifteen times.

The *Sons of Liberty* returned to WWTC on August 27, 2011, defiantly challenging GOP leaders in the legislature to come on the show and explain why they condemned the prayer at the Capitol. Bradlee told his audience that "the real target" of his critics was Michele Bachmann.

It remains to be seen whether Bradlee Dean will become Michele Bachmann's "Pastor Problem."

CHAPTER 7

Bachmann's "Frank Vennes" Problem

In 2006, during orientation for freshman Congress members, a *Star Tribune* reporter asked Michele Bachmann what her goal was as a new representative. Bachmann gave a puzzling answer: "My No. 1 goal is to not go to jail."

Bachmann has so far achieved that goal, but many of her colleagues and associates have run afoul of the law—a startling number for a presidential candidate. Bachmann's close associate in the Minnesota Legislature, Mark Olson, was convicted of assaulting his wife in 2007. Bachmann's first campaign manager and mentor, Bill Pulkrabek, was arrested on Memorial Day 2011, also on assault charges.

Yet this chapter and chapter 8 are about the financial fraudsters who helped Bachmann climb to the top of the fund-raising heap. First up is Frank Vennes, a convicted felon and Bachmann's top donor in 2006. Bachmann lobbied for a pardon for Vennes. This chapter follows the trail of dirty money to Bachmann's campaign.

Pardongate

The big money contributions for Senator Michele Bachmann's bid for Minnesota's 6th Congressional District seat were not from residents of the 6th Congressional District. Nor did they live in her hometown of Stillwater or even in the State Senate district she represented. Rather, according to an analysis of Bachmann's 2005 first-quarter campaign contributions by *Dump Bachmann*, the largest bloc of financiers bankrolling Bachmann's fledgling campaign came from out of state or resided in wealthy Lake Minnetonka enclaves.

In fact, 56 percent of Bachmann's congressional campaign contributions through March 31, 2005, came from individuals *outside* the 6th Congressional District, the district Bachmann chose to represent. That's $33,005 out of a total $59,032. Even more revealing, 27 percent of Bachmann's money came from the area including Minnetonka, Wayzata, Long Lake, Orono, and Deephaven. The money she received from these donors put her ahead of her rivals who were seeking to become the Republican candidate for the 6th Congressional District.

The *Dump Bachmann* crew found it rather odd that Senator Bachmann's initial support would come from wealthy people not even living in the district she wanted to represent in Congress. We never suspected that much of those contributions came from a single source—an enormous Ponzi scheme.

In September 2008, while we were blogging about the race between Elwyn Tinklenberg and Michele Bachmann, an executive at the Petters Worldwide Corporation in Minnetonka, Minnesota, was secretly recording conversations in her boss's office for the FBI. In a wire recording from September 8, 2008, government witness Deanna Coleman recorded Tom Petters talking about an investor in their corporation, Frank Vennes Jr. Petters was in deep trouble. His $3.8 billion Ponzi scheme was unraveling, and he was desperately looking for a way out. Petters told Deanna Coleman that Vennes would be saved from the consequences because he was going to receive a presidential pardon "next year."

When a *Star Tribune* business reporter revealed that Michele Bachmann had written a letter to the U.S. Department of Justice's Office of the Pardon Attorney in support of the pardon for Frank Vennes, team *Dump Bachmann* rolled up its sleeves and began to dig.

Frank Vennes Jr.'s Rap Sheet

On April 20, 2011, convicted money launderer and cocaine/gun runner Frank Vennes Jr., a close personal friend and a major campaign contributor of Minnesota presidential candidates Michele Bachmann and Tim Pawlenty, was indicted on federal fraud and money-laundering charges for his alleged role in the Tom Petters Ponzi scheme.

To do full justice to this convoluted story, we think it's best to begin at the beginning.

According to federal court documents, Vennes's legal troubles began on the plains of North Dakota in August 1986:

> IRS agents investigating suspected money laundering
> by certain North Dakota car dealers were told that

Vennes, a Bismarck pawnshop owner, had made numerous trips to Switzerland and might have experience in transferring funds to a foreign country. An undercover agent, posing as a Chicago investor, contacted Vennes and asked for help in transferring cash abroad. Vennes later admitted that in the next three months he and his codefendants received $370,000 from the undercover agent and transferred it, minus their substantial commissions, to the Bahamas, the Isle of Man, and Switzerland without complying with federal currency transaction laws.

Frank Vennes Jr. was charged in May 1987 with multiple counts of money-laundering charges and illegal firearms and drug offenses. The first firearms offense alleged that Vennes arranged to illegally transfer an automatic weapon from an acquaintance to a federal agent; the second involved the illegal sale of a firearm to a Mexican national, who subsequently took the weapon out of the country. The cocaine trafficking charge was related to the use of an interstate telephone to facilitate the sale of cocaine. The charges stemmed from an undercover operation in which Vennes and his codefendants received $370,000 from federal agents and deposited the money in bank accounts in Switzerland, the Bahamas, and the Isle of Man in a series of transactions. In the last transaction, Vennes personally delivered $100,000 to Switzerland, where his associates allegedly either lost or stole it.

Vennes pleaded guilty to one count of money laundering and no contest to the firearms and cocaine charges. The remainder of the money-laundering charges were dismissed. He was sentenced to five years in prison—three years for money laundering and one year each for the firearms and drug convictions—and restitution of $100,000, which was later reduced to $50,000.

Vennes was sentenced to five years in the Sandstone (Minnesota) Federal Correctional Facility. He served thirty-eight months in prison; was released on parole on December 12, 1990; and completed his sentence on September 25, 1992. Vennes claimed to have found God in prison and played that card on many occasions.

In December 1990, Vennes moved to Minneapolis, started Metro Gem, and built a successful business dealing in precious stones and rare coins. Along the way, he became involved in prison ministries.

Following his release from prison, Vennes did not appeal his sentence or conviction, but he commenced a "Bivens action" against the federal government, seeking $10 million in damages from "unnamed federal agents for entrapment, outrageous conduct, and willful violation of the tax laws."

According to a judicial opinion from the 8th Circuit Court of Appeals, Vennes testified that at the prompting of undercover agents posing as Chicago businessmen in North Dakota, "he made two trips to Switzerland to launder money provided by the agents. Vennes successfully laundered $100,000 on the first trip, but on the second trip, associates of Vennes made off with the other $100,000.

"When Vennes returned without the money," the opinion stated, "the Chicago businessmen revealed themselves to be members of the Mafia and threatened . . . to dismember his children if he failed to recoup this money (perhaps suspecting that their superiors would be none too pleased at the loss of $100,000 of government money). These newly revealed mobsters then suggested that Vennes engage in illegal drug and firearms transactions in an effort to recoup the money and thereby avoid serious bodily harm to him and his family. Vennes did so, the efforts to recoup the money were unsuccessful, and Vennes was eventually charged with a panoply of crimes."

Vennes told the court that "I did get involved with some drug deals, but I lost money on those too, or got ripped off, so that there was never any money to repay the agent."

The District Court acknowledged, "the underlying factual situation . . . is wondrously bizarre. Especially fascinating is speculating about the scene which occurred when the undercover agents tried to explain the loss of $100,000."

Yet Vennes failed to convince the court that he was entrapped, most notably because he pleaded either guilty or no contest to the charges. In dismissing Vennes's claims, North Dakota U.S. District Judge Patrick Conmy wrote that "The record reveals that at one point, Vennes purchased cocaine from his own source in Florida after haggling with an undercover agent supplier about price and speed of delivery. This is not the conduct of one coerced or entrapped into crime."

In addition, at sentencing, according to the appeals court record, "Vennes's attorney stated that the presentence report was complete, fair and thoroughly professional. He further stated that he was not 'in any way indicating that these government agents acted in an improper fashion.'"

Vennes argued that he pleaded guilty and no contest on the advice of his attorney, whom he accused of "ineffective assistance."

Vennes appealed the District Court's decision to the 8th Circuit Court of Appeals and lost, and he was denied appeal to the U.S. Supreme Court. His claims were ultimately rejected in 1994.

The Petters Ponzi Scheme

It didn't take long after his appeals were rejected for Vennes to fall into bad company again. In May 1995, Vennes began a business association with Tom Petters, the now-convicted mastermind behind a massive Ponzi scheme that Petters had hatched just two years earlier. Vennes eventually would make tens of millions of dollars in commissions for steering investors—many of them evangelical Christian groups and investors—to Petters's Ponzi scheme.

Court documents state that Vennes raised money from investors directly and also induced hedge funds to raise money from investors to purchase short-term, trade finance promissory notes in Petters's company, PCI. In return, Vennes allegedly earned more than $105 million in commissions from 1995 to 2008.

The PCI notes were represented to investors as being used to finance the purchase of electronic goods and other consumer goods from suppliers for resale by PCI to big-box retailers.

"In reality," the indictment states, "the transactions underlying virtually all PCI notes were fictitious. Documents evidencing the purported transactions were fabricated by Petters' criminal associates, and the purported suppliers of the electronics goods were shell companies acting in concert with Petters. No retailers participated in the transactions underlying the PCI notes and there were no purchases and resales of consumer electronics or other consumer merchandise. Instead, Petters diverted hundreds of millions of dollars to his own purposes and paid purported profits to investors with money raised from the sale of new notes.

"Petters' inventory finance operation was a Ponzi scheme," the indictment charges.

Around 2002, according to the indictment, Vennes introduced Petters to David William Harrold and Bruce Francis Prevost, the owners and managers of Palm Beach–based and offshore hedge funds, referred to as the "Palm Beach Funds." Vennes described himself to Harrold and Prevost as "Petters' financier" and said that he "knew Petters' business intimately," according to the indictment.

Vennes recruited the two to raise money for Petters and PCI and, court documents state, from 2002 through September 2008, the Palm Beach Funds invested approximately $8 billion in PCI notes. The arrangement netted Harrold and Prevost more than $58 million in fees under their agreements with the Palm Beach Funds. Vennes earned more than $60 million in commissions paid by Petters and/or PCI for the Palm Beach Fund investments, based on a percentage of the money he attracted.

According to the indictment, Vennes had a similar arrangement with another hedge fund from which he obtained more than $45 million in commissions on money he raised for PCI. The grand jury indictment also names Harrold and Prevost as defendants and alleges that they, along with Vennes, made false representations to Palm Beach Fund investors about the PCI investments and also failed to notify investors about delayed payments and approaching defaults on the PCI notes.

Instead, beginning in February 2008, the three allegedly engaged in a series of "note swaps," in which they exchanged PCI notes that were on the verge of defaulting with other PCI notes that had later maturity dates. Harrold and Prevost, through Vennes, engaged in more than thirty-five of these "note swap" arrangements, involving more than 250 PCI notes worth about $1 billion, according to the indictment.

"They created the appearance that the PCI notes had not defaulted, and were intended to conceal [from Palm Beach Funds investors] PCI's inability to pay," court documents state.

Later, the indictment charges, "Instead of receiving cash payments and then reinvesting that cash in new PCI notes as they had done in the past, Harrold and Prevost, aided and abetted by Vennes, simply exchanged old PCI notes for new ones in a cashless exchange of paper."

From February 2008, when the "note swaps" began, through September 2008, when the Petters Ponzi scheme came crashing down, Vennes convinced Harrold and Prevost to raise more than $75 million in new investor money, the indictment states.

On April 20, 2011, Vennes, Harrold, and Prevost were charged with four counts of securities fraud. On April 21, Harrold and Prevost pleaded guilty and indicated that they were cooperating with prosecutors in their case against Vennes. Vennes was also charged with one count of money laundering involving a check he wrote to the law firm of Howse & Thompson, P.A., for $98,814.12. The money was derived from securities fraud, according to the indictment. Craig Howse had formerly been Vennes's personal lawyer.

Did Frank Vennes Jr. Try to Buy a Pardon?

Let's backtrack to 1998, at which point Vennes had been a "business associate" of Tom Petters for three years.

A decade or so after his release from Sandstone Federal Correctional Facility in Minnesota, Vennes began to lay the groundwork for a presidential pardon: cultivating Washington, D.C., power brokers; currying favor with Minnesota politicians by making hefty campaign contributions; and eventually soliciting them for letters of recommendation.

Besides each taking tens of thousands of dollars in campaign cash from Vennes, his family, and his personal lawyer, Michele Bachmann and Tim Pawlenty—along with former Minnesota senator Norm Coleman and former Minnesota GOP chair Ron Ebensteiner—unsuccessfully sought a presidential pardon from President George W. Bush for Vennes's federal crimes from the 1980s. Vennes donated heavily to Bachmann's congressional campaign, Pawlenty's gubernatorial campaign, Coleman's senatorial campaign, the state House Republican Campaign Committee, the Minnesota GOP, and other GOP candidates, all during the time the four Republicans heartily endorsed his candidacy for a pardon.

The timing of Vennes's largesse led many to speculate that it was part of a "pay-for-pardon" plot.

Vennes's first foray into politics was a $2,000 contribution to Ted Mondale's gubernatorial campaign on August 28, 1998. Mondale had joined the Petters Group as an executive vice president in 1998. According to a top Washington lobbyist who wrote Vennes's first letter of recommendation for a pardon in 2000, it was through Ted Mondale, who worked with Vennes, and the connections of his father, former vice president Walter Mondale, that Vennes first sought assistance for his presidential pardon.

Frank Elroy Vennes Jr. filed his application for executive clemency—a presidential pardon—with the U.S. Department of Justice Office of the Pardon Attorney on July 12, 2000.

On that same day, John D. Raffaelli, one of Capitol Hill's leading lobbyists with the Washington Group, sent a letter to Bruce R. Lindsey, the assistant and deputy counsel to President Bill Clinton, in support of Vennes's petition for a pardon.

Raffaelli had spent four years as counsel to Senator Lloyd Bentsen (D-TX). He got to know Vennes through Walter Mondale, who as a U.S. senator was good friends with Bentsen. Mondale had asked Raffaelli to help Vennes with his pardon petition at the request of his son, former state senator Ted Mondale, who knew Vennes.

Ted Mondale did not respond to phone and e-mail requests for an interview about Frank Vennes Jr. Walter Mondale's Minneapolis law office, Dorsey & Whitney, said Mondale was too busy for an interview.

"My involvement with Frank Vennes began and ended in 2000," recalled Raffaelli. Walter Mondale had asked Raffaelli to "help [Vennes] figure out how Washington works" as a favor for Ted. "I met [Vennes] several times in the process. He came to D.C., told me his story, gave me his materials."

Vennes's story had impressed Raffaelli. "I was touched by him and thought it was certainly worth it to look at it." Vennes told him he needed a pardon because "at that time, he was doing a prison ministry thing. He couldn't go into any federal prison because of his conviction."

After examining the record of his conviction, Raffaelli had said, "It really does look like a pretty strong case of entrapment."

Raffaelli referred Vennes to Margaret Colgate Love, a private practice attorney who served as U.S. Pardon Attorney under the Clinton administration from 1990 to 1997. Love represented pardon applicants, and she ended up representing Vennes in his pardon petition process.

"I didn't have any idea how the pardon process works," said Raffaelli. "I had never been asked to recommend one before. . . . I compared it to trying to get the church to approve an annulment."

Raffaelli wrote his letter of recommendation for Vennes to the White House on July 12, 2000—the same day the OPA received Vennes's pardon application.

"There are a number of unusual and questionable governmental actions surrounding the original conviction of Mr. Vennes," Raffaelli wrote. "But more importantly, since his release from prison, he has been a model citizen and humanitarian. His story is very compelling. . . . I am confident that President Clinton will find him a worthy applicant for a pardon."

President Clinton never acted on Vennes's pardon petition.

Vennes's pardon petition was referred to the U.S. Attorney's Office on November 6, 2000; was returned to the Office of the Pardon Attorney on November 27; and then was referred to the FBI on March 29, 2001. It already had been referred to Vennes's probation officer and the U.S. Attorney's Office in North Dakota where he was prosecuted—standard steps in preliminary investigations of pardon petitions.

When he first met with Vennes, Raffaelli said, "He seemed like a guy who was pretty proud of what he did in business. I talked to him quite a bit. I probed him quite a lot about what he was doing. I guess he was a pretty good talker."

When recently informed of the details of Vennes's April 2011 indictment on fraud and money-laundering charges, Raffaelli replied sorrowfully, "I'm still just shocked . . . I'm really sick about Frank."

Pawlenty and Vennes

While Vennes raked in tens of millions from his association with Tom Petters and his Ponzi scheme, he continued to press for his pardon. By 2001, he also began donating to political candidates and parties in earnest, including tens of thousands of dollars to former Minnesota governor Tim Pawlenty, Congresswoman Michele Bachmann, former U.S. senator Norm Coleman, former state senator Ted Mondale, former congressman Mark Kennedy (MN-06), U.S. senator Amy Klobuchar, the Minnesota House Republican Campaign Committee, and the Republican Party of Minnesota.

Vennes made his second political contribution on October 25, 2001—$1,000 to Minnesota Republican Norm Coleman, who was running in his first campaign for the U.S. Senate. He followed up with another $1,000 to Coleman two days later, and his brother Gregory Vennes gave another $1,000.

Vennes made his first donation to Tim Pawlenty in December 2001 ($250), and his and his brother's family dropped another $8,000 into Pawlenty's campaign in January 2002. Vennes's personal lawyer, Craig Howse, gave $550 to Pawlenty in February.

In 2002, Vennes, his family, and his personal lawyer continued to donate heavily to Pawlenty. Kimberly Vennes (Frank's wife), Gregory Vennes, Stephanie Vennes (Gregory's wife), and Colby and Denley Vennes, who have shared an address with Frank and Kimberly, each donated $2,000 to the Pawlenty for Governor

Committee, making a total of $10,000 given by Vennes and his family to Pawlenty's gubernatorial campaign in 2002.

On May 1, 2002, Vennes took the unusual step of making restitution to the federal government on the remainder of the $100,000 he lost in the money-laundering scheme. Restitution had been reduced to $50,000, which Vennes had paid off in 1996.

"Since his release from prison, Mr. Vennes has been very active in the Christian faith and in conveying the teachings of Jesus Christ and the Bible to others," wrote Leo F. J. Wilking, Vennes's lawyer, in an affidavit to the U.S. District Court in North Dakota.

"Although Mr. Vennes is under no legal obligation to make any further payment on the Order for restitution," Wilking noted, "he has the financial resources to do so and feels he has a moral obligation to make such a payment."

"The defendant's motion is indeed a pleasant surprise," wrote District of North Dakota U.S. Attorney Drew Wrigley in a May 2, 2002, response to Vennes's payment. "Mr. Vennes had no legal obligation of any kind to make this offer. His willingness to do so represents genuine rehabilitation."

Vennes cut a check to the U.S. Treasury for $47,822.64. A copy of the affidavit and the check were placed in his pardon petition file.

The Vennes money pipeline continued to flow to Republicans. In June 2002, Vennes gave $10,750 to the Minnesota House Republican Campaign Committee (HRCC), $8,000 to Norm Coleman's Rally for Leadership Fund in July, and $3,000 to the Republican Party of Minnesota in August. Colby Vennes, Frank's son, chipped in $2,000 to Pawlenty's gubernatorial campaign in August.

Vennes's pardon petition was referred back to the U.S. Attorney's Office on September 4, 2002.

The Karl Rove Connection

On December 20, 2002, just weeks after he was elected, Pawlenty, along with Coleman and former Minnesota GOP state chair Ron Ebensteiner, sought a presidential pardon for Vennes in a letter that Coleman sent to "President George W. Bush c/o Mr. Karl Rove." Rove was then senior adviser to President Bush.

By then, Vennes and his family and lawyer had contributed more than $35,000 to Coleman, Pawlenty, and Republican Party committees.

Coleman, who had received a total of $16,000 from Frank Vennes and his brother, wrote, "Being well-acquainted with Frank and his wife Kim, I want to encourage President Bush to give Frank a pardon. Frank is a very successful businessman, known for his integrity and fine character. He has shared his success with others by being seriously involved in a number of faith-based outreach organizations and being a more than generous financial contributor to those organizations. His efforts and contributions have had a significant influence for the good of Minnesota. Frank is indeed an example of successful rehabilitation."

Coleman went on to write that he wanted to join "my friend, [former Minnesota GOP Chairman] Ron Ebensteiner and Governor-Elect Tim Pawlenty in urging President Bush to grant Frank Vennes a Presidential Pardon."

Pawlenty received a total of $28,550 from Vennes, his family, and his lawyer during his Minnesota political career, and he has other connections to the convicted money launderer as well.

The roles of Pawlenty and Ebensteiner in seeking a pardon for Vennes are unclear. Freedom of Information Act requests did not turn up pardon letters from either. Pawlenty has refused to respond to repeated requests for explanations of his relationship with Frank Vennes Jr. or his role in Vennes's pardon request.

This wasn't the first time that the paths of Pawlenty, Coleman, and Rove had crossed. Pawlenty and Coleman each came to their respective races in 2002 as a result of Rove's and Vice President Dick Cheney's intervention in 2001. Pawlenty originally had intended to challenge Paul Wellstone for the U.S. Senate, but then on April 18, 2001, according to a *Star Tribune* report, Rove called Pawlenty and urged him not to run for the Senate. Pawlenty intended to go ahead with his plans, but a second call from the White House—this one from Dick Cheney—changed his mind.

"On behalf of the president and the vice president of the United States, [Cheney] asked that I not go forward. . . . For the good of the party, for the good of the effort [against Wellstone] I agreed not to pursue an exploratory campaign," Pawlenty said at a news conference.

The White House confirmed that Bush, Cheney, and Rove had discussed the Minnesota Senate race and that Coleman enjoyed strong support in the White House. Less than a month later, after Coleman sent his first letter of support for Vennes to Rove, Vennes's file was referred to the Deputy Attorney General.

Vennes wrote a $10,000 check to the House Republican Campaign Committee in May 2003.

Normally, according to sources familiar with the process, the Deputy Attorney General would sign off on the OPA's recommendation and send it on to the White House. In this case, however, Deputy Attorney General Larry Thompson sat on it for six months and then returned it to the OPA.

Vennes made an end-of-the-year 2003 campaign contribution of $5,000 to Coleman's Northstar Leadership PAC, and the spigot kept flowing from various members of the Vennes family to Pawlenty and the GOP. Frank Vennes dumped another $10,000 on the HRCC in August 2004. Frank, Kimberly, Gregory, Stephanie, Colby, and Denley Vennes each contributed $250 to Pawlenty in 2004.

On December 3, 2004, Coleman wrote a second letter urging approval of a presidential pardon for Vennes, this time to Samuel

Morison and Roger Adams in the Office of the Pardon Attorney. "I personally know Mr. Vennes and find him to be trustworthy, extremely dedicated to his community and compassionate about serving others less fortunate than himself, and a talented successful businessman," Coleman wrote.

Coleman touted Vennes's numerous business endeavors and his work with faith-based groups and prison ministries. He stated unequivocally that "Mr. Vennes' moral and ethical standards more than justify your consideration of his pardon application; the pardon will eliminate the continuing stigma of a conviction which limits Mr. Vennes' ability to reach out and share with others in similar situations as Mr. Vennes' past. Mr. Vennes' faith is very real."

Four weeks later, the Vennes file was referred back to the FBI for a second time, where it stayed for only a week before being returned to the OPA on January 6, 2005.

On April 11, 2005, Frank, Gregory, and Stephanie (Gregory's wife) Vennes gave $5,000 each to the HRCC.

On April 29, Frank's file was sent back to the Deputy Attorney General, and Roger Adams in the OPA sent a memo to Deputy Attorney General James B. Comey with an apparent recommendation to approve it.

Then, on June 30, four members of the Vennes family, including Frank, made their only donations to a Democrat—$2,000 each to U.S. Senate candidate Amy Klobuchar.

Vennes's file was referred back to the Office of the Pardon Attorney from the Deputy Attorney General in December 2005—an attempt to get the Pardon Office to recommend another denial?

Vennes's lawyer, Craig Howse, and his wife, Lisa, contributed a total of $5,600 to Pawlenty's gubernatorial campaigns from 2002 to 2006. Howse—a partner in the law firm through which Vennes allegedly laundered ill-gotten Petters Ponzi money—continues to be associated with Pawlenty. Shortly before leaving office in 2010,

Pawlenty circumvented the Commission on Judicial Selection and appointed Plymouth lawyer Jamie L. Anderson to the 4th Judicial District Court. Anderson was a lawyer in Howse's firm and also the wife of Pawlenty's chief of staff, Paul Anderson.

Pawlenty and Vennes have another common interest: Minnesota Teen Challenge. Besides steering Minnesota Teen Challenge investments to Petters's company, Vennes served on the Minnesota Teen Challenge Board of Directors with Mary Pawlenty, Tim Pawlenty's wife. And in 2009, Pawlenty donated nearly $86,000 from his defunct gubernatorial campaign fund to Minnesota Teen Challenge.

Vennes and Teen Challenge

Vennes's lawyer, Craig Howse, was also the chairman of the Fidelis Foundation, a nonprofit organization "organized to assist Christians in discerning, clarifying and implementing God's call and direction in their life," according to the group's tax filings. Fidelis invested more than $27 million in the Petters Ponzi scheme, more than $4 million of it from Minnesota Teen Challenge. Fidelis also donated more than $1.4 million to Minnesota Teen Challenge.

In earlier lawsuits, Vennes is alleged to have been used by Petters to lure primarily Christian organizations into investing in Petters's companies through Metro Gem—one of Vennes's companies—or through the Fidelis Foundation. Among those investors was Minnesota Teen Challenge, which allegedly lost $5.7 million in investments in Petters's companies.

"In true Ponzi scheme fashion," one lawsuit filed by investors against Petters and his associates alleged, "each time one of Plaintiff's promissory notes expired, Petters secured a new note via Metro Gem and, again via Metro Gem, paid the interest due on the old note, presumably with funds obtained from other investors."

The investment connection between the Fidelis Foundation, Petters, and Teen Challenge is detailed in a federal affidavit authorizing the seizure of Petters's assets. The affidavit states that Petters implicated Vennes in his alleged fraud scheme in recorded phone conversations.

"In these recordings, Petters repeatedly admits executing the fraud scheme by providing fraudulent information to investors," the affidavit states. "Petters also attributes knowledge of, and participation in, the fraud scheme to (Deanna) Coleman, (Robert) White, Vennes (investor broker), and (Larry) Reynolds (vice president of NIR). Petters states that Vennes told Petters that they are 'a little paper manufacturing plant.' On one occasion, Petters states that he and Vennes would be jointly implicated in a scheme to defraud investors out of $130 million."

In the recordings, the affidavit states, "Vennes cautions that if investors send auditors out to visit warehouses where the merchandise is located, that the scheme would implode. Vennes also asks that Coleman prepare purchase orders to be submitted to investors so that the investors will extend the due date on a debt."

The affidavit states that evidence shows Vennes was the broker for five investors who were owed approximately $1.2 billion by Petters and his companies, and that as a broker he earned at least $105 million in commissions for delivering investors to Petters and PCI.

Coleman, White, Reynolds, and Michael Catain (another Petters associate) all pleaded guilty to charges in the fraud investigation and all fingered Petters as the kingpin in the massive Ponzi scheme.

Minnesota Teen Challenge was forced to lay off twenty-two employees because of losses from its investments in Petters's businesses. The organization only obliquely referred to its endangered investments in an oddly worded letter posted on its website: "About seven years ago, one of our major donors recommended that we consider building a strong reserve fund for Teen Challenge—a nest egg—for use in case of emergency or for program expansion. The donor suggested that we work with the Harvest Fund, and later the Fidelis Foundation, organizations that work with many other Christian ministries, and consider investing some of his large charitable gifts in the Petters Companies, a once strong, respected corporate entity in Minnesota."

The letter went on to note that "For seven years this investment bore a healthy return and helped us expand our programming and outreach." Yet it made no mention of the precarious situation those investments were in, nor did it name the mysterious "major donor" who recommended the investment in Petters's company.

Campaign Cash for Bachmann

Michele Bachmann's political relationship with Vennes began in December 2005. Bachmann got on the Vennes gravy train with a whopping $16,800 in contributions from Frank, Kimberly (Frank's wife), Gregory, and Stephanie Vennes before the end of the year—$4,200 apiece. Bachmann told WCCO's Esme Murphy in an October 19 interview that she met Vennes through Minnesota Teen Challenge.

"Frank Vennes is an individual here in the Twin Cities who had a remarkable record of rehabilitation in his own life," Bachmann told Murphy. "He was a person who put a lot of money in the community, Teen Challenge, for instance, which I believe very strongly in. It does a wonderful job taking people who are alcohol- or drug-addicted and trying to get them clean and sober.

> And I knew Frank Vennes through Teen Challenge and saw that he had made a remarkable transformation in his life, and he told me his goal was to give as much

money as he could to charity so that more people could find freedom in their life. And I thought that was great, so I supported him.

All this time, Frank Vennes Jr. and his family kept supporting Bachmann with campaign cash. In 2006, Frank—who has never lived in Bachmann's congressional district—dumped another $10,000 into her campaign coffers.

In addition, six members of the Vennes family, along with Vennes's lawyer Craig Howse, jump-started Tim Pawlenty's 2006 gubernatorial campaign with $2,000 each in January. In March, Vennes's case was referred to the FBI for a third time. That was followed by a flurry of activity in April between the FBI, the Pardon Attorney, and the Deputy Attorney General.

On April 10, 2006, Roger Adams in the Office of the Pardon Attorney sent a memo to Deputy Attorney General Paul J. McNulty with what appears to be a recommendation to deny Vennes's pardon and asking for "your review and signature."

On April 18, Adams sent a memo to Harriet Miers, the counsel to the president, which appears to recommend denying pardons in two separate cases.

"Attached are two letters of advice signed at the direction of the Deputy Attorney General recommending that the President (redacted) pardon in the following cases," Adams wrote. Because the Pardon Attorney signed them, it appears the recommendation to the White House was to deny both pardons. Vennes's was one of them.

On June 1, 2006, a little more than a month after his petition was referred to the White House, Frank Vennes gave $50,000 to the Minnesota House Republican Campaign Committee. On June 28, he dropped another $10,000 to the Bachmann Minnesota Victory Committee. Lisa Howse, Craig Howse's wife, donated a total of $9,200 to Bachmann's campaign committee and victory

PAC that same day. And on July 26, Frank Vennes threw another $10,000 at the Minnesota GOP. In the midst of all of these political contributions, Karl Rove appeared at a July 21 fund-raiser for Bachmann in Stillwater, Bachmann's hometown.

It appears that Vennes's case was referred back to the Pardon Office by the White House in July 2007 and then to the FBI for a fourth time, according to OPA documents.

U.S. Office of the Pardon Attorney (OPA) documents obtained by *Ripple in Stillwater* suggest that the politically charged presidential pardon of Frank Vennes Jr. went through several unusual permutations of approval and denial as it was volleyed back and forth between the Pardon Office, the FBI, the deputy attorney general, and the White House for nearly eight years before it was ultimately recommended for approval in 2008.

Based on the sequence of events outlined in those documents, it appears that something happened at the White House regarding Vennes's pardon petition sometime between April 2006, when the OPA recommended that the White House deny the pardon, and the summer of 2007, when it appears the White House returned Vennes's pardon case to the OPA and asked that the OPA "take a second look at" it.

Vennes and his family were among Michele Bachmann's biggest campaign contributors. After Bachmann received a total of $33,000 in campaign contributions from the Vennes family and Frank's lawyer's family during the previous twenty-four months, she wrote a glowing letter of recommendation for Vennes's pardon on December 10, 2007, even though Vennes, a resident of Shorewood, Minnesota, and Jupiter, Florida, was not and never had been a constituent. Vennes, his wife, and his brother and sister-in-law had already donated $26,800 to Bachmann's congressional campaigns when she wrote the letter; Vennes's personal lawyer, Craig Howse, and his wife had donated another $6,200 to Bachmann's campaign; and by June 2008, the Vennes and Howse families would pour another $12,200 into Bachmann's campaign coffers, for a total of $45,200.

In the December 2007 letter, Bachmann used the power of her congressional office to recommend a presidential pardon of Vennes: "As a U.S. Representative, I am confident of Mr. Vennes' successful rehabilitation and that a pardon will be good for the neediest of society," Bachmann wrote to the Office of the Pardon Attorney. "Mr. Vennes is seeking a pardon so that he may be further used to help others. As I know from personal experience, Mr. Vennes has used his business position and success to fund hundreds of nonprofit organizations dedicated to helping the neediest in our society."

Bachmann noted that Vennes needed a pardon because he "still encounters the barriers of his past and especially in the area of finance loan documents." Bachmann has refused to further explain the nature of her "personal experience" with Vennes or provide clarification of the finance loan documents to which she refers in her letter.

On June 30, 2008—six months after Bachmann wrote her pardon recommendation for Vennes—he and his wife gave another $9,200 to Bachmann's campaign.

So Close

Former federal officials who were familiar with the pardon process and who examined documents obtained by *Ripple in Stillwater* through the Freedom of Information Act confirmed that Vennes's pardon was headed for approval after it went to the White House for the final time on July 1, 2008.

Then on September 24, 2008—less than six weeks before the election—federal agents raided Vennes's $5 million Shorewood home on Lake Minnetonka in connection with the $3.8 billion Tom Petters Ponzi scheme and seized "boxes and buckets of silver and gold coins, trays of jewelry, five stacks of $100 bills, boxes of gem stones, silver plates and Rolex watches," along with diamond rings and artwork. Two days later, Vennes's $6 million oceanfront home in Jupiter, Florida, was also raided and among the items seized was a briefcase containing "256 $20 gold pieces dated 1904, and eight uncirculated one-half dollar pieces."

This was not good news for Bachmann, who was in the midst of a tough reelection fight against DFLer Elwyn Tinklenberg. One of her top campaign contributors and personal friends for whom she had solicited a presidential pardon for earlier crimes of money laundering was now implicated in the largest Ponzi scheme fraud in the history of Minnesota.

Eight days later, on October 2, 2008, Bachmann withdrew her letter of recommendation for Vennes's pardon. Coleman, while also engaged in a tight reelection race with Al Franken, never withdrew his letters of support for Vennes.

Bachmann wrote to the Office of the Pardon Attorney, "I had known Mr. Vennes for some time and was familiar with his good works with local charity organizations. Like so many others, I was under the impression that he had turned his life around and was seeking to do the right thing by those less fortunate. Regrettably, it now appears that I may have too hastily accepted his claims of redemption and I must withdraw my previous letter."

Bachmann's motives in withdrawing her recommendation of a pardon for Vennes without his ever having been indicted—other than to distance herself from a convicted felon and a heavy campaign contributor in an election year—are unclear. She has never responded to the inquiries of *Dump Bachmann* about her relationship with Vennes or why she sought a presidential pardon for a convicted money launderer who wasn't even a constituent.

She told WCCO's Murphy, however, that "when the Tom Petters affair came open and Frank may have had a part in that affair, it wasn't appropriate for me to recommend a pardon anymore.

And so my office issued a letter, and we pulled that pardon back, because we don't know what the answers are right now about his involvement with Tom Petters."

On October 3, 2008, the day after Bachmann withdrew her pardon recommendation, she tried to symbolically wash her hands of Vennes's most recent campaign contributions by donating the sum of $9,200—an amount equal to Frank and Kimberly Vennes's donations to Bachmann earlier that year—to Minnesota Teen Challenge. That didn't work out so well for the congresswoman, either. Minnesota Teen Challenge returned the donation to Bachmann two weeks later.

"We didn't want to be involved if it was dirty money," said Rich Scherber, the executive director of Minnesota Teen Challenge. Scherber personally suffered a loss of $423,759 in the Petters Ponzi scheme after investing with Vennes, according to court documents.

Scherber said that when Bachmann's office made the donation, Bachmann's employees explained the connection between the campaign's charitable contribution to Teen Challenge and Vennes's campaign contributions to Bachmann. Scherber's staff brought the matter to the organization's chairman, and he brought it before the board.

"The board had decided they weren't going to take the check," Scherber continued. "They sat on it for two weeks and we just returned the check."

Bachmann ultimately donated the $9,200 to R3, a collaborative of Christian recovery groups that included Minnesota Teen Challenge.

Documents obtained from the OPA indicate that this was the first that this office—and the White House—had known of Vennes's alleged involvement in the Petters Ponzi investigation.

On October 3, 2008, Ronald Rodgers in the OPA sent an e-mail to Kenneth K. Lee, the associate legal counsel for the White House who handled pardon applications.

Ken, this is a pardon case that you asked us to take a second look at and we sent it through the wickets anew and then over to you on or about 1 July 2008 (redacted) no action by the President has been taken on the case.

We just got a call from Congresswoman Michele Bachman's [*sic*] office: they wanted to withdraw their letter of support that they submitted on behalf of the guy, though they didn't specifically disclose the reason for it. It appears he is under investigation for a securities and/or wire fraud matter and they executed a search warrant last week in which he was implicated.

Rodgers sent Lee a link to a September 26 *Star Tribune* report on the Petters raid that named Vennes.

On October 3, 2008, the OPA also sent a two-page fax, the contents of which are unknown, to Bachmann with the subject line "per your request." The fax wasn't sent to the congresswoman's office, however, from which her pardon letters had been sent. It was sent to Bachmann's campaign office in Minnesota.

Just days later, on October 6, 2008, the assets and the records of Vennes, Petters, Petters's companies, and other Petters associates were frozen by a federal judge. Most of Vennes's assets were eventually liquidated to repay some of the victims of his alleged fraud under a court-ordered "work-out plan" issued in January 2011.

On October 6, 2008, Rodgers e-mailed Lee at the White House with more details on Vennes's involvement in the unfolding Petters investigation. That afternoon, Lee responded from the White House: "Ron—Wow—quite a surprising turn of events. Thanks. Ken"

On October 24, Vennes withdrew his request for executive clemency, the White House returned his case to the Office of the Pardon Attorney, and the case was "no actioned" and closed.

Bachmann went on to win reelection with the Vennes' substantial financial support and barely a mention of her close relationship with the convicted money launderer and Ponzi suspect in the local mainstream media. Coleman lost to Al Franken in the closest statewide election in Minnesota history. Tim Pawlenty ran a brief and ill-fated campaign for president in 2011 after leaving the governor's office. And as of this printing, Bachmann is still running for the Oval Office.

Yet now that Bachmann has entered the presidential arena, she is facing renewed scrutiny of her relationship with Frank Vennes Jr., particularly since things turned for the worse for the convicted money launderer last spring.

On April 20, 2011, thirty-three months after his homes were raided and his assets seized by federal agents, Vennes was indicted for his alleged role in the Tom Petters Ponzi scheme. He pleaded not guilty and was released on $100,000 bond on May 3.

The Justice Department filed a superseding indictment against Vennes in U.S. District Court in Minneapolis on July 19, 2011, that brings to twenty-four the number of fraud, money laundering, and false-statement charges the politically connected former felon now faces. The charges include the four counts of fraud and the one count of money laundering in the April 20, 2011, indictment filed against him.

His trial on fraud and money-laundering charges stemming from the Petters Ponzi scheme is scheduled to begin in February 2012—right in the thick of the presidential primary season.

Take a Second Look

If Vennes was going to be granted his pardon by President Bush before he left office, as Vennes claimed, that means that it was headed for denial until the White House asked the Office of the Pardon Attorney to "take a second look" at it.

Was it President Bush himself who asked for that second look when he saw a kindred soul in Vennes's deep involvement with Teen Challenge? Or was someone else running interference for Vennes at the White House?

Also, if Vennes was going to be granted a pardon, how did he pass muster with the FBI only five months before the feds recorded Tom Petters implicating him in the Ponzi scheme? It's hard to fathom that Vennes wasn't on the FBI's radar until those recordings were made.

One government official who was familiar with the pardon process concurred that the record didn't reflect well on the FBI. "I think it's quite strange that the FBI didn't give the Pardon Attorney a head's up, at a time when the FBI had to know that Vennes was the target of an ongoing investigation," the former official noted. "Instead, the Pardon Attorney had to learn about it from the press, like everyone else. I have no reason to think that it was anything other than the left hand not knowing what the right hand was doing, that the Pardon Attorney asked the background unit to address a narrow issue and the FBI didn't think to check any further.

"But even so, that's hardly an excuse. The FBI's failure to connect the dots nearly resulted in a pardon that would surely have been a great embarrassment to the president, which is one of the reasons that supposedly justifies the Justice Department's advisory function in the first place."

OPA Meddling?

The pardon process of Frank Vennes Jr. points up other long-standing concerns about undue influence on the way the Office of the Pardon Attorney operates.

After looking at the documents produced under FOIA, a former federal official familiar with the pardon process said that "it appears that someone with influence must have contacted the White House about the case between the time DOJ sent its denial report in April of 2006 and the time the White House told the Pardon Attorney to 'take another look' at the case (code for 'we want a different recommendation') in July of 2007. But that sort of lobbying happens all the time, and there really isn't anything wrong with it. In fact, I think the White House showed quite a lot of respect for the Justice Department's process by sending the case back for reconsideration.

"What is more interesting is what the documents reveal about the extensive and inefficient meddling with the Pardon Attorney by the Deputy Attorney General's office, which delayed the processing of Vennes's application for years and showed no respect for the official whose job it is to make recommendations to the president. The DAG sent the case back to OPA at least three times between 2002 and 2006, and finally had to direct the Pardon Attorney to change what had been a favorable recommendation to a denial. In 2008, after the White House indicated that it wanted to grant the pardon, the DAG again interfered, this time directing a new Pardon Attorney to make a favorable recommendation.

"Honestly, it is a real shame that the Pardon Attorney can't command more respect in his own agency—which is precisely what has made the Justice Department so unhelpful to the president in clemency matters over the past twenty years."

Questions Remain

Many questions remain unanswered about the apparently close relationship Frank Vennes Jr. once had—and may still have—with three of Minnesota's most visible Republican politicians. Two of them—Bachmann and Pawlenty—ran for president. And Coleman just landed a job with one of Washington, D.C.'s, top lobbying law firms.

Bachmann, Pawlenty, and Coleman have been contacted multiple times in the past to respond to questions about Frank Vennes

Jr. All were contacted with written questions for this story as well. Bachmann, Pawlenty, Coleman, or their spokespersons have never responded.

Was there a "pay-for-pardon" scheme at work? At this time, there's no evidence to prove this. Yet Vennes clearly was trying to curry financial favor with the same politicians who would later write pardon recommendations on his behalf. It's also not known whether Vennes solicited Bachmann, Pawlenty, and Coleman to write pardon endorsements on his behalf or whether they volunteered the services of their offices. All have been asked, and none have responded.

Then there was the matter of what to do with Vennes's campaign contributions, which, like his other assets, almost certainly could be linked to illegal Petters Ponzi money. Bachmann gave away only $9,200 of the $27,600 she took from Vennes and his wife. Pawlenty spent his $23,500 in Vennes family contributions on his campaigns and never claimed to give any of it away. The donations to other politicians and party units go well into six figures.

When Petters was indicted, most politicians couldn't dump their contributions from him fast enough. Will they do the same for Vennes, whose contributions allegedly came from the same poisoned well, now that he's been indicted?

George W. Bush left office without ever pardoning Vennes. So the question remains: Would a President Bachmann pardon her close personal friend Frank Elroy Vennes Jr.?

So far, she hasn't been any too anxious to talk about it.

Follow the Money

The role of political money in Vennes's pardon story also is troubling.

During the course of a decade, from 1998 to 2008, Vennes, members of his family, his personal lawyer, Craig Howse, and his wife donated a total of $212,800 to Michele Bachmann, Tim Pawlenty, Norm Coleman, Amy Klobuchar, Ted Mondale, the Minnesota House Republican Campaign Committee, and the Republican Party of Minnesota. During eight of those ten years, Vennes was pursuing a presidential pardon through the same politicians and political entities who were benefiting from his largesse.

"In part, the failure lies with the Justice Department for failing, as a matter of routine policy, to not look at this issue," says one former federal official. "They deliberately don't look at it because they don't want to know."

Checking Federal Election Commission records for donations made to politicians by pardon applicants for whom those politicians have written letters of recommendation should simply be a part of the pardon investigation process, the official suggests. "How can you judge the credibility of one of these letters if they don't know that important information?"

Some in the academic and legal community who follow presidential pardons closely fear that cases such as Vennes's could taint the process so that less politically connected pardon candidates won't get a fair shake. Or that politicians will fear recommending a pardon for anyone, regardless of the merits of their case.

Payback

The day after Election Day 2010, Frank Vennes Jr. filed a motion in U.S. District Court to approve a "work-out plan" to repay victims of the Petters Ponzi scheme through the liquidation of most of his assets. In return, Vennes and his investment business, Metro Gem, would receive a release from all liability related to financial losses from the Petters scam—a scam that Vennes claimed he knew nothing about.

Vennes invested heavily in Petters's company notes on behalf of his Metro Gem investors from 1995 to 2008. When federal agents swooped down on Petters in September 2008, Metro Gem had more than $130 million in unpaid investments in Petters's notes.

Vennes's court filings list his total debts at $55.4 million.

His millions of dollars in assets, which included gold and silver coins and figurines, artwork, Harley-Davidsons, and properties in Minnesota, North Dakota, Ohio, and Florida, have been frozen and in receivership since the Petters scheme came crashing down more than two years ago. Some properties already have been liquidated.

The November 3 timing of Vennes's first motion seeking relief in more than two years is curious—especially given his close political and personal ties to Bachmann, who was engaged in an expensive reelection battle with Tarryl Clark until November 2. Revisiting the story of Bachmann's relationship with a convicted money launderer during the election would not have helped Vennes's former beneficiary.

Coleman, Pawlenty, and the state GOP did not return any of Vennes's allegedly "dirty money." None of the recipients of Vennes's tens of thousands of dollars in political contributions have ever responded to inquiries about their relationships with the convicted money launderer.

Listed among Vennes's secured creditors in his proposed workout plan is Richard Scherber, the executive director of Minnesota Teen Challenge. Documents filed with Vennes's proposal show that Scherber was owed $910,000 when the Petters scheme ended. Minus the returns he had received on his investments with Vennes, Scherber had an out-of-pocket loss of $423,759, according to court documents. Under Vennes's proposed work-out plan, Scherber would receive only $173,741.

Also listed among Vennes's secured creditors is the locally owned First State Bank of Bayport, shown as a cocreditor on four individuals' IRAs. Total out-of-pocket losses shown for those IRAs is $1.4 million. Under Vennes's proposal, those IRAs would recover only $574,067 of their combined out-of-pocket losses.

"The work-out plan represents the best opportunity for Mr. Vennes' creditors to receive meaningful financial recovery for their losses sustained as a result of the Petters fraud," Vennes's motion states.

Vennes noted that he was under "no compulsion" to enter into any agreements with creditors. Because he had not been charged with any crime at that point, he was not facing a forfeiture or a restitution order and said he could just as easily have filed for bankruptcy, leaving his creditors with little or nothing.

Vennes is the subject of a $2.7 billion "clawback" lawsuit in the bankruptcy proceedings of Petters's estate; however, Vennes proclaimed his innocence in the Petters Ponzi scheme and has filed claims against Petters.

"Metro Gem, Inc., and I were victims of the Petters fraud," Vennes stated in court documents filed with his work-out proposal motion. "I was not a co-conspirator of Thomas J. Petters or anyone else in that fraud."

On January 25, 2011, U.S. District Judge Ann D. Montgomery ruled on the motion.

The *Star Tribune* reported that the investors with Frank Vennes would get 35 to 74 cents on the dollar. Three banks with loans secured by Vennes got 65 percent to 74 percent of their losses, or $11.4 million. Investors with personal guarantees got 50 percent of their investment, while investors without personal guarantees received 35 percent. It was very odd that a court would recognize the personal guarantee of a convicted felon.

Mr. Vennes didn't do too bad, either . . . from Judge Montgomery's decision. According to the court-ordered "work-out" plan, Vennes would be left with his personal effects, an automobile, one year's living expenses of $62,400, some money to cover legal expenses, and reimbursement for the expenses he incurred while assisting the liquidating trustee in the sales or other dispositions of assets and the carrying out of the asset distribution plan.

The Next Step

Vennes, now of Cocoa Beach, Florida, was indicted on April 20, 2011, on four counts of securities fraud and one count of money laundering. He entered a not-guilty plea on May 3. Two other defendants charged with securities fraud along with Vennes—David William Harrold and Bruce Francis Prevost—already have pleaded guilty and reportedly are cooperating with federal authorities.

The federal government piled on in a superseding indictment on July 19, 2011, with additional charges that brought to twenty-four the number of fraud, money laundering, and false-statement counts he now faces.

Vennes's fraud and money-laundering trial is scheduled to begin in U.S. District Court in Minneapolis on February 6, 2012—right in the middle of presidential primary season. That might focus enough attention on Vennes's pardon to get Bachmann and other politicians to explain their cozy relationship with him. It might also spur the media to address the concerns expressed in this chapter about flaws in the pardon process itself.

Stay tuned—things could get very interesting before this is all over. Team *Dump Bachmann* will be covering the trial from start to finish.

CHAPTER 8

Bachmann's "Bobby Thompson" Problem

According to law enforcement officials, "Bobby Thompson" is not his real name. Nobody seems to know who "Bobby Thompson" really is. What we do know is that he contributed boatloads of money to Republican candidates such as Michele Bachmann. As it turned out, the money came from a sham veterans' charity. What happened to the rest of the money? Nobody knows—"Bobby Thompson" is on the lam.

This chapter is based on an award-winning investigative series by Karl Bremer, which began in July 2010 and traces the developing story.

The $10,000 Photo

At a Minneapolis event with former half-term governor Sarah Palin on April 7, 2010, Michele Bachmann received a $10,000 campaign donation from a man known as Bobby Thompson. The sum, which was to be shared with the Republican Party of Minnesota, would have qualified him for a table for ten at the fund-raiser, as well as a photo shoot with the two Tea Party queens. Thompson, one of only six individuals to pony up the money for a picture, was the founder of the U.S. Navy Veterans Association (USNVA), a national charitable veterans organization.

Within a month his organization was under investigation by six states, as well as by the IRS at the request of Senator Jim Webb (D-VA), and Thompson had vanished. The last place he was thought to have been was at the fund-raiser, although Bachmann's campaign has refused to confirm or deny whether Thompson actually attended her big-bucks affair.

The investigations were spurred by a major series of articles published the month before the Minneapolis event by Florida's *St. Petersburg Times*. They had uncovered little evidence that the group was a nationwide charity, despite billing itself as a "'nationally recognized U.S. Department of Veterans Affairs Veterans Service Organization,' with 41 state chapters, more than 66,000 members and $22.4 million a year in income that it says it uses for gifts to military personnel, veterans and their families." The paper reported that all but one of "its officers, directors and auditors were nowhere to be found, its offices a network of rented mailboxes, its records kept secret."

That one was Thompson, who, the *Times* reported, "lived in a $600-a-month Ybor City, FL, duplex" and "said he is a retired Navy lieutenant commander and 'trust fund baby' who poured more than $180,000 of his own money into political campaigns."

Thompson had spread the wealth around. In addition to giving $10,000 to Bachmann, he gave:

- $21,500 to Norm Coleman's Senate reelection campaign between 2006 and 2008
- $5,000 to the Minnesota House Republican Campaign Committee in 2008
- $10,400 to the Republican Party of Minnesota from 2008 to 2010—most recently on May 6, 2010

He was later found to have given $500 each to two Minnesota Republicans, former representative Marty Seifert's Seifert for Governor campaign in 2009 and David J. Carlson's Citizens for David Carlson committee in House District 67B in 2008.

Thompson also had ties to Stillwater lobbyist Edwin E. Cain, a close friend of Bachmann's. Cain, who was hired as a consultant by the USNVA to lobby for the group in Virginia in 2010, and a Mary Cain from the same Stillwater address, also a lobbyist, donated $500 each to David Carlson's House campaign on the same day that Thompson's donation was recorded. Thompson and the Cains represented three of the top six individual donors to Carlson's campaign that year.

The question the series couldn't answer was, Why? Why was so much Florida money pouring into Minnesota?

The Investigation

The Minnesota chapter of the U.S. Navy Veterans Association took in a total of $1.56 million in contributions from 2005 to 2009 and claims to have distributed $1.06 million of that to needy veterans and other charitable causes in those same years. Yet Thompson disappeared just as the nationwide investigation of the group by the *St. Petersburg Times* was getting started, and the Minnesota chapter of the USNVA dissolved mysteriously in May 2010.

The U.S. Navy Veterans Association has been shut down by state attorneys general in Hawaii, New Mexico, and Ohio. Investigations into the group are under way in Florida, Missouri, and Virginia. U.S. senator Jim Webb (D-VA) has asked the IRS to begin an investigation into the organization; however, Minnesota attorney general Lori Swanson's office has not responded to repeated inquiries about the organization's Minnesota activities or the reason for its dissolution.

The address for the Minnesota chapter of the navy vets group that was registered with the Attorney General's Office and the IRS led to a UPS store on Grand Avenue in St. Paul, an apparent violation of the state's requirement to file a physical address for the organization in addition to its mailing address. As of July 10, 2010, the Minnesota phone number listed for the group still carried a recorded message as if it were still operating in Minnesota. The address listed for the Minnesota chapter's Commander John Clinton and Lieutenant Commander Reint Reinders on the group's 2008 IRS filing was the same Grand Avenue UPS store. The address listed for CFO Bobby Thompson led to another UPS mailbox, in Washington, D.C.

The navy vets group innocently described its mission in its Minnesota Attorney General filing as "to assist disabled and needy war veterans and members of the U.S. Armed Forces and their dependents, and the widows, widowers and orphans of deceased veterans." Yet the investigations of the *St. Petersburg Times* and state attorneys general have found numerous instances of alleged fraud, fictitious names, and other misrepresentations of its charitable activities in the group's chapters across the country.

Bachmann Dumps PAC after *Dump Bachmann* Dumps on PAC

The Minnesota-Bachmann Victory Committee PAC was suddenly terminated on July 13, 2010, a week after *Dump Bachmann*'s exclusive July 6 report that Bobby Thompson, a $10,000 donor to the PAC, was wanted by attorneys general nationwide in an investigation into his allegedly fraudulent veterans organization.

PAC treasurer Daniel G. Puhl filed the termination papers with the FEC on the same day that Bachmann's finance director, Zandra Wolcott, left the campaign abruptly.

It's not known whether investigators contacted the Bachmann campaign regarding the whereabouts of Thompson. The Bachmann campaign did not respond to an inquiry about Thompson.

The Minnesota-Bachmann Victory PAC reported total receipts and disbursements through June 30 of $268,455 each, for a zero balance at the end of the 2010 second quarter reporting period.

The PAC claimed operating expenses of $147,094. That included such items as:

- $20,672 to Elliot Aviation Flight Services, Moline, Illinois, for air transportation
- $948 for one room at the downtown Minneapolis Hilton Hotel and two other rooms at the rates of $644 and $546 a night.
- $54,201 to the Hilton Hotel for event space and catering
- $25,000 to Fundraising Associates, Edina, Minnesota

The PAC hauled in $100,729 for the Bachmann for Congress campaign and $20,631 for the Republican Party of Minnesota in its nearly five-month existence.

Washing Her Hands

In late July 2010 Bachmann's campaign manager told the *St. Paul Pioneer Press* that Bachmann's campaign had "frozen" the $10,000 donation it had received from Bobby Thompson, "pending the results of the investigations." She went on, "Congresswoman Bachmann believes people are innocent until proven guilty. However, she wants to ensure her campaign is above reproach and maintains the highest of ethical standards."

Meanwhile, the nationwide search for Bobby Thompson also went on.

Bachmann spokesperson Gina Countryman told the *Pioneer Press* that Bachmann didn't know Bobby Thompson. It's not known whether the Bachmann campaign or Bachmann herself was contacted by investigators or attorneys general seeking information about the whereabouts of Thompson.

A spokesperson for the Minneapolis law firm of Gray Plant Mooty, which represented the U.S. Navy Veterans Association Minnesota Chapter in 2007, declined to say whether the firm still represented it.

"We don't disclose who our clients are," he said.

On July 27, 2010, an Ohio judge allowed lawyers for the group to withdraw from legal proceedings there because Thompson, the group's only known remaining board member, could not be found. The group's attorneys last heard from him on June 20. The judge also issued an injunction that sealed a UPS mailbox that the U.S. Navy Veterans Association used as an address for its Ohio chapter—just as it had done in Minnesota for five years without being questioned by anyone.

Another Ohio judge had frozen the USNVA's bank accounts there, and Ohio Attorney General Richard Cordray ordered the organization to cease soliciting in the state.

Cordray charged that the USNVA used charitable contributions to the group to make political contributions in Ohio and other states. The navy vets group denied that.

The group's primary fund-raiser, Associated Community Services of Southfield, Michigan, also jumped ship from the navy vets group, on July 7, 2010. The Minnesota Chapter of the USNVA paid Associated Community Services $186,025 for fund-raising services from 2006 to 2009. The group did not claim any fundraising expenses for the Minnesota chapter in 2005.

On July 20, 2010, messages left at the Minnesota chapter's phone number in St. Paul were not returned. A message left July 19, 2010, on a Tampa, Florida, phone number that was once Thompson's and featured a gruff male voice saying, "Bobby," on the voicemail also was not returned.

John Markman was named as the USNVA Minnesota Chapter's CFO on the group's 2009 federal tax filing that was filed with the IRS on April 15, 2010, and its 2009 annual report filed with the Minnesota Attorney General's Office on May 17, 2010. Bobby Thompson, who had been listed as CFO and "Contact Person" of the Minnesota chapter until that time, disappeared from the group's state and federal filings in 2009 as quickly as he disappeared from his Florida duplex that same year.

The signature on the Minnesota chapter's dissolution resolution, dated May 4, 2010, also appeared to be Markman's.

If the Minnesota Attorney General's Office was interested in contacting John Markman—beyond the Washington, D.C., UPS drop box he gave as his address on the Minnesota chapter's federal tax filing—it should have to look no further than the Ohio Attorney General's Office. Markman was served with a summons and a complaint by certified mail on June 28, 2010, in the investigation under way there by Cordray.

What was Attorney General Lori Swanson waiting for?

October, it turned out. That's when her office, according to spokesperson Ben Wogsland, began "looking into this," he told *Ripple in Stillwater*.

Minnesota was at least the eighth state to be looking into the USNVA. The others included Hawaii, New Mexico, Oregon, Missouri, Ohio, Virginia, and Florida. Attorneys general in several states shut their operations down, and in Ohio, a judge froze the organization's bank accounts.

That summer, agents from the IRS, as well as the Veterans Administration and the Florida Department of Agriculture and Consumer Services, seized computer records and documents—some already shredded—from the Tampa-area offices of associates of Bobby Thompson. The seizures were made in connection with investigations into the organization by the three agencies.

Finally, after considerable negative publicity over Bachmann's connection to the alleged fraudster, her campaign reportedly gave her $4,800 portion of the proceeds to other veterans' groups. The Republican Party of Minnesota claimed it was going to donate its remaining portion of the dirty money to charity as well.

There was no indication that other recipients of Thompson's largesse intend to dispense of their contributions.

$1.56 Million from a P.O. Box

The USNVA operated for more than five years in Minnesota out of a UPS drop box on Grand Avenue in St. Paul in apparent violation of state charities laws.

State law requires charitable organizations such as the USNVA to register with the Attorney General's Office and file annual reports listing both a "mailing address" and a "physical address." Yet since it started soliciting funds in Minnesota in 2005, the USNVA never registered any physical address at all with the Attorney General's Office or the IRS—a clear violation of that requirement. Every address listed in the group's state or federal filings led to drop boxes at UPS stores in St. Paul; Washington, D.C.; and Tampa, Florida.

Even though the Minnesota chapter of the USNVA officially dissolved in May 2010, its St. Paul–area phone number listed with the Attorney General's Charities Division—(651) 645-4570—still carried a message as of October 3, 2010, that said "we are away from our desk" and suggested the group was still operating here.

Out of more than $1.14 million that the U.S. Navy Veterans Association Minnesota Chapter claimed to have spent on charitable programs and services in Minnesota since 2004, only $26,300 can be positively accounted for: two $10,000 donations to a St. Paul Veterans Center in 2007 and one $6,300 donation to Twin Cities Public Television in 2008.

The rest of the money from the organization that went to benefit individuals was allegedly spent to provide such generic things as "direct cash assistance," food, clothing, publications, "care packages" for service members, and "psychological counseling and comfort" for survivors of veterans. Yet there is little evidence or documentation of those services in records filed with the state or the IRS. Furthermore, the officers for the Minnesota chapter of the USNVA could not be found, nor could any address be located for the group, other than UPS drop boxes in St. Paul and several other states.

The Ohio arrest warrant was issued by Hamilton County Municipal Court and ordered Thompson to appear on charges of identity fraud. A detective's affidavit accompanying the arrest warrant alleged that Thompson fraudulently used the Florida identification card of a Bobby Charles Thompson now living in Washington to open a UPS post office box in Cincinnati in April 2003. It also alleged that Thompson fraudulently solicited charitable contributions in excess of $100,000 in Ohio from 2003 to 2010; fraudulently filed annual reports with the state; and falsely stated that the UPS drop box was the organization's primary Ohio office.

"Our investigators have determined that this individual stole the identity of someone else and used that as the centerpiece of an apparent scam that has continued for seven years and involved tens of millions of dollars," Ohio Attorney General Richard Cordray said. "The real Bobby Thompson, whose identity was stolen, including his Social Security number and date of birth, has absolutely no connection to the U.S. Navy Veterans Association. We don't know who this individual is yet, but we do know that he is not Bobby Thompson."

Cordray suggested that money collected under the guise of the USNVA may have been used to finance political contributions made by Thompson. An August 5 press release from Cordray's office stated,

> There appears to be very little evidence that the organization spent money actually helping veterans or their families. Yet public records do show hundreds of thousands of dollars in political contributions to various candidates made by "Bobby Thompson" personally or through the political action committee he created and to which he was the sole contributor, NAVPAC.

Virginia Attorney General Ken Cuccinelli, another Republican officeholder, recently announced that he was finally giving away $55,700 in campaign contributions he received from Thompson, but it took a firestorm of public protest for him to do it. The story received national attention when it appeared on *ABC Nightly News* on November 10, 2010.

As the nationwide manhunt for the fugitive commander of the U.S. Navy Veterans Association (USNVA) known as Bobby Thompson widened, the alleged fraudster's connection to Minnesota Republicans deepened.

Ripple in Stillwater learned that following Thompson's controversial $10,000 donation to a Michele Bachmann fund-raiser in Minneapolis on April 7, 2010, featuring former Alaska half-term governor Sarah Palin—the last known contribution the donor-on-the-lam made—he gave $5,000 to a Republican-leaning, Minnesota-based political action committee called Patriot PAC on April 26, 2010.

Patriot PAC was formed in 2009 by Joey Gerdin, a Republican political operative who served as its chair. Gerdin was the finance director of the Minnesota House Republican Campaign Committee (HRCC) from 2007 to 2008, during which time the man known as Bobby Thompson gave $5,000 to the HRCC and attended a Republican National Convention HRCC event in St. Paul. Next to Gerdin, who donated $11,100 to her own PAC, Thompson is Patriot PAC's second largest contributor.

Gerdin said she doesn't remember how she became connected with Thompson. Because of his donation to her PAC, she was contacted by the Ohio Attorney General's office, which had a nationwide arrest warrant out on Thompson for identity fraud.

The Ohio Attorney General's office aggressively pursued the case and claimed that donations to the USNVA weren't used to aid veterans but instead diverted to political causes by Thompson. It earlier had a nationwide arrest warrant out on Thompson for identity fraud and more recently indicted Thompson and an alleged accomplice on corruption, money laundering, and theft charges.

The Ohio AG's office also released a number of photos of the man known as Bobby Thompson posing with prominent Republican politicians such as George W. Bush, John McCain, and John Boehner, as well as Republican operative Karl Rove.

A Typical RNC Patriot

To Gerdin, Thompson was just another political donor prospect. When raising money for the HRCC, Gerdin said, "I would just call anyone and everyone. I honestly don't even remember if I cold-called him or he cold-called me. He was coming in for the RNC [2008 Republican National Convention], and I was having a fund-raiser downtown with the House caucus."

Gerdin said she met the alleged con man in St. Paul at the fund-raiser she hosted. "He seemed like a nice guy, completely congenial, supportive of veterans. Seemed like your typical patriot to me."

The Ohio Attorney General investigator asked her about bank records for the donation to her PAC, she said. "The check that I got came from him personally, that I know."

Although some politicians—including Bachmann and reportedly the Republican Party of Minnesota—have donated money they received from Thompson to other veterans groups following the glare of bad publicity, Gerdin said she has no intention of doing so at this time.

"The money was given to me from an individual who wanted to elect veterans to office . . . that's what I basically used it for." She said she will eventually look further into the matter once things settle down with her current duties as finance director for 8th District congressman-elect Chip Cravaack.

Meanwhile, Blanca Contreras, an alleged coconspirator of Thompson's, was arrested and arraigned by Ohio authorities on charges of racketeering, money laundering, and theft of more than $1 million. According to court documents, Contreras "personally withdrew $416,000 in cash from a single USNVA account" between October 2007 and June 2010.

Contreras was being held on $2 million bail.

Although Ohio Attorney General Richard Cordray was the most aggressive in pursuing the man known as Bobby Thompson, that could change. Cordray lost in the November 2 election to Mike DeWine, who once received a $500 political contribution in a U.S. Senate campaign from Bobby Thompson.

State Campaign Finance Board Fines
Bobby Thompson

In June 2011, the Minnesota Campaign Finance and Public Disclosure Board (CFB) fined the man representing himself as Bobby Thompson $21,000 for making seven campaign contributions with a false identity in an attempt to circumvent state campaign finance laws.

The CFB conducted an extensive investigation of its own and confirmed what Karl Bremer's series had already revealed about Bobby Thompson and the U.S. Navy Veterans Association: that Thompson allegedly ran a sham organization in Minnesota that collected more than $1.5 million from unsuspecting Minnesotans using nothing more than a UPS drop box and a forwarded telephone recording for an office.

The CFB subpoenaed records for the USNVA's UPS box and phone records from Qwest Communications and procured documents from the State of Ohio courts, the Attorney General's office, and Minnesota campaign committees that received donations from Thompson.

Diane Johnson, the treasurer for the Seifert for Governor Committee, provided the CFB with a copy of a $500 money order and a handwritten note on USNVA letterhead that came with it. The note read "Marty: With my compliments, Bobby." Yet the name on the money order was "Maria D'Annuzio," a name that the CFB determined was also fake and used by Bobby Thompson to circumvent campaign finance laws.

Johnson also provided the CFB with a copy of a $500 check to the Seifert for Governor Committee drawn on the personal account of Bobby Thompson, located in Florida. There is an individual limit of $500 in aggregate donations to candidates for governor in nonelection years.

The CFB found that the two $500 donations made to the Seifert for Governor Committee under the names of "Bobby Thompson" and "Maria D'Annuzio" likely came from the same source and thus exceeded donation limits; they also violated Minnesota statutes prohibiting such donations to be delivered (bundled) together. Yet it accepted Johnson's explanation that the campaign assumed the two were spouses and thus the bundled donations legitimate, so it did not levy a penalty for the violation.

Among the items used to secure the USNVA's St. Paul UPS box was a business card for "Bobby Thompson" bearing a photo and a Social Security number. The Social Security number led to a Bobby Thompson in Bellingham, Washington—the same Bobby Thompson the State of Ohio found whose identity had been stolen by the USNVA's Bobby Thompson. The Ohio Attorney General's office issued a nationwide arrest warrant for Thompson for identity fraud. Thompson was also wanted on a warrant for his arrest on an Ohio grand jury indictment for money laundering and aggravated theft.

The Ohio Attorney General charged that donations to the USNVA found their way into political contributions. Yet the CFB noted that "While other investigators have concluded that the individual known as Bobby Thompson misappropriated funds from the U.S. Navy Veterans Association, the scope of the Board's investigation did not include determining the source of the funds used for the donations to Minnesota committees."

What about the Dirty Money?

The CFB did address the disposition of campaign contributions received from Bobby Thompson.

"The Board recognizes that, with the benefit of this and other investigations, some committees that accepted contributions from the individual claiming to be Bobby Thompson may find it inconsistent with their policies or philosophy to retain those contributions," it wrote. It noted that Minnesota statutes limit campaigns' charitable contributions to $100 per charity per year.

Campaign committees also may make unlimited donations to the state's general fund to salve their conscience for accepting "dirty money."

GOP operative Joey Gerdin, who was the HRCC finance director in 2008 when Thompson made his initial $5,000 donation to the committee and the founder and chair of the GOP-leaning Patriot PAC, which received a $5,000 donation from Thompson in 2010, wasn't interested in talking about Thompson, however.

She hung up the telephone without responding to a request for a comment on the CFB findings or the disposition of the $5,000 in allegedly fraudulent campaign contributions her PAC took from Thompson last year.

Minnesota Speaker of the House Kurt Zellers, the chair of the HRCC, and Jenifer Loon, the HRCC treasurer, did not respond to telephone and e-mail requests for comments on the CFB findings or on the disposition of the $7,000 in allegedly fraudulent campaign contributions that Thompson made to the HRCC.

According to the CFB's final report, its investigation did not include contributions to the Republican Party of Minnesota through federal political action committees; however, according to Federal Election Commission reports, the state GOP received a total of $10,400 from Bobby Thompson through committees run by Michele Bachmann's and Norm Coleman's campaigns.

Deputy Minnesota GOP chair Michael Brodkorb did not respond to telephone and e-mail requests for comments on the CFB findings or on the disposition of the $10,400 in allegedly fraudulent campaign contributions given by Thompson to the Republican Party of Minnesota.

No Help from the Attorney General

It's not likely that any of the duped donors to the U.S. Navy Veterans Association Minnesota Chapter will ever recover their money, particularly if the attorney general fails to investigate the organization.

The CFB findings ordered the CFB executive director to "monitor other states' efforts to locate the individual using the name 'Bobby Thompson' to make political contributions in Minnesota." If he's located, the CFB director is to work with the attorney general to try to collect the $21,000 in penalties levied.

Meanwhile, the Minnesota Attorney General's office has refused repeated requests for information about its own investigation—if any—into Bobby Thompson and the whereabouts of the $1.5 million he collected from Minnesotans under the guise of a charitable veterans organization. Republican recipients of Thompson's largesse no longer seem interested in talking about him or his money either.

Thanks to the diligence of former Ohio Attorney General Richard Cordray, Bobby Thompson's accomplice, Blanca Contreras of Tampa, Florida, was sentenced in August 2011 to five years in prison for her role in the navy veterans fraud.

Contreras admitted falsifying documents and cashing nearly $500,000 in checks from fraudulent U.S. Navy Veterans Association accounts. She pleaded guilty in June 2011 to engaging in a pattern of corrupt activity, aggravated theft, money laundering, and tampering with records in connection with her four-year involvement with the sham veterans organization, which Cuyahoga County Court of Common Pleas judge Kathleen Ann Sutula described as a "criminal enterprise of mammoth proportions."

Michele Bachmann isn't the only presidential candidate to take money from alleged fraudster Bobby Thompson. Besides Bachmann, one other Republican candidate for president can be found on Bobby Thompson's contribution list: former Massachusetts governor Mitt Romney.

Bobby kicked in $2,300 to the Romney for President campaign in 2007.

CHAPTER 9

Bachmann's Bathroomgate

Michele Bachmann's freak-out in a public women's rest-room in Scandia, Minnesota, on April 9, 2005, in the Scandia Town Hall caused a small sensation in the local media and the blogosphere. Here are some of our blog posts about the incident.

An Eyewitness Account

On April 9, 2005, Jan Hogle, a resident of Scandia, provided us with an eyewitness account of what happened in that bath-room.

> State Sen. Michele Bachmann and Rep. Ray Vandeveer were in Scandia Saturday morning for a town meeting

with their constituents. Usually the senator and representative expect a half dozen folks to show up for a comfortable chat. Not so on April 9th, when 36 area residents seated themselves firmly before their elected officials and demanded accountability on issues ranging from educational funding to the controversial "defense of marriage" amendment.

Saturday's meeting was stiffly cordial until the room erupted in applause at the suggestion that higher taxes were acceptable, if such taxes were valid expenditures used to keep Minnesota's quality of education at a premium level. Stating that "the quality of education is integral to what Minnesotans consider their high quality of life," several audience members asserted that Governor Pawlenty's "No New Taxes" pledge is leaving the state poorer with regard to education, social services, and overall economic stability.

While the representative and senator replied to questions with growing impatience and formulaic responses, their bodies squirmed in discomfort at the unexpected chilly reception in rural Washington County. During several comments, Rep. Vandeveer turned away from the audience member speaking to him, and spoke under his breath to the senator. Frequently the two exchanged smirks during audience remarks.

Mr. Vandeveer commented later that audience members were rude and disrespectful.

The audience then moved to contest the Defense of Marriage Act, stating that several people in the room were gay or lesbian and requesting clarification from the two officials as to why persons with alternative lifestyles were considered so threatening. Ms. Bachmann was asked to cite an actual study, which showed that children were harmed by exposure to couples with alternative life styles. She responded by referring vaguely to conclusions that children are best raised in a household with a mother and a father, to which the audience suggested making divorce illegal.

When asked why families who had lived in this country since before it was the United States and who had for generations volunteered to fight to defend this country were not worthy of equal representation because they believed in a different God than the Senator believes in, Ms. Bachmann had no response.

Apparently this was more than Rep. Vandeveer could handle, as he then stood up and began backing away from the audience. Stating that he and Ms. Bachmann had to leave, he tried to convince the audience that the meeting time was over. Audience members shouted in protest and held up their hands, indicating at least 5 minutes remained, but to no avail. The meeting was over.

After the meeting, some attempted to speak further with Bachmann and Vandeveer to emphasize the hurtful consequences of the narrow political policies. Even among the few conservatives in attendance, it was commented that the Defense of Marriage Act was a political waste of time perpetrated by Republicans to divert attention from more pressing issues. One retired farmer remarked, "I'm straight, but God made gays and I don't have any problem with them. The Defense of Marriage thing is a waste of time. They have more important business at the legislature."

Senator Bachmann retired to the restroom and residents began moving toward the exit. Less than a moment later, piercing screams were heard from the ladies' washroom. "Help!!!! HEEEELLLLLLPPPPPP!!!!!" With everyone's attention riveted on the door, Senator Bachmann emerged in a crouching run, crying, "I was being held against my will!" Two women were seen standing behind her, one tall and elderly, the other young and petite, both unassuming and bewildered.

The women reported afterward they had followed the senator into the restroom to continue to question her about education. One had her hand on the door handle, ready to open it, which she immediately did when Senator Bachmann became frightened and began screaming.

Mused one bystander, "I'm guessing our Senator won't be returning to Scandia any time soon."

Rep. Vandeveer spirited Senator Bachmann away from the unfriendly gathering in his shiny gas guzzling SUV in an apparent effort to either protect her from the raving liberals or save fuel on their drive to the next gathering in Hugo.

—Jan Hogle (April 9, 2005)

The Vandeveer Version

In the various and conflicting ways that Senator Michele Bachmann (R-Stillwater) described the town hall meeting she and Representative Ray Vandeveer (R-Forest Lake) held on April 9, 2005, at the Scandia Town Hall, you'd think she barely escaped with her life ahead of an angry mob of pitchfork-wielding homosexuals. Yet Vandeveer's account of events, as told to the Washington County Sheriff's Office (WCSO), sounded as if he was at an entirely different meeting altogether.

Bachmann told the *St. Paul Pioneer Press* that she ended that meeting early when "tensions elevated beyond reasonable levels."

By the time she talked to the *Star Tribune*'s Katherine Kersten, her story had grown to "about 35 self-described supporters of the gay/lesbian/bisexual/transgender community surrounded her and noisily took over the meeting." In yet another version of her story, however, Bachmann told WCSO that when attendees wanted to continue the meeting until its allotted time, she argued with them for fifteen minutes more and "then walked out of the main room and into the bathroom in an effort to get away from the groups of people so they would leave the area."

Vandeveer, in an interview with WCSO, had this to say about that angry mob that supposedly surrounded Bachmann and took over the meeting: "You expect it to be, when you have some controversial issues, to be a little rancorous. So, they were a little bit out of line, but I didn't get a sense that they were violent."

When asked whether he could relate anything about the incident following the meeting in which Bachmann claimed to have been imprisoned in the bathroom against her will by two of the aforementioned "gay activists," Vandeveer told WCSO, "I can't because I was, the bathrooms are off the hall. This is in the room. I was in the room kind of herding people toward the door because we were late. There were quite a few people—I would guess forty or so—and they were talking and stuff so I didn't hear anything, and I didn't see anything until Sen. Bachmann came over and just told me what happened. So I can't help there."

Were "tensions elevated beyond reasonable levels," as Bachmann charged? Not according to Vandeveer's version. "She came out and I kind of got a little more 'Well, we all have to go now.' And everybody went now. They moved out, 'cause we had to clear it out and lock it up. They didn't want to go, but when it came down to it they did, so I can't say, there wasn't anything outside of the bathroom incident to report."

Although Bachmann characterized the meeting as being stacked with members of "the GLBT group" who were encouraged to attend by DumpBachmann.com, Vandeveer mentioned nothing to the WCSO about the makeup of the group or of anyone surrounding the senator or taking over the meeting.

He did note that one woman he described as "maybe seventy," who was later identified as one of the women in the bathroom with Bachmann, approached them as they were in his truck preparing to leave and attempted to apologize to Bachmann.

"She said something about 'I didn't mean to scare you,' or something like that. I can't remember the exact words—and she said she was from Scandia," Vandeveer told WCSO.

In Bachmann's hyperventilating report to WCSO, she made no mention of any further contact with either woman after the bathroom incident or that one of them had apologized to her immediately afterward. Instead, she said she located Vandeveer and "indicated to Vandeveer that she was unable to drive as she was too shaken up and was absolutely terrified and has never been terrorized before as she had no idea what those two women were going to do to her."

Bachmann also never referred to her alleged captors as constituents in her sheriff's report, only that she suspected they were "with the GLBT Group, which is a gay and lesbian activist group." According to Vandeveer's version, however, Bachmann knew full well that at least one of them was a constituent, because he said the woman identified herself to both of them after the meeting as being from Scandia.

Bachmann's various accounts of the meeting also conflict with those of Jan and Gary Hogle of Scandia, who were present at the meeting and for the events that followed. Bachmann's description of the group as a bunch of militant gay activists, Gary Hogle said, "is just a bald-faced lie. I'm an election judge up there. I know these people."

Added Jan Hogle, "There were no more than six people out of

thirty-eight [who were GLBT], and they were just residents of this area. So it was not a GLBT group, and I do not know what led her to believe that. Because neither of the women involved [in the bathroom incident], at any point when I was standing there, identified themselves as being gay or lesbian."

Likewise, the Hogles said, Bachmann's description of the meeting as "contentious" was grossly inaccurate. "The meeting that we had was very calm and orderly," Gary told Washington County deputy Wayne Johnson. "There were no raised voices. There were a couple of protests when Rep. Vandeveer tried to shut the meeting down early, but other than that, there was no contention." Concluded Gary Hogle, "If she's trying to contend that people were verbally attacking her—not at all the case."

Deputy Johnson seemed to agree: "Well, that kind of seems to fit with what I'm getting from every other source," he told Hogle. The likelihood of any charges resulting from Bachmann's complaints appeared to be slim, according to Johnson.

"I think this is one of those things that, once I get completed with my report and ship it over to the county attorney's office for an opinion, I think it's just going to go away quietly," he told Hogle.

Yet questions still remain about the discrepancies in the different accounts of events given by Bachmann to the Washington County Sheriff's Office and various media outlets. Some Bachmann constituents have expressed an interest in pursuing charges against Bachmann of filing a false police report.

"Bachmann's overblown version of events during the town hall meeting seems inconsistent with that of her own legislative colleague who co-chaired the event," said Eva Young of DumpBach mann.com.

All previous quotes were taken from Washington County Sheriff's Office interviews with Senator Michele Bachmann, Representative Ray Vandeveer, and Jan and Gary Hogle.

Bachmann's Shifting Accounts

Michele Bachmann's report to the Washington County Sheriff's Office of being "prevented from leaving the bathroom" after a town meeting in Scandia differed considerably from accounts of the story that she gave to the media, and even from Bachmann's own version of events as reported to the sheriff in a follow-up interview. That led us at *Dump Bachmann* to wonder what other "facts" may have been misconstrued—or misreported—by Bachmann in this bizarre tale.

According to Bachmann's initial report to the WCSO, Bachmann "was preparing to leave near 1100 hours" and "used the rest room." In her follow-up interview, though, Bachmann claimed that she continued arguing with others for "an additional fifteen minutes" after the meeting was over and "then walked out of the main room and into the bathroom in an effort to get away from the groups of people so they would leave the area." And in media reports, Bachmann said she ended the meeting when "tensions elevated beyond reasonable levels."

Bachmann also reported that the women who "held her against her will" were "with the GLBT group, which is a gay and lesbian activist group," when in fact they both were constituents of hers from Scandia, and she knew that at least one of them was.

So which was it, Senator? Did the meeting end at 11 a.m. as scheduled, and you merely "used the bathroom," as you stated in your initial complaint? Or did you try to end the meeting fifteen minutes early and then run in the bathroom to hide from your constituents when they wanted the meeting to continue to its allotted time, as you admitted in your second interview?

Bachmann also complained to the WCSO that "there is a website dumpbachmann.com and on the website it is giving her locations of where she is going to [be] publicly speaking." Although DumpBachmann.com was pleased that Senator Bachmann was reading our website regularly, we wondered when it became a crime to report on an elected official's upcoming public events? There was another place where you could find Senator Bachmann's public events: her official state Senate website.

Bachmann also told police that she was held in the bathroom until she screamed for help, at which time "she took the opportunity to run between the two of them and grabbed the door handle away from them." Yet according to *Star Tribune* columnist Katherine Kersten, "It was not until she called out for help that the startled women let her through."

So which was it, Senator? Did you have to wrest the door handle from the two women, as you told police? Or did the two women let you out, as you told Kersten?

We also found it curious that Bachmann gave her capitol office address when filing her report and not her home address, which was in the phone book if anyone really wanted it. In addition, significant discrepancies exist between Bachmann's version of events in the WCSO report and those of Pam Arnold and Nancy Cosgriff, who were with Bachmann in the bathroom that fateful day.

At that point, it didn't appear that any charges would be forthcoming from the WCSO as a result of Bachmann's complaint, but *Dump Bachmann* suggested that authorities investigate whether Senator Bachmann filed a false police report in light of her shifting versions of her story. No charges were ultimately filed.

Meanwhile, we anxiously awaited the version of events as reported to the WCSO by Representative Ray Vandeveer, who to that point had been silent on the whole tawdry affair.

It is worth noting the law—Chapter Title: CRIMINAL CODE Section: 609.505

> Falsely reporting crime.
> Whoever informs a law enforcement officer that a crime has been committed, knowing that it is false and

intending that the officer shall act in reliance upon it, is guilty of a misdemeanor. A person who is convicted a second or subsequent time under this section is guilty of a gross misdemeanor.

Over the years, Bachmann supporters have defended Bachmann's account of the incident. This is from a Prayer Transformation ministries e-mail.

> Friday night Sen. Bachmann was terribly harassed at a town meeting and after, as she was in the rest room, was verbally attacked by two from the gay group who held the door so she couldn't get out. Michele started screaming for help so they moved a side. She was verbally shaken and crying as she left. I say all this to say that she needs much more prayer now than ever. Her husband Marcus also has pneumonia so please lift him up in prayer also.

EdWatch posted an account of the April 11, 2005, incident on their website that claimed supporters of same-sex marriage "stepped over the line of civil debate into threatening behavior that has the potential for personal safety being put at risk." The EdWatch article went on to say Bachmann and Vanderveer were met with an "unruly group who turned out to be largely a gay/lesbian crowd" from out of town who had invaded Scandia after reading that an announcement "steeped in highly abusive language had been posted on the Internet detailing the Scandia meeting and the vehicle Bachmann drives." The florid EdWatch version goes on to describe how "the same-sex marriage contingent" dominated the meeting using "tactics of intimidation" toward the author of the infamous constitutional amendment:

When the meeting was over, the boisterous crowd refused repeated requests for them to leave. Sen. Bachmann was verbally harassed and, for a time, was refused exit from a restroom by two women who blocked the doorway.

Star Tribune columnist Katherine Kersten weighed in with her opinion on June 13, 2005 ("Tolerance Should Be Extended to All"), as to what occurred in the bathroom. Kersten claimed the citizens at the meeting were using "strong-arm tactics" to intimidate Bachmann at the urging of bloggers. The unnamed bloggers, Bachmann apparently told Kersten, were "crashing" the community meetings Bachmann was holding in her district. Kersten's account, via Bachmann, adds a few dramatic touches to the incident:

> At a senior citizens center in Scandia, Bachmann reports, about 35 self-described supporters of the gay/lesbian/bisexual/transgender community surrounded her and noisily took over the meeting. When she left and went to the bathroom, two women followed her in and belligerently accosted her.
>
> When Bachmann tried to leave, the women leaned against the door and blocked her way. "I could hear a crowd gathering outside. I didn't have my cell phone, and no one knew where I was," says Bachmann. It was not until she called out for help that the startled women let her through.

In 2009, Bradlee Dean claimed that Bachmann was "locked in a bathroom."

The story about what happened in that bathroom in Scandia resurfaced only briefly after Michele Bachmann announced her run for the presidency.

CHAPTER 10

Bachmann's Secretary of State: Jesus

When Michele Bachmann prayed for Bradlee Dean's ministry at a fund-raiser in 2006, she professed her belief that we were in the End Times. The End Times, to put it simply, is the doomsday scenario in the Bible that foretells a struggle between Good and Evil, with Jesus returning to gather up the faithful for a happy ending in Heaven (and a not-so-happy ending for everyone else). Several incidents in Michele Bachmann's political career would indicate that she is looking forward to the final showdown in Armageddon. Many of Bachmann's End Times–supporting flock believe the return of the Messiah requires that Jews be in control of the real estate mentioned in the Bible.

Those Jews in Israel who do not convert to Bachmann's faith at the sound of the last trumpet will be judged and condemned to eternal damnation . . . an unpleasant notion when you think about President Bachmann having access to the launch codes for the U.S. nuclear arsenal.

Bachmann on Nuking Iran

Before she won the Republican endorsement for the 6th Congressional District, Michele Bachmann gave an interview to Minnesota Public Radio. In a short segment on Iran, Bachmann threatened Iran with a "nuclear response." Bachmann also threatened to go after Venezuela.

The question was, "If diplomacy should fail to stop Iran's nuclear program, what should we do?"

Bachmann replied,

> I think that at this point diplomacy is our option. And we certainly don't want to move toward a nuclear response any time soon or without an abundance of caution.
>
> Iran is at a point right now where America has to be very aggressive in our response. We can't remove any option off the table. And we should not remove the nuclear response.
>
> However, we must proceed with an abundance of caution. Because we know that Iran is very precarious. And I think we should take very seriously the threats coming out of Iran right now. But again, there are other nations including Venezuela that we need to keep our eyes on as well.

Chilling.

Bachmann's Night with the King

In a lecture at an EdWatch conference in 2004, Bachmann talked about how the gay marriage issue "fueled the reelection of George Bush." Bachmann then proceeded to make a odd biblical reference: "I just cannot help but think of the Book of Esther . . . with Haman who built a device to hang the powerful Jewish ruler and then to exterminate all the Jews."

The Book of Esther is about the ancient Israelites' exile and captivity in Babylon. The Persian ruler (Xerxes) Ahasuerus divorces his queen and chooses a new queen, Esther, from a roster of "fair young virgins." Esther is a foster kid living with her cousin Mordecai who hangs out at the palace. A Jew-hating bad guy, Haman, tries to talk Ahasuerus into unleashing a Persian-style pogrom. Haman and Ahasuerus are unaware that Queen Esther is a Jew. With some prompting from cousin Mordecai, Esther convinces Ahasuerus to turn the tables on Haman, and an Old Testament–style bloodbath ensues, wiping out Haman and his tribe forever.

Does Bachmann see herself as a modern-day Esther? The media should ask her about that. Who is the modern-day Haman?

According to author Sarah Posner, the Queen Esther fantasy is a mainstay of fundamentalist woman such as Bachmann and Palin. There's even a Christian bodice-ripping film version of the Esther story called *One Night with the King*, which was produced by a film company run by Matthew Crouch, the son of fundamentalist preacher Paul Crouch.

In the biblical worldview of some Christian dominionists, modern-day Persia is Iran and the present-day incarnation of Haman is Iranian president Mahmoud Ahmadinejad. Keep that in mind every time Bachmann rattles the sword for war with Iran.

If Michele Bachmann is the present-day Esther, is her husband Marcus the present-day Mordecai? And who's the king?

Bachmannistan

Bachmann gave a podcast interview to *Saint Cloud Times* reporter Larry Schumacher on February 9, 2007. Bachmann told Schumacher this curious tale of Iranian meddling in Iraqi affairs:

> Iran is the trouble maker, trying to tip over apple carts all over Baghdad right now because they want America to pull out. And do you know why? It's because they've already decided that they're going to partition Iraq.
>
> And half of Iraq, the western, northern portion of Iraq, is going to be called the Iraq State of Islam, something like that. And I'm sorry, I don't have the official name, but it's meant to be the training ground for the terrorists. There's already an agreement made.
>
> They are going to get half of Iraq and that is going to be a safe haven zone where they can go ahead and bring about more attacks in the Middle East region and then to come against the United States because we are their avowed enemy.

A bizarre claim, even for Bachmann: Iran and al-Qaida wanted to partition Iraq, and the al-Qaida–controlled part would be used to attack Israel and other nations.

Star Tribune reporter Eric Black picked up the story and posted it on the *Star Tribune*'s *The Big Question* blog. After being linked from the *Drudge Report* and mentioned by Rush Limbaugh, Eric Black's blog post logged 200,000 hits. On an average day, the blog averaged 5,000 visits.

To this date, nobody knows where Bachmann got her information about the plan to partition Iraq. Eric Black was unable to contact Michele Bachmann again.

Appreciating Everyone's Values and Cultures

Bachmann doesn't offer much in the way of solutions to the problem of illegal immigration, but she isn't above spreading a lot of fear about immigrants. As of August 30, 2001, Bachmann's congressional website had a statement about immigration putting an "unfair strain on our country's job markets" and that she wanted Congress to "work to secure our nation's borders and enforce the immigration laws already in place."

In a debate recorded in November 2005 by the Minnesota-based video news outlet *The Uptake*, Bachmann responded to a question about rioting in France and assimilating foreign cultures:

> Only in France can you have suburban youth rioting because welfare benefits aren't generous enough. . . . What we are seeing is the fruits of leftism. It's suburban kids watching cable TV. In a lot of these high-rises where a lot of these suburban youth are rioting, they have cable TV and they are watching Al Jazeera. And they are being encouraged and prompted to start these riots all over France.
>
> There is a movement afoot that is occurring and part of that is this whole philosophical idea of multi-cultural diversity, which on the face sounds wonderful. Let's appreciate everyone's values and cultures.
>
> But, guess what? Not all cultures are equal. Not all values are equal.
>
> And one thing we are seeing is in the midst of this violence that is being encouraged by Al Jazeera and the Jihadists, is those that are coming into France, which had a beautiful culture, the French culture is actually diminished. It's going away.

Bachmann exploited a tragic incident that happened in Cottonwood, Minnesota, in February 2008, when an undocumented immigrant from Guatemala, Franco del Cid, ran a stop sign and crashed into the side of a school bus, killing four children.

Although the incident didn't occur in Bachmann's district, she was invited onto Bill O'Reilly's show to talk about it being an example of what was wrong with the nation's immigration policy. Bachmann said it was an issue of "law versus anarchy." During a debate in October 2008 with DFL (Minnesota Democratic-Farmer-Labor Party) candidate Elwyn Tinklenberg, Bachmann again used the incident to spread fear about immigrants:

> Without having some sort of a barrier at the border, we're going to continue to have the kind of problems that we've had with Olga Franco that we saw most recently in the tragic death of four children in the accident.
>
> These are preventable and we need to do that with sealing America's borders.

Bachmann also claimed that illegal immigrants were "bringing in diseases, bringing in drugs, bringing in violence" (*Star Tribune*, October 17, 2008).

Compulsory Divorce

On November 17, 2010, Michele Bachmann appeared at a press conference called by her pal Larry Klayman at his Freedom Watch symposium titled "National Security, Freedom, and Iran—Is It Time for U.S. and Western Intervention?" Bachmann voiced her support for the People's Mujahideen Organization of Iran (MEK, PMOI), asking that it be removed from the U.S. State Department's Current List of Designated Foreign Terrorist Organizations (FTOs).

The People's Mujahideen Organization of Iran is a bizarre, cult-like organization that participated in the Iranian revolution of the 1970s. The U.S. State Department claims that the MEK assassinated at least six U.S. citizens during the revolution and supported the takeover of the U.S. embassy in Tehran. The leader of the MEK, Massoud Rajavi, fell out of favor with the new regime and fled to France. The MEK collaborated with Saddam Hussein against Iran during the 1980–1988 war. In April 1992, the MEK carried out terrorist attacks on thirteen Iranian embassies around the world. The U.S. government listed the MEK as a terrorist organization in 1997.

Human Rights Watch (HRW) issued a report on the MEK that said the People's Mujahideen Organization of Iran required its members to divorce their spouses:

> The leadership asked the members to divorce themselves from all physical and emotional attachments in order to enhance their "capacity for struggle." In case of married couples, this phase of the "ideological revolution" required them to renounce their emotional ties to their spouses through divorce.

When a reporter asked Bachmann about the lack of trust Iranian dissidents have for the People's Mujahideen Organization of Iran, Bachmann replied with this money quote: "Not every vehicle is a perfect vehicle, and we don't want to defeat the good because we are in search of the perfect."

In two videos posted on YouTube, recorded at Klayman's presser, Bachmann proclaimed her support for the People's Mujahideen Organization of Iran, asking that they be removed from the U.S. State Department's List of Designated Foreign Terrorist Organizations. Alan Keyes, who said the United States should declare war on Muslim "imperialism," followed Bachmann.

The Price of Michele Bachmann's Vote

Michele and Marcus took a little jaunt over to Israel, a weeklong junket in August 2007, courtesy of the nonprofit arm of the American Israeli Public Affairs Committee (AIPAC), which cost nearly $18,000 for the Bachmanns alone. But then, when you're flying business class and staying in $436/night hotels, you can run up quite a bill in no time.

Airfare for the happy couple was estimated at $4,600 apiece. Meals were estimated at $625 per person, and the cost for other incidentals such as "security, ground transportation, guide, honoraria and entrance fees" was pegged at another $1,230 apiece.

Although the junket was sponsored by the American Israel Education Foundation, the first order of business on arrival was an "orientation and political update" from AIPAC. According to SourceWatch, "One strategy adopted by AIPAC for building political support is by organizing tours to Israel. In August 2003, an AIPAC foreign policy associate in Jerusalem told CNSNews.com that in that month alone, approximately 10 percent of the members of the U.S. House of Representatives had visited Israel on their tours. "AIPAC is associated with the American Israel Education Foundation (AIEF), which sponsors fact-finding trips for many members of Congress." Indeed, twenty other members of Congress—Republicans and Democrats—joined the Bachmanns on this trip, and nearly forty more were scheduled to go on later trips.

When Bachmann was asked about her trip on KKMS radio, this is what she remembered: "The marvelous thing—I think everyone who went on this trip was a solid born again believer in Jesus Christ—and we had one Jewish member of Congress."

One has to wonder whether Michele "perfected" any Jews along the way, as her hero Ann Coulter advocates?

In her congressional travel approval form, Bachmann explained her reason for participating: "As a freshman member of Congress who votes on legislation affecting the U.S.-Israel relationship and the region more broadly, I have an interest in learning more about the issues facing the U.S.-Israel relationship."

What Bachmann didn't explain was why Marcus went along. Was it common for spouses to accompany members of Congress on official lobbying, er, "educational" junkets? Or was this just a way for AIPAC to double its investment in members?

Either way, it's simply another symptom of a system that's rotting from the inside out.

Bachmann Claimed God Will Curse the United States If It Won't Support Israel

In a speech to the Republican Jewish Coalition in Los Angeles in 2010, Michele Bachmann said the following:

> I am convinced in my heart and in my mind that if the United States fails to stand with Israel, that is the end of the United States. . . . [W]e have to show that we are inextricably entwined, that as a nation we have been blessed because of our relationship with Israel, and if we reject Israel, then there is a curse that comes into play. And my husband and I are both Christians, and we believe very strongly the verse from Genesis [Genesis 12:3], we believe very strongly that nations also receive blessings as they bless Israel. It is a strong and beautiful principle.

A candidate for president of the United States with a foreign policy based on God's curses and blessings?

CHAPTER 11

Bachmann's Boondoggles

B achmann is better known for her extremist views on the "social issues," such as same-sex marriage and abortion, but her positions on transportation are just as far out of the mainstream. Despite her claim to be a fiscal conservative, Bachmann favors expensive boondoggle projects over less expensive, conventional transportation projects.

Michele Bachmann and the Stillwater Bridge

Michele Bachmann has been a big supporter of highway expansion and an opponent of transit. It's no wonder the Sierra Club put her in its 2002 "Toxic Twelve" list of Minnesota legislators with the worst environmental voting records.

Bachmann loves highways so much, she has said she will support an increased gas tax to pay for more highway construction . . . even if it means breaking her 2000 no-tax pledge to the Taxpayer's League. Bachmann told the *Forest Lake Times* in 2002, she would consider supporting a gas tax increase and bonding to build and maintain roads and bridges.

From her old website:

> As your District 52 State Senator, I will work hard to add capacity to Minnesota highways. . . . This is my personal commitment to you." Michele believes a successful transportation policy must put an end to the diversion of scarce funds to impractical and expensive rail transit programs that will have no direct benefit for area residents and will cost millions of dollars in the future for operating subsidies. She has called for dedicating 100 percent of the sales tax on vehicles to road construction.
>
> When weighing transportation options, it becomes readily apparent that the most effective way to reduce traffic congestion, make our roads safer, and get us home from work to spend time with our families is by expanding and improving our metro highway system. Since we're talking about transportation, I can't leave out one important local issue that I've been an advocate for—the Stillwater bridge project. I simply want to express to you my dedication to keeping up the momentum we've achieved on getting a new bridge built.

The Taxpayers for Common Sense included the Stillwater Bridge in their 2004 *Road to Ruin Report*, citing taxpayer concerns that it was unnecessary because the Interstate 94 (I-94) bridge crosses the St. Croix only six miles to the south. The estimated

$200 million price tag of the proposed Stillwater Bridge was excessive and called for consideration of alternatives. The *Road to Ruin Report* also cited community concerns. A big, four-lane bridge would encourage sprawl in western Wisconsin and drain people, tax base, and jobs from Minnesota. In fact, the growth and land-use plans of communities in Wisconsin were based on the bridge being built. The bridge would also induce congestion on Highway 36 leading to Saint Paul.

The report also listed environmental effects: "Construction of the new bridge and related highway improvements would destroy five wetlands and 130 acres of farmland, triple the amount of paved surface, and increase the amount of polluted runoff flowing into local streams and wetlands." The immense size of the span, stretching from the tops of the bluffs on either side, would "alter the character of the St. Croix River, the only Wild and Scenic River in Minnesota, and set a damaging precedent for similar rivers nationwide. In 1997, NPS (National Park Service) ruled against the bridge under the Wild and Scenic Rivers Act, a stance it has since reversed."

In the years since the *Road to Ruin Report* came out, Michele Bachmann and bridge advocates continued to lobby for the bridge boondoggle, always playing loose with the facts on the St. Croix River.

In 2011, Bachmann charged that opposition to the new bridge was coming from "radical environmental groups." She took time out from the Tea Party rubber-chicken circuit in February 2011 to breeze by the capitol and drop a bill in the hopper to exempt the St. Croix River from the National Wild and Scenic Rivers Act.

Meanwhile, the fledgling Coalition for St. Croix River Crossing, a pro-bridge consortium of St. Croix Valley government and business groups on both sides of the river, was touting two previous projects exempted from the Wild and Scenic Rivers Act as being comparable to the proposed Stillwater Bridge when, in fact, the exemptions weren't even for bridges. They were for projects designed to preserve the fisheries of two protected rivers and had absolutely nothing to do with transportation. Yet that didn't stop the coalition from perpetuating this myth through the media, presenting it as a precedent for exempting the Bachmann boondoggle from the act.

One of the "radical environmental groups" in our midst is the National Parks Conservation Association (NPCA). The NPCA was established in 1919—three years after the National Park Service came into being—to serve as an advocate for the protection of America's national parks. The NPCA Midwest Office oversees forty-eight National Park sites in eleven states, including the 93,000-acre St. Croix National Scenic Riverway.

"We aren't an environmental group," said NPCA Midwest regional director Lynn McClure. "We were established in 1919 by the director of the Park Service as an independent organization fulfilling the function of advocate/watchdog for the parks. We did some educational outreach for the Park Service originally. But today, we're the only dedicated national group that is the voice of the National Parks in Washington."

Just how radical is it?

"I'd wager we have more Republicans on our board than Democrats," McClure said. "It's pretty darn close. We have a lot of fiscally conservative Republicans on our board. But they understand the preservation side of things and they will stand with the parks. They're not banging the radical environmental drum."

The NPCA was one of twenty-six state and national organizations that sent a letter to Governor Mark Dayton urging him to "shelve plans for a new bridge that would cost over $640 million, damage the Riverway's scenic and natural resources, and accelerate sprawl into rural western Wisconsin. Instead," the groups asked, "we urge you to quickly seize this opportunity to identify, with leadership from the Minnesota Department of Transportation and in collaboration with stakeholders, an alternative proposal for a new, modestly-scaled bridge—one that would dramatically reduce the impact on the Lower St. Croix, while serving the needs of Minnesota and Wisconsin residents and saving taxpayers hundreds of millions of dollars. At the same time, we urge you to oppose efforts to move the current unworkable proposal forward."

Dayton responded that "all possibilities have been reopened for consideration" with regard to bridge options.

"Our first instincts are to find the best solutions that both protect the national parks and bring a local community together around it," said McClure. "We understand the role national parks can play in economic development. But sometimes, you have to say you need to weigh in on this picture."

The St. Croix River has long been considered one of the more unique rivers in the Wild and Scenic Rivers system because of its close proximity to a major metropolitan area.

"That's primarily the reason we got involved in the bridge issue," McClure explained. "The St. Croix is an extreme point of pride for the National Park Service." When she's in Washington, McClure said, the St. Croix is often mentioned in the same breath as Yellowstone or Glacier national parks. "The director understands the critical nature of this bridge if it were to go in."

The Wild and Scenic Rivers system, created in 1968, protects more than 11,000 miles of 166 rivers in thirty-eight states and Puerto Rico—barely more than one-quarter of 1 percent of the nation's rivers. The Upper St. Croix, from its source to Taylor's Falls, was among the first rivers designated under the act; the Lower St. Croix, from Taylor's Falls to Prescott, Wisconsin, was added to the system in 1972.

"You don't grant exemptions to the act lightly," McClure stressed.

Which brings us to the exemptions hailed by the Coalition for St. Croix River Crossing as precedents for granting an exemption to the act for the proposed four-lane, 65-mph freeway bridge at Stillwater.

William Rubin is the executive director of the St. Croix Economic Development Corporation (EDC) in Hudson and a member of the Coalition for St. Croix River Crossing. The coalition was incorporated in Minnesota in December 2010 and lists the Stillwater City Hall as its address.

At the time of this writing, August 29, 2011, the St. Croix EDC website features a news release detailing the pro-bridge coalition's goals and notes that two previous exemptions have been granted from the Wild and Scenic Rivers Act. Other news reports about the coalition state that the two exempted projects were "similar" to the proposed Stillwater Bridge or that they actually were for bridges.

When I asked Rubin for specifics about the previous two exemptions from the Wild and Scenic Rivers Act that his group cited, he didn't have a clue as to what they were.

"Maybe you should ask the Department of Transportation," he replied.

When reminded that the reference to the exemptions was information put out by his group and not by the Department of Transportation, Rubin became irritated.

"We deal in economic development here. Maybe our journalistic skills aren't all that they should be," Rubin said.

There was a good reason why Rubin didn't want to talk about the exemptions: because they don't even remotely resemble the proposed Stillwater Bridge project and couldn't under any reasonable circumstances be compared to it.

According to Dan Haas, a U.S. Fish and Wildlife planner who sits on the federal Interagency Wild and Scenic River Coordinating Council, "There have been only two exemptions to the Wild and Scenic Rivers Act after the fact." Neither of them were bridges, nor were they even transportation-related.

One exemption was for a sea lamprey barrier on the Pere Marquette River in Michigan. This electric fish barrier features bottom-mounted electrodes on a wooden deck. It works in conjunction with a fish bypass channel and a lamprey trap to block the upstream migration of Atlantic sea lamprey into trout-spawning habitat on the river. The lamprey are diverted, trapped, and electrocuted, eliminating the need for chemicals to rid the river of them.

The other exemption was for a temperature-control tower built upstream from Cougar Dam on the South Fork of the McKenzie River in Oregon. The tower takes in warmer waters from the surface of Cougar Reservoir above the dam to maintain consistent temperatures downstream from the dam. This allowed for the return and revitalization of Chinook salmon populations on the South Fork of the McKenzie, which had stopped migrating up the river due to cold waters flowing out from the bottom of the reservoir following construction of the dam in 1963. The reservoir was drained for the tower's construction, but once it was refilled, the tower was submerged. The exceptions were approved to mitigate human-made problems, not to create new problems.

The only bridges that have been built over designated Wild and Scenic Rivers have been built in the same corridor as the old bridges, and then the old bridges were torn down on completion of the new ones.

Rubin and the Coalition for St. Croix River Crossing weren't the only bridge proponents misrepresenting the facts. Not surprisingly, Bachmann played fast and loose with them as well. Besides painting opponents of her billion-dollar boondoggle as "radical environmentalists," Bachmann also claimed her critics were lying about what her bill would do.

"It has also been claimed that my bill exempts the Lower St. Croix from the Wild and Scenic Rivers Act," said Bachmann. "This is wrong. My bill points to the 2005 National Park Service decision stating the proposed four-lane bridge construction is consistent with the Wild and Scenic Rivers Act. . . . These groups and I may never agree on what the river crossing should look like, but I am calling on them to stop lying about my legislation."

Evidently, Bachmann's pals in the Coalition to Support St. Croix Crossing didn't get her memo. In its news release, it stated that the group "will work with federal legislators from Wisconsin and Minnesota and the Federal Highway Administration (FHWA) to exempt the river crossing from the Wild and Scenic Rivers Act."

Although Bachmann would prefer that the history of the National Park Service and the Stillwater Bridge began in 2005, the fact is, the NPS opposed the bridge in 1996 before it supported it in 2005. It's no coincidence that the NPS reversed itself during the Bush administration, yet Bachmann was silent on that flip-flop. In a lawsuit filed by the Sierra Club, U.S. District Judge Michael Davis ruled in March 2010 that the NPS 2005 policy reversal ignored its 1996 decision against a similar bridge and must be revisited. On review of the 2005 decision, the NPS announced in October 2010 that it had determined that the bridge as proposed could not be built without causing "direct and adverse effects that cannot be avoided or eliminated," a violation of Section 7(a) of the Wild and Scenic Rivers Act.

So Bachmann not only was seeking to exempt the bridge from the Wild and Scenic Rivers Act by declaring its most recent application null and void, she apparently was trying to exempt the project from judicial review as well.

In April 2010, just a month after District Judge Davis ordered the NPS to revisit its 2005 policy reversal, Bachmann sent a letter to House Natural Resources Committee chair Nick Rahall, sounding the alarm about "the growing trend of radical environmentalist groups like the Sierra Club abusing the Wild and Scenic Rivers Act to pursue their ideological ends" and suggesting "possible revisions to the Wild and Scenic Rivers Act to ensure it is not misused."

Bachmann's legislative end-run on the courts, the NPS, and the Wild and Scenic Rivers Act was only one salvo in this long-running battle to preserve the St. Croix River and the integrity of the act itself. Bachmann introduced essentially the same bill in 2010 and attracted no cosponsors. In 2011, Wisconsin Republican Sean Duffy and Wisconsin Democrat Ron Kind have signed on.

Minnesota's two Democratic senators, Amy Klobuchar and Al Franken, are supporting a Senate version of Bachmann's bill authored by Klobuchar, a politically motivated move some feel is designed to blunt a potential challenge from Bachmann for her Senate seat in 2012.

Bridge opponents can take heart in the fact that despite her high visibility as self-appointed congressional leader of the Tea Party caucus, the ineffective Bachmann has not passed one piece of legislation in her entire congressional career; her tenure in the Minnesota State Senate was equally unproductive.

There's also the niggling little detail of the bridge's nearly $700 million-and-climbing price tag—$300 million more than Alaska's infamous "Bridge to Nowhere"—which flies in the face of Bachmann's alleged fiscal conservatism. The federal government is hardly flush with cash these days, and neither Minnesota nor Wisconsin has a few hundred million lying around for anything, let alone a bridge whose need is dubious.

Ironically, Bachmann wrote an editorial for the Hill's Congress blog (1/12/2010) in which she asked, "When will the President and Democrat [sic] leadership learn that spending money we don't have isn't always the remedy to fix whatever problem confronts us?"

Although Bachmann claimed that the new bridge was needed to create jobs, in that same opinion piece, she railed against President Obama for making the same claim: "A federal spending surge of more than $20 billion for roads and bridges in President Obama's first stimulus has had NO EFFECT on local unemployment rates, raising questions about his argument for billions more to address an 'urgent need to accelerate job growth.'"

If the latest pronouncements from disingenuous pro-bridge forces are any indication, the arguments for building the Bachmann boondoggle are likely to get even more specious.

"I don't see Michele and that group backing down," said the NPCA's McClure. Yet she remains optimistic, given the latest turn of events. "I think it would behoove everyone to take a step back and look at the transportation issues."

She pointed to alternatives such as the replacement bridges that were built over other Wild and Scenic Rivers—called "low and slow" bridges because they cross at river level, rather than at bluff level, and are built for slower traffic speeds to minimize their impact on the river.

"I do think there's a solution out there," she concluded.

Bachmann Said Liberals Want to Force Everyone to Ride the Light Rail

"This is their agenda, I know it is hard to believe, it's hard to fathom—but this is 'mission accomplished' for them. They want Americans to take transit and move to the inner cities. They want Americans to move to the urban core, live in tenements, [and] take light rail to their government jobs. That's their vision for America" (*One News Now*, August 6, 2008).

Michele Bachmann: "Drill Here, Drill Now"

During the summer of 2008, as gas prices soared to new heights, all that we heard from the congresswoman from Minnesota's 6th District was "Drill, baby, drill."

Bachmann predicted gasoline prices would top five dollars a gallon if Barack Obama were elected president. Her message was simple: we needed to dramatically increase the supply of oil by drilling everywhere, regardless of the environmental implications—"Drill here, drill now."

Michele Bachmann became a loyal defender of Big Oil, calling for more offshore oil drilling and for drilling in the Arctic National Wildlife Refuge (ANWAR). Bachmann claimed in 2008 that drilling in ANWAR would enhance the habitat for wildlife "because of the warmth of the pipeline." Bachmann claimed that the existing pipeline had become a meeting ground and a "coffee klatch" for the caribou.

During the 2010 Gulf of Mexico oil spill, Bachmann showed her loyalty to Big Oil on radio and television. As oil spilled into the Gulf, Bachmann leaped to the defense of British Petroleum, saying that BP would be "chumps" to get "fleeced" by paying into an independently monitored compensation fund for the victims of the spill. Bachmann called efforts to hold BP to account "extortion."

When asked later whether she would retract her extortion charge, Bachmann replied, "In the context of which I was speaking, the government has been doing a lot of overreaching and that was the context of my concern. Government should not overreach in the areas where they have no business."

Bachmann's Pod People

Perhaps the most bizarre and least reported legislative endeavor of Michele Bachmann was her bill to permit local governments to sell bonds to build a Personal Rapid Transit (PRT) testing facility.

Personal Rapid Transit (PRT) is a futuristic fifty-year-old, pod-monorail-like concept that has sucked down hundreds of millions of public and private dollars for nothing. Bachmann was joined in this effort by two of Minnesota's troublesome politicians—Mark Olson and Dean Zimmermann—both still promoting the pods. Mark Olson is a lobbyist for a company that is proposing a $100 million PRT project in Coon Rapids. Dean Zimmermann is a volunteer representative of Citizens for Personal Rapid Transit.

PRT is a transportation concept that is supposed to consist of thousands of little pods on an elevated monorail-like structure with many off-line stations. After thirty years and hundreds of millions of dollars spent on PRT research, there are no true PRT systems in revenue service anywhere in the world, although there have been many failed attempts.

PRT has a solid thirty-year record of controversy and failure. Its main purpose in recent years seems to have been to provide a cover that enabled its proponents to spread misinformation about real, workable transit systems. Except for the occasional laboratory-scale prototype, PRT actually "exists" largely in computerized illustrations, in promotional brochures, and in scores of animated simulations on the Internet.

Michele Bachmann wrote legislation for PRT and was featured in an article about the pods on Minnesota Public Radio back in 2004:

> Supporters range from Minneapolis City Council member Dean Zimmerman, a Green Party member, to Republican Sen. Michelle Bachmann of Stillwater. Bachmann says personal rapid transit, like many political issues, creates strange bedfellows.
>
> People on the right, people on the left, we have the common goal of moving people with transit, but doing it in the most cost-effective manner, in fact, in a manner that may end up costing no government subsidy, it may end up paying for itself.

Reporters didn't bother to ask Bachmann or her cosponsor Mark Olson exactly how PRT could pay for itself only through, as PRT promoters claim, fares—and few have examined the long history of failed PRT projects.

For instance, in the middle to late 1990s, PRT "visionary" and former University of Minnesota professor J. Edward Anderson convinced the Regional Transportation Authority (RTA) of Illinois to fund a PRT project for an industrial park in Rosemount, Illinois. The military contractor Raytheon agreed to build it. The project was discontinued in the late 1990s, due to cost overruns and technical snafus. Total losses in public and private investment in the Raytheon PRT project are estimated at $67 million.

J. Edward Anderson's Fridley-based corporation Taxi 2000 tried to get city after city to fund a PRT testing facility. In Cincinnati, promoters of PRT managed to convince Republican senator Jim Bunning of Kentucky to release $500,000 in federal money for a PRT project they called Skyloop. A regional planning committee rejected Skyloop after engineers found the PRT concept to be unsafe and infeasible. The Skyloop website remains on the Internet to this day.

In the twenty-first century, bills and amendments were introduced into the Minnesota legislature by Michele Bachmann and Mark Olson that granted bonding, regulatory, and tax advantages to develop a PRT industry in Minnesota. Not one of these bills survived the legislative process, but along the way the PRT bills provided a platform for antitransit, pro-highway politicians, mostly Republicans, to complain about the cost of two reality-based transit projects, the Hiawatha Light Rail Line and the Northstar Commuter Line between Minneapolis and Big Lake.

For more than thirty years, PRT had support from antitransit, pro-highway groups such as the Citizens League in Minnesota. PRT had no support from traditional grassroots transit advocacy groups such as Transit for Livable Communities and the Sierra

Club North Star. The Sierra Club North Star resolution is still on their website and TLC President Barb Thoman reaffirmed her organization's opposition to public funding of PRT at a Minnesota Department of Transportation workshop on August 18, 2010.

Perhaps the high point for PRT promoters at the Minnesota Legislature was the 2004 session when a PRT bonding bill for $4 million was passed by the House, only to be extinguished in a conference committee. Things went quickly downhill for PRT promoters after that.

Late in 2004, Professor J. Edward Anderson was prevented from regaining control of Taxi 2000 Corp. One bitter shareholder wrote in a letter to the *Pioneer Press*, "I was present at all of the relevant shareholder meetings and can affirm without reservation that this company was taken over by a gang of political opportunists led by one Morrie Anderson." Morrie Anderson, a former chief of staff to Governor Arne Carlson, had replaced J. Edward Anderson as the CEO of Taxi 2000.

In 2005, Taxi 2000 Corp. filed a lawsuit against J. Edward Anderson and two associates. The lawsuit was settled and J. Edward Anderson formed his own PRT company, located in Fridley as well, called PRT International.

Also in 2005, one of PRT's most energetic promoters, Minneapolis councilman Gary Dean Zimmermann, was investigated and charged by the U.S. Attorney's Office with soliciting and accepting bribes from a developer. Zimmermann subsequently lost his seat on the council to Robert Lilligren, a supporter of conventional transit. Zimmermann was tried and convicted on three counts of bribery and served a two-and-a-half-year sentence in a federal correctional facility.

PRT has since lost its support among liberal and moderate Minnesota politicians. An attempt by Representative Mark Olson to attach a PRT amendment to a bonding bill in the Minnesota House on April 12, 2006, was voted down, 26 to 107. Mark Olson was reelected on November 7 but was arrested and jailed for domestic assault five days later. Olson was expelled from the Republican caucus and lost his House seat in 2008.

Personal Rapid Transit hucksters attempted to grab more public dollars in 2010 when the City of Winona announced a plan to build a PRT testing facility. The Minnesota Department of Transportation and former governor and one-time presidential candidate Tim Pawlenty announced their support for PRT and spent more than $100,000 on studies and meetings. Taxi 2000 Corporation spent nearly $80,000 on lobbying in Minnesota from 2004 to 2009. Taxi 2000 lobbyist and Bachmann pal Ed Cain also lobbied for the phony U.S. Navy Veterans Association charity (see chapter 8, "Bachmann's 'Bobby Thompson' Problem").

PRT promoters will likely put in another request for local bonding or another government pork subsidy when the Minnesota Legislature puts together the biannual Omnibus Transportation bill in 2011–2012.

Reporters need to ask candidate Bachmann whether she will support PRT if she becomes president.

Michele Bachmann's Trashy Adopt-a-Highway Saga

Michele Bachmann has rarely passed on an opportunity to use her public office to promote herself. Whether it's illegally appropriating the State Senate chambers to make a cheesy promotional video for a commercial business or mailing out campaign-style literature from her office at taxpayer expense, the career politician treats public office as if it's a public relations agency for Michele Bachmann.

The most shameless example of all, though, was Bachmann's attempt to turn the Washington County Adopt-a-Highway Program into a year-round campaign sign for herself.

Bachmann had "adopted" a stretch of Stonebridge Trail in Still-water Township since 1995, and when her highway adoption came up for renewal in 2001, Bachmann requested that Washington County's Department of Transportation and Physical Development change her signs to credit "State Senator Michele Bachmann" for cleaning up the road. So at taxpayer expense, Bachmann's Adopt-a-Highway signs were changed to accommodate her self-serving interests. The total cost was about $125, according to county officials.

Unfortunately for Bachmann, when the *St. Paul Pioneer Press*'s Mary Divine looked into the matter after the new signs went up in January 2002, she found that Minnesota Department of Transportation rules expressly prohibit politicians from using the signs as permanent campaign signs.

The *Pioneer Press* reported that the guidelines, adopted in 1998, clearly state, "Adopt-A-Highway signs may not promote any message, whether political, social or advertising," and specifically say, "No political candidates in office or running for office. Individual names are OK, but not titles (i.e. John Smith, not Senator John Smith)."

"If the county wants to take the name 'State Senator' off [the sign], that's certainly fine," Bachmann told the *Pioneer Press*. "Whatever they determine is fine with me. I'm going to keep my adopted highway and continue to do that, but if they want it to just be 'Michele Bachmann,' that's fine. It doesn't have to be 'State Senator.'"

So once again, at taxpayer expense on account of Bachmann's flaunting of the law, the signs were ordered to be changed to remove "State Senator." Another $125 hit for the taxpayers.

Bill Pulkrabek, the Washington County Board chair at the time and Bachmann's first campaign manager, jumped to her defense and suggested that the county could set its own sign guidelines.

"The [MnDOT] guidelines are not legally binding," he told the *Pioneer Press*. "We could snub our noses at them. The board will have to decide whether they want to follow it or not." He added, "Anybody that would complain about such a petty item needs to seriously get a life."

Most recently, Pulkrabek's life has involved being charged with misdemeanor domestic assault.

Eventually, when Bachmann set her sights on running for Congress in 2005 and lost any interest she ever had in her Senate district, she also lost interest in picking up her section of Stonebridge Trail. In May 2005, *Dump Bachmann* founder Eva Young of Minneapolis said she got word that the road "was looking kind of trashy," so she marshaled some *Dump Bachmann* volunteers to pick up after the lackadaisical state senator. The group collected seven large bags of trash and other miscellaneous items and dropped it all off at the Washington County Department of Transportation shop nearby.

Young told the *St. Paul Pioneer Press* that Bachmann "can find the time to jet out to Washington, D.C., for fundraisers with Phyllis Schlafly, but she can't find the time to fulfill her trash-collection obligations on her adopted road right here in her own district."

Bachmann claimed that she had the trash pickup on her adopted highway scheduled, but she was too busy at the capitol to do it. "I'm delighted that the group took care of the spring cleaning for me, and I thank them for their work to help keep Washington County roads cleaned," she told the *Pioneer Press*.

A Washington County official said it was the first time in the fourteen years of the program she could remember this happening.

APPENDIX

THE QUOTABLE
BACHMANN

Never before has a politician been so prolific in malapropisms, barely believable gaffes, and pants-on-fire lies as Michele Bachmann. Over the years, the *Dump Bachmann* blog's comments would frequently light up with exclamations of "Did you hear what she said today?" Often the *Dump Bachmann* team discovered these bizarre quotes embedded like rough gems in the dross of right-wing radio interviews or sermons to theocratic groups such as EdWatch or Mac Hammond's megachurch. The *Dump Bachmann* team had a difficult time keeping up with the tsunami of crazy and abandoned the task of keeping a list years ago. For this book, we have gone back through the six thousand–plus posts on *Dump Bachmann*, looking for additional quotes from those special moments when Michele Bachmann let all of her flying monkeys loose.

This is hardly an exhaustive compilation. Bachmann says so much that's either false or just plain nuts, it's certain she will have added to the list since this book went to press.

On Her Career Aspirations

"My No. 1 goal is to not go to jail."

 —Star Tribune, 2006

On the Persecution She's Suffered

"Nancy Pelosi came into my city, went before the microphones, and called me a disgrace to the Congress. It literally felt like somebody had marched me into the public square, given me a public flogging for eighteen days straight."

 —Interview with Marc Levin, November 2008

"My opponent has just so brazenly and blatantly lied about what I said. So this shows you that right out of the gate, that these people are not telling the truth, they have no plans to and so if they are altering how I look and coloring my teeth, that tells you who they are and how low they are."

 —Interview with Chris Baker, KTLK-FM, July 11, 2010

"Is there no longer freedom of speech in this chamber, Mr. President? Mr. President . . . MR. PRESIDENT? You can turn my microphone off now."

 —May 16, 2004, last day of the 2004 legislative session

"I had high heels on and I just couldn't stand anymore. I was not in the bushes."

 —Star Tribune, 2004

"Help!!!! HEEEELLLLLLLPPPPPP!!!!! I was being held against my will!"

> —Women's restroom in Scandia, Minnesota,
> April 9, 2005

On Work

"Literally, if we took away the minimum wage—if conceivably it was gone—we could potentially virtually wipe out unemployment completely because we would be able to offer jobs at whatever level."

> —Jobs, Energy, and Community Development Committee,
> Minnesota State Senate, January 26, 2005

"Many teenagers that come in should be paying the employer because of broken dishes or whatever occurs during that period of time. But you know what? After six months, that teenager is going to be a fabulous employee and is going to go on a trajectory where he's going to be making so much money, we'll be borrowing money from him."

> —Jobs, Energy, and Community Development Committee,
> Minnesota State Senate, January 26, 2005

"I was wondering, if most employers are already doing this anyway, isn't minimum wage really just superfluous? Why do we even have one?"

> —Jobs, Energy, and Community Development Committee,
> Minnesota State Senate, January 26, 2005

"If raising the minimum wage to $7.00 an hour is a good idea, then why don't we just raise it to $20.00 an hour, that must be even better."

> —Jobs, Energy, and Community Development Committee, Minnesota State Senate, January 26, 2005

"I am so proud to be from the state of Minnesota. We're the workingest state in the country, and the reason why we are, we have more people that are working longer hours, we have people that are working two jobs, we have more women in the workforce than any other state."

> —News conference, 2008

"We're running out of rich people in this country."

> —Interview with Chris Baker, KTLK-FM, 2009

On Evolution

"I look at the Scripture and I read it and I take it for what it is. I give more credence in the Scripture as being kind of a timeless word of God to mankind, and I take it for what it is. And I don't think I give as much credence to my own mind, because I see myself as being very limited and very flawed, and lacking in knowledge, and wisdom and understanding. So, I just take the Bible for what it is, I guess, and recognize that I am not a scientist, not trained to be a scientist. I'm not a deep thinker on all of this. I wish I was. I wish I was more knowledgeable, but I'm not a scientist."

> —Interview with Todd Fiel at KKMS, as quoted in the *Stillwater Gazette*, September 29, 2003

"Something that I think sometimes people don't like to hear is that secular people can be sometimes even more dogmatic in beliefs than people who are not secular. . . . In some ways, to believe in evolution is almost like a following; a cult following—if you don't believe in evolution, you're considered completely backward. That seems to me very indicative of bias as well."

—*Stillwater Gazette*, September 29, 2003

"No one that I know disagrees with natural selection—that you can take various breeds of dogs . . . breed them, you get different kinds of dogs," she said. "It's just a fact of life. . . . Where there's controversy is [at the question] 'Where do we say that a cell became a blade of grass, which became a starfish, which became a cat, which became a donkey, which became a human being?' There's a real lack of evidence from change from actual species to a different type of species. That's where it's difficult to prove."

—*Stillwater Gazette*, September 29, 2003

"There are hundreds and hundreds of scientists, many of them holding Nobel Prizes, who believe in intelligent design."

—6th District Debate, October 2006

On Gay Marriage

"On the morning of December 7, 1941, local St. Paulite Orville Ethier was aboard the USS Ward, a boat manned by 82 Navy reservists from St. Paul, when a small Japanese sub appeared near the entrance to Pearl Harbor. The Ward fired two shots, one of which struck and sank the sub, which constituted the first American shots of World War II. The commander of the Ward relayed a message about the incident back to military headquarters in Honolulu. The message stated, 'We have attacked, fired upon and dropped depth charges upon submarine operating in defensive sea area.' The message, sent more than an hour before the 8 a.m. attack on Pearl Harbor, went unheeded.

"You are a type of Orville Ethier—a patriot looking to secure American freedoms. The question is, will the Senators of Minnesota act like the Honolulu military headquarters and ignore your message? Today we face perhaps the greatest attack on the family in our lifetime. Now is OUR time to stand up and send a message to avert an equally impending disaster. Please visit www.mnmarriage.com to read my recent column on the threat that legalized gay marriage poses to our civil and religious liberties and, to tax exempt organizations in particular."

> —E-mail to supporters, 2004

"Because, Jan, this is an earthquake issue, this will change our state forever. The immediate consequence if gay marriage goes through is that K–12 little children will be forced to learn that homosexuality is normal and natural and that perhaps they should try it. And this will take away the civil rights of little children to be protected in their innocence—so it will take away the rights of parents to control and direct their child's education and step on their sincerely held religious beliefs.

"It will take away the right of the taxpayers because they will be forced to pay for same-sex benefits at school district level, county, city level. And also private businesses will immediately have to begin paying same-sex health care benefits—whether they want to or not. Plus this will end up resulting in loss of religious liberty and privileges and I can go into that."

> —Interview with Jan Markell on KKMS,
>   March 20, 2004

"So the impact of Civil Unions, and of Domestic Partnerships from a legal perspective from the point of view of the force of law is exactly the same. That's what happened in Canada. They have the civil unions. And now today in Canada we're seeing the words *mother* and *father* and *natural parent* are being struck from the books, so no longer will natural parents have any rights over their children. This has profound implications, no one would even think it would go this far."

—Interview with Joyce Harley, April 15, 2005

"This is a radical transformation. We're not talking about extending benefits to a few people. We're talking about transforming marriage. That's why we need to think of these profound implications that occur. We can't have a quilt where we have one state that has marriage defined one way and another state where marriage is defined another way. The United States Supreme Court in *US vs Reynolds* made that very clear with polygamy cases. Utah could not be admitted to the union because they had a different standard for marriage."

—Interview with Joyce Harley, April 15, 2005

On the Constitution

"I never wanted to amend the Constitution."

—Calling in to Tom Barnard, KQRS-FM, May 12, 2005

"I believe in the constitutional amendment, but also one thing I do know on the DOMA law, that's the Defense of Marriage Act, President Obama has said as the president of the United States who swore that he would faithfully execute the laws of the United States, he said he would pick and choose and not select, not enforce laws that are on the books. That's why we are seeing a movement toward a federal marriage amendment because President Obama won't even stand up for a law that President Clinton signed and passed into law and that's the Defense of Marriage Act, which would preserve marriage between one man and one woman."

> —*Good Morning America*, June 14, 2011, in response to George Stephanopoulos asking whether she believed in a constitutional amendment to overturn state laws allowing gay marriage

On Kissing President Bush

"Karl Rove said, 'Now run, chase him.' So I run after in my pink high heels. And the president—he's absolutely buff—he's like you, Jason, he's got one percent body fat. . . . I ran up behind him and it was the experience of a lifetime."

> —*Jason Lewis Show*, KLTK-FM, State Fair, August 2006

"With the president's poll numbers, he could use a little encouragement. It was absolutely spontaneous."

> —On her State of the Union kiss, January 2007

"He kissed me in Minnesota, too."

> —*Star Tribune,* January 2007

"The president and I enjoy a great relationship. When he and I were back visiting the collapsed bridge, he reached over because he wanted to give me a kiss when we were down at the site. I pulled back and he said, 'What? You don't want to embrace?' I said, 'The people of Minnesota love you, Mister President, but one kiss was enough.' . . . We were just joking. It was light-hearted. It was fun.'"

—WCCO interview, September 19, 2007

On Muslims

"So to see the specter of our president apologizing for American activity, bowing before the king of Saudi Arabia, which to me was highly symbolic, that he did that . . . and then now denying it, and then lying about it, and then also, our president is saying to the world that we are not a Christian nation, during Holy Week. Saying we are not a Christian nation, that we're merely citizens with shared values. That is not true, it's not reflective of our history."

—April 9, 2009, interview with KSFO, San Francisco

"The imams, the imams were actually attending Congressman Keith Ellison's victory celebration, when he won as a member of Congress. And the imams went to the Minneapolis airport to leave and go home. While they were there, they were shouting phrases anti-Bush, anti-America and they laid their prayer shawls, their prayer rugs out on the floor in the airport terminal, were having their prayers, and were making these statements and when they got aboard the airplane, they switched seats, they didn't go to their proper seats, and they went in the pattern of the 911 terrorists who were on the airplanes, and they all asked for seatbelt extenders on their seats, in the airplane, and these weren't large people."

—April 9, 2009, interview with KSFO, San Francisco

On the Natural World

"Carbon dioxide is portrayed as harmful. But there isn't even one study that can be produced that shows that carbon dioxide is a harmful gas."

—House speech, April 2009

On President Obama

"I find it interesting that it was back in the 1970s that the swine flu broke out under another, then under another Democrat president, Jimmy Carter. I'm not blaming this on President Obama, I just think it's an interesting coincidence."

—Interview on Pajamas TV, April 28, 2009

"Take this into consideration. If we look at American history, between 1942 and 1947, the data that was collected by the Census Bureau was handed over to the FBI and other organizations at the request of President Roosevelt, and that's how the Japanese were rounded up and put into the internment camps. I'm not saying that that's what the administration is planning to do, but I am saying that private personal information that was given to the Census Bureau in the 1940s was used against Americans to round them up, in a violation of their constitutional rights, and put the Japanese in internment camps."

—Interview on the *Sue Jeffers Show*, KTLK-FM, April 4, 2009

"I believe as dangerous as the president has been on economic policy, I think the president has been more dangerous on foreign

policy. In many ways, he's disregarded our allies and empowered our enemies."
—Interview with Scott Hennen, June 20, 2011

"The president wanted to change the mission of NASA and the focus of NASA to be no longer on space but instead be an outreach to the Muslim community."
—Interview with the blog *The Shark Tank*, May 12, 2011

"From the time when George Washington took the presidency on his first day to the day George W. Bush left as president of the United States, all forty-three presidents, if you take all of the debt combined of all of those 43 presidents, do you know that all of that debt is less than the debt that was accumulated by Barack Obama in one year? That is the level of debt and spending that we have engaged in. So this isn't hyperbole. This is facts."
—At an Iowans for Tax Relief event, January 21, 2011

"What people recognize is that there's a fear that the United States is in an unstoppable decline. They see the rise of China, the rise of India, the rise of the Soviet Union, and our loss militarily going forward. And especially with this very bad debt ceiling bill, what we have done is given a favor to President Obama and the first thing he'll whack is five hundred billion out of the military defense at a time when we're fighting three wars. People recognize that."
—*Jay Sekulow Life* radio show, August 18, 2011

"Well I think we know that just within a day or so the president of the United States will be taking a trip over to India that is expected to cost the taxpayers $200 million a day. He's taking two thousand people with him. He'll be renting out over 870 rooms in India. And these are 5-star hotel rooms at the Taj Mahal Palace hotel. This is the kind of over-the-top spending; it's a very small example, Anderson."

> —Interview with Anderson Cooper, CNN, November 3, 2010 (Factcheck.org said there was "simply no evidence to support" the claim.)

On Our Nefarious Government

"I'm a foreign correspondent on enemy lines, and I try to let everyone back here in Minnesota know exactly the nefarious activities that are taking place in Washington."

> —WWTC interview, March 23, 2009

"We change the economy by changing the tax code. How many of you love the IRS? No! It's time to change it. I went to work in that system because the first rule of war is 'know your enemy.' So I went to the inside to learn how they work because I wanted to beat them."

> —Rally in South Carolina, August 19, 2011

"Unlimited credit cards for our elected leaders have become an entitlement like Speaker Pelosi, who has been busy sticking the taxpayer with her $100,000 bar tab for alcohol on the military jets that she's flying."

> —Values Voter Conference, September 18, 2010

"I wish the American media would take a great look at the views of the people in Congress and find out: Are they pro-America or anti-America?"

—Interview with Chris Matthews, MSNBC, 2008

"This is their agenda, I know it is hard to believe, it's hard to fathom—but this is 'mission accomplished' for them. They want Americans to take transit and move to the inner cities. They want Americans to move to the urban core, live in tenements, [and] take light rail to their government jobs. That's their vision for America."

—On congressional Democrats, interview with *One News Now*, August 6, 2008

"FDR applied just the opposite formula—the Hoot-Smalley Act [sic—Smoot-Hawley], which was a tremendous burden on tariff restrictions, and then, of course, trade barriers and the regulatory burden and tax barriers. That's what we saw happen under FDR. That took a recession and blew it into a full-scale depression. The American people suffered for almost ten years under that kind of thinking."

—Speech on the the House floor, 2009

"Does that mean that someone's thirteen-year-old daughter could walk into a sex clinic, have a pregnancy test done, be taken away to the local Planned Parenthood abortion clinic, have their abortion, be back and go home on the school bus? That night, mom and dad are never the wiser."

—Speech on the House floor, October 2009

"I don't know how much God has to do to get the attention of the politicians. We've had an earthquake; we've had a hurricane. He said, 'Are you going to start listening to me here?' Listen to the American people because the American people are roaring right now. They know government is on a morbid obesity diet and we've got to rein in the spending."

> —*St. Petersburg Times*, August, 30, 2011
> (The next day, Bachmann claimed she was joking.)

On Energy

"I'm pro-choice on lightbulbs, you bet I am. Pro-life on babies, but pro-choice on lightbulbs."

> —Interview with Jason Lewis, KTLK-FM, St. Paul, Minnesota,
> March 26, 2008

"[Nancy Pelosi] is committed to her global warming fanaticism to the point where she has said that she's just trying to save the planet. We all know that someone did that over 2,000 years ago, they saved the planet—we didn't need Nancy Pelosi to do that."

> —Interview with *One News Now*, August 2008

"I want people in Minnesota armed and dangerous on this issue of the energy tax because we need to fight back. Thomas Jefferson told us 'having a revolution every now and then is a good thing,' and the people—we the people—are going to have to fight back hard if we're not going to lose our country. And I think this has the potential of changing the dynamic of freedom forever in the United States."

> —WWTC interview, March 23, 2009

"Under President Bachmann you will see gasoline come down below $2 a gallon again. That will happen."

  —On the stump, Greenville, South Carolina, August 16, 2011

On the Man

"Michael Steele, you be da man! You be da man!"

  —Conservative Political Action Conference (CPAC),
    February 26, 2009

On the Middle East

"Iran is the trouble maker, trying to tip over apple carts all over Baghdad right now because they want America to pull out. And do you know why? It's because they've already decided that they're going to partition Iraq.

And half of Iraq, the western, northern portion of Iraq, is going to be called the Iraq State of Islam, something like that. And I'm sorry, I don't have the official name, but it's meant to be the training ground for the terrorists. There's already an agreement made.

They are going to get half of Iraq and that is going to be a safe haven zone where they can go ahead and bring about more attacks in the Middle East region and then to come against the United States because we are their avowed enemy."

  —Interview with Larry Schumacher, *St. Cloud Times*,
    February 10, 2007

"Iran is at a point right now where America has to be very aggressive in our response. We can't remove any option off the table. And we should not remove the nuclear response."

  —Debate, May 3, 2006

"There is not a plan that they're bringing forward, other than surrender. That's the only plan they've come up with."

— On the Democrats' approach to the Iraq War, 2007

On God's Will

"And in the midst of that calling, God then called me to run for the United States Congress. And I thought, what in the world would that be for. And my husband said, 'You need to do this.' And I wasn't so sure. And we took three days, and we fasted and we prayed. And we said, 'Lord, is this what you want, are You sure? Is this Your will?' And after—along about the afternoon of day two, He made that calling sure. And it's been now twenty-two months that I've been running for United States Congress. Who in their right mind would spend two years to run for a job that lasts for two years? You'd have to be absolutely a fool to do that. You are now looking at a fool for Christ. This is a fool for Christ."

— Living Word Center, 2006

"And from there, my husband said, 'Now you need to go and get post-doctorate degree in tax law.' Tax law? I hate taxes. Why should I go and do something like that? But the Lord says: Be submissive, wives, you are to be submissive to your husbands."

— Living Word Center, 2006

On History

"When they were about 150 miles west of Greenland, they got an alert that there were German U2 boats."

— Bachmann at a Sean Hannity Freedom Concert in August, 2010, speaking about a World War II incident involving a German submarine (not the British rock group)

"You're the state where the shot was heard around the world at Lexington and Concord. And you put a marker in the ground and paid with the blood of your ancestors."

—Manchester, New Hampshire, March 12, 2011

"Before we get started, let's all say 'Happy Birthday' to Elvis Presley today. Happy birthday! We played you a little bit of 'Promised Land' when we pulled up. You can't do better than Elvis Presley, and we thought we'd celebrate his birthday as we get started celebrating taking our country back to work."

—Spartanburg, South Carolina, August 15, 2011,
the 34th anniversary of Elvis's death

"It didn't matter the color of their skin, it didn't matter their language, it didn't matter their economic status, it didn't matter whether they descended from known royalty or whether they were of a higher class or a lower class, it made no difference. Once you got here [to the United States] you were all the same. Isn't that remarkable? . . . That is the greatness and essence of this nation. We know we were not perfect. We know there was slavery that was still tolerated when the nation began. We know that was an evil and it was scourge and a blot and a stain upon our history. But we also know that the very founders that wrote those documents worked tirelessly until slavery was no more in the United States. And I think it is high time that we recognize the contribution of our forebears, who worked tirelessly, men like John Quincy Adams, who would not rest until slavery was extinguished in the country."

—At an Iowans for Tax Relief event, January 21, 2011